SCHOCKEN BOOKS

The Secret of the
HITTITES
The Discovery of
an Ancient Empire

C.W.CERAM
Gods, Graves, & Scholars

author of

SCHOCKEN PAPERBACKS ON ARCHAEOLOGY

CERAM, C. W., *ed.*
Hands on the Past: Pioneer Archaeologists Tell Their Own Story

CERAM, C. W.
The Secret of the Hittites: The Discovery of an Ancient Empire

KENYON, KATHLEEN
The Royal Cities of the Old Testament

WELLARD, JAMES
Babylon

Descriptive catalogs may be obtained by writing to Schocken Books

THE SECRET OF THE HITTITES

THE SECRET OF
THE
HITTITES

The Discovery of an Ancient Empire

by C. W. CERAM

TRANSLATED FROM THE GERMAN BY
RICHARD AND CLARA WINSTON

p 21

SCHOCKEN BOOKS • NEW YORK

PREFACE

HITTITOLOGY is the newest branch of the science of archaeology. The story of its development, which is the subject of this book, abounds with the ludicrous errors, perplexing difficulties and unexpected triumphs which make the probing of the past such an exciting business. The excavator has passed through periods of soaring hope and of intense disappointment, and the decipherer has endured endless frustration and perhaps one brief moment of blessed insight, before the historian's work can begin.

The discovery of the Hittites has been an unusually stirring adventure of the human spirit. In slightly more than a century a people of whom nothing but a name was known has become an integral part of the history of our civilization. Much still remains to be learned about the Empire of the Hittites, but a good beginning has been made.

In the orthography of names complete confusion reigns throughout the scholarly literature. Phonetic rendering of classical and modern Turkish names naturally produces differing results in every language. Moreover, even scholars using the same language disagree. We find the name *Boghazköy* variously spelled *Boğazköy* and *Boghaz-keui*. The uninitiated reader will have no way of knowing that what is meant is the spot where Hittite *Hattusas* (or *Hattuscha* or *Hattuša*) was situated. For consistency's sake I have therefore used Dr. O. R. Gurney's orthography, which to my mind represents the most readable compromise between the German and the English usages. If, as often happens, there exist radically different spellings for the same name (*Sendschirli* for *Zinjirli* or *Zendjirli*), I have included all versions in the index, with references to the spelling used in this book. I have followed a similar practice with the modern names of ancient places; under Tell Atchana, for example, there will be a reference to Alalakh.

In conclusion, a few words of gratitude. It would have been quite impossible for me to have brought this account up to date, in regard to researches even now being pursued, if I had not had the opportunity to visit the scenes of important excavations. I am indebted to Professor Carl Rathjens of the University of Hamburg for an invitation to attend the Twenty-second Congress of Orientalogists at Istanbul. There I had the opportunity to engage in a great many extremely stimulating conversations, which in turn led to my participating in several scientific excursions into the Empire of the Hittites.

Thus I was able to inspect Alaja Hüyük under the guidance of the excavator, Dr. Hamit Zübeyr Kosay, former Director General of Turkish Museums and Antiquities. The Kültepe excavation was explained to me by the excavator's wife (at that time herself director of the expedition), Dr. Nimet Özgüç. I am indebted to Professor Kurt Bittel, now Director of the German Archæological Institute in Istanbul, for making possible my first inspection of Boghazköy and Yazilikaya, where he labored from 1931 to 1939. It was Professor Bittel also who, in the course of long talks in Istanbul, provided me with a first systematic survey of Hittite history in general and the latest Hittite excavations—fields into which it is virtually impossible to break without some initial assistance.

I imagine my greatest debt is to Professor Helmuth T.

Bossert of the University of Istanbul, the discoverer and excavator of Karatepe. From the very start he has shown the warmest interest in my undertaking. In the fall of 1951 I was the guest of his expedition until the start of the rainy season. (In thanking him I automatically include the Turkish Historical Society, the General Directorate of Turkish Museums and Antiquities, and the Literary Faculty of the University of Istanbul—the institutions which made these excavations possible.) I shall never forget his hospitality in the wilderness, the cordiality in that atmosphere of hard work, the evening round-table discussions accompanied by the distant howls of the jackals. Nor can I forget the long talks about the new finds with Dr. U. Bahadir Alkim and Dr. Halet Çambel, with another guest of the expedition, with Father O'Callaghan, who has since died in an unfortunate accident near Bagdad, and with Dr. Muhibbe Darga, Professor Bossert's youngest student.

I am especially indebted to Dr. Bahadir Alkim and his wife, Handan Alkim. Not only were they the most charming of hosts during my second stay at Karatepe in 1953, but Dr. Alkim has also had the kindness to examine a first brief outline of this book. To him, as well as to Dr. Franz Steinherr, now of the German Embassy at Ankara, I owe many important suggestions.

When the book was completed Professors Bossert and Bittel, as well as Dr. Margarete Riemschneider once again gave of their time to look through the proofs and help me correct a number of the errors which have inevitably crept into a work of this sort.

I am indebted to the generosity of many scientists and museums for the abundance of illustrative material. The photographer Max G. Scheler, who was the amiable com-

panion of my second trip to Turkey, offered me my choice
of all the photographs he had taken in Anatolia. Seventeen of them are reproduced in this book. Sources for all
illustrations will be found in the lists of plates and line
drawings, pages xiii–xxi.

October 1955.   C. W. CERAM

CONTENTS

I THE ENIGMA OF THEIR EXISTENCE

II THE RIDDLE OF THE SCRIPTS

III THE SECRET OF THEIR POWER

CITADEL, STATUES, RELIEFS, AND INSCRIPTIONS. THE
MISTAKE. NOCTURNAL ENCOUNTER WITH KARATEPE.

LIST OF PLATES

LINE DRAWINGS IN THE TEXT

A NOTE ON QUOTATIONS

ALMOST ALL the translations from Egyptian and Hittite sources quoted here exist in several versions which vary rather widely according to the personal views of different scholars and the state of the science at the time each translation was made. For the purposes of this book they have been stripped of their learned commentaries and run together to form continuous texts. The quotations from the Egyptian are based on the work of Adolf Erman, Günther Roeder, Hermann Ranke, Alexander Scharff, and Siegfried Schott; those from the Hittite primarily on translations by H. T. Bossert, Johannes Friedrich, and Heinrich Zimmern, some of whose texts have been reproduced in books and papers by Anton Moortgat and Margarete Riemschneider. The reader who is interested in pursuing the subject will find further references under these names in the Bibliography (Groups 1 and 6).

Part I

THE ENIGMA OF A PEOPLE

HITTITE WARRIOR WITH BOW
AND ARROW, ON A BEAR HUNT.
FROM KARATEPE.

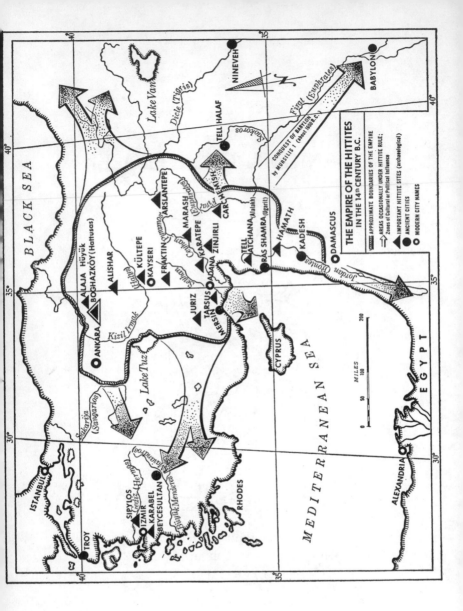

THE EMPIRE OF THE HITTITES
IN THE 14th CENTURY B.C.

APPROXIMATE BOUNDARIES OF THE EMPIRE

AREAS OCCASIONALLY UNDER HITTITE RULE;
Zones of Cultural or Political Influence

IMPORTANT HITTITE SITES (archaeological)

ANCIENT CITIES

MODERN CITY NAMES

CONQUEST OF BABYLON
by MURSILIS I. (About 1600 B.C.)

BLACK SEA

MEDITERRANEAN SEA

EGYPT

BABYLON

NINEVEH

TELL HALAF

Dicle (Tigris)

Lake Van

Zagros

Firat (Euphrates)

CARCHEMISH

MARASH

ARSLANTEPE

FRÄKTIN

KÜLTEPE

KAYSERI

KARATEPE

ZINJIRLI

ALAJA Hüyük

BOGHAZKÖY (Hattusas)

ALISHAR

ANKARA

Kizil Irmak

Halys

Seyhan

Ceyhan

Pyramos

TELL ATCHANA (Alalakh)

RAS SHAMRA (Ugarit)

HAMATH

KADESH

DAMASCUS

Jordan (Jordanes)

ADANA

TARSUS

MERSIN

JURIZ

Lake Tuz

Sakarja (Stangarios)

CYPRUS

RHODES

TROY

ISTANBUL

IZMIR

SIPYLOS

KARABEL

BEYCESULTAN

Gediz (Hermos)

Büyük Menderes

(Kaimaros)

ALEXANDRIA

MILES
0   50   100   200

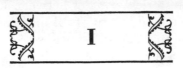

DISCOVERY AND WILD SURMISE

W<small>HEN IN DIM, FAR-OFF DAYS</small> young Leander swam the Hellespont to rest in the arms of his beloved Hero, he was swimming from Asia to Europe. The Dardanelles, as we now call this strait connecting the Mediterranean Sea with the Sea of Marmora, has always served as a link rather than as a dividing-line between Asia Minor and Southeast Europe. Across this strait the Ægeans invaded Greece. The great Persian king, Xerxes I, struck out in the same direction in 480 B.C. A hundred and fifty years later Alexander the Great brought Greek arms and culture back across the narrow waterway into Asia Minor. This land, which is now Turkey, has from the beginning been a highway for armies, a battleground, and a melting-pot of nations. Here history played itself out in its full savagery, and the stakes were death or survival—as they have always been down to our own day whenever East and West have collided. That is why for us of the twentieth century *after* the birth of Christ there is a strange contemporaneity about what took place in this arena twenty centuries *before* Christ, when the Indo-European Hittites descended into Asia Minor. For "this was the first time," to quote the Hittitologist Albrecht Götze, "that European peoples penetrated the civilized world." He adds that this invasion was "the first historical conflict between East and West."

It is one of the oddest twists of history that the people responsible for this epochal clash were "discovered" by historians only a few decades ago. It verges on the miraculous that archæologists are already able to interpret the language and script and to write a fairly full history of this nation that passed away more than three thousand years ago.

How scholars contrived by excavation, by research, and by the subtlest reasoning to build such an astonishing body of knowledge in so short a time—that is the subject of this book.

If we wish to know the status of any branch of science at a given time, we will do well to turn to an encyclopædia. For ever since the publication of the first great lexicon of the sciences and arts in the middle of the eighteenth century, the historic French *Encyclopédie*, encyclopædias have embalmed the knowledge of an era. Let us therefore glance at the article on Hittites in the 1871 edition of Meyer's *Neues Konversationslexicon*, the classic German encyclopædia. No more than a glance is necessary, for the article reads:

"Canaanite tribe encountered by the Israelites in Palestine; dwelt in the vicinity of Hebron along with the Amorites; later are found further to the north in the region of Bethel, at which time they were made tributary by Solomon. Still later an independent Hittite tribe under a monarchic government lived even further north, near Syria."

That is all. The Hittites are accorded just *seven lines*. The article is not only pitifully brief; it is also wrong in all essential points. These seven lines do nothing but summarize the sparse information given by the Bible.

In other words, in 1871 historians knew hardly anything about the Hittites. Today we are aware that in the second millennium B.C. this nation was a Great Power whose sway extended over all of Asia Minor as far as Syria, who conquered Babylon and fought successful wars against Egypt. From our present vantage point it seems utterly incredible that such a dominant political force, with a culture, a script, ₹nd a legal code of its own, should have become an unknown, forgotten people and have escaped the notice of archæologists and historians down to our twentieth century A.D. Its re-discovery was sudden and dramatic. A handful of scholars pioneering in the bare tablelands of Asia Minor resurrected this unknown civilization. How they did it is a fascinating tale. To be sure, from the turning of their first spadeful of earth, they were attended by enormous luck. But before we speak of that, let us look at the land whose past we shall unearth side by side with the scholars.

Asia Minor is an appendix to the great Continent of Asia. It is not only a tailpiece, but also a miniature image. The Ancients called it Asia Minor because, they believed, its outlines and general form corresponded to that of the larger continent: tableland in the center, high mountains around the rim, sloping terraces on all sides. The resemblance is not quite complete, but then the Ancients had no knowledge of the northern and eastern ends of Asia.

Nowadays railroads, trucks, buses, and American-built automobiles carry the traveler across Asia Minor. But it is a land meant to be traversed by horse. Seated upon the creaking wooden saddles the natives use, you see this land in its true aspect—in its timeless aspect. Even today in Central Anatolia (the name means "land toward the rising sun") you still encounter oxcarts whose wheels are solid wooden discs that screech like banshees as they move across the windswept wastes. The gray villages crouch under the hot sun just as they did more than thirty-five hundred years ago when the first Assyrian merchants went forth from rich Assur, "that great city," to ply their wares in the heart of Anatolia. The buildings which make up these villages are still constructed of bricks of unfired clay —bricks which crumble under the baking sun and slowly dissolve under the sparse rain. The poorer and the more neglected the village, the more it looks like the inspired creation of a bizarre imagination. Such adobe houses seldom last more than twenty years. When they fall apart, sons and grandsons build anew upon the ruins. That is how "archæological strata" are created.

Asia Minor is no larger than Spain, Germany, or the State of California; it is smaller than the Australian province of Queensland. Kayseri, which is geographically in the center of Asia Minor, is said to have a winter like that of northern Germany, a summer like that of southern France. Among the gorges of the Taurus Mountains bears still prowl, packs of wolves attack sheepfolds, and dangerous snakes sun themselves on rocks. And when darkness falls the hyena slinks through the jungles of prickly broom and the jackal howls his nocturnal serenade.

In the northeast tea is raised, in the southeast cotton and citrus fruits. Near Adana I once watched a peasant cultivating a tiny grove of lemon trees which were sheltered from the wind by the remains of ancient walls; and in Yazilikaya, a Hittite religious sanctuary near Boghazköy, I saw a peasant bringing his wife onions from a planting he had made along a wall lined with gods sculptured in relief. In the river valleys and along the narrow coastal strips, tobacco and poppies, wheat and olives, are grown. But how few green valleys there are!

There is not a single navigable river in all of Asia Minor. The largest stream is the Kizil Irmak, known in ancient times as the Halys. This is the river that Crœsus hesitated to cross until he had consulted the oracle at Delphi. The oracle informed him that if he made the crossing, a great empire would be destroyed. Its words came true: Crœsus lost his own empire instead of destroying that of the Persians. Coming from the East, the Halys swings in a great bend into Central Anatolia, then cuts through the

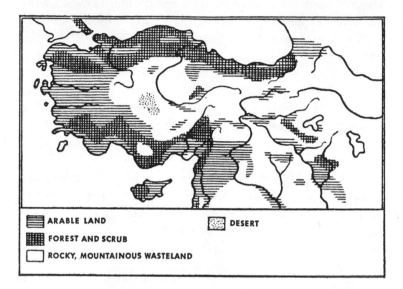

ARABLE LAND　　　　　　DESERT

FOREST AND SCRUB

ROCKY, MOUNTAINOUS WASTELAND

VEGETATION MAP OF ASIA MINOR.

northern mountains and empties into the Black Sea.

One third of Asia Minor is plateau, parched tableland with little vegetation out of which naked rocks rise up; the barrenness is broken only here and there by the gleam of blue water—huge salt lakes. There is a sublime monotony about this landscape; all the colors seem dried up, as if burned to a hard enamel. It also has a terrifying quality. If you encounter a solitary rider, you feel a thrill of danger. As you approach a chain of mountains, you are aware of a distinct sense of menace, of unknown perils awaiting

you. When you come upon a settlement of mud huts, it
strikes you at first as a ghost town; under the flickering
heat waves the doorways stare at you like lifeless eyes.
Then men emerge; no women are to be seen, and a scatter-
ing of inquisitive children are driven away with a gesture.
The men approach slowly, their immobile faces showing
no signs of curiosity. They form a ring around you and
gaze at you in silence. A glass of tea is handed to you, the
stranger, and as you sip it you look around the taciturn
circle with a feeble smile of embarrassment. There is none
of the noisy importunity of the Levant, nor the colorful
splendor of a fairy-tale Orient. The people here have a
rare kind of dignity that seems singularly appropriate to
this landscape. It is as if the landscape had formed their
temperament.

The peoples who fought for Asia Minor were so numerous and so diverse that throughout early antiquity
they never—with a single exception—coalesced into large
kingdoms that lasted for any length of time. As far back
as the fourth millennium B.C. the inhabitants formed mu-
tually hostile hordes, tribes, and small nations. . . .

Only once in the early history of this divided land one
people succeeded in uniting all those heterogeneous tribes
and founding a confederacy which swiftly rose to be one
of the Great Powers of the Near East. The cultural influence of that new state extended as far as the world of
the Greeks—and perhaps permeated Greek civilization to
depths that as yet we cannot even guess.

Back in the thirties of the last century a certain
Frenchman made everything ready for a journey into the
area. He was much handicapped by the fact that he was
planning in the dark. In the course of his preparations he
had frequent occasion to complain that the reports of
other travelers yielded few facts about the region. After

his arrival in Turkey he noted: "Although all information was exceedingly incomplete, I set out with my caravan on July 18, 1834, heading north."

Some time later, after a solitary ride through the majestically bare tablelands, he came to the little village of Boghazköy, in the great bend of the ancient Halys River. Near this village he suddenly came upon ruins that took his breath away. However, he was at a loss to determine where in history any such ruined city could have fitted.

This venturesome traveler, Charles-Felix-Marie Texier, was one of those delvers into the past whom the nineteenth century produced in such numbers. Their work was, so to speak, an outgrowth of the emotional needs of their century. Technology was opening up such tremendous prospects for the future that the existing historical footing seemed to be crumbling under the weight of man's new destiny.

Searching for the ancient town of Tavium, where invading Celts had been settled in Roman times, Texier had collected a few hints in the village of Boghazköy, and decided to check them. He clambered up a rutted road lined by crumbling mud hovels, ascended higher and higher into more and more rugged hills, and suddenly:

There before him lay gigantic blocks of stone in long, straight rows. Though worn by centuries of time, they unmistakably formed the outline of a building, a huge, strangely rambling, complex layout. He climbed on, came upon the remains of a fortification wall, and paced it off. It was miles long.

When he reached the peak of the hill, he paused and let his eyes sweep over the view. Mentally he drew a circle around all the ruins in sight, and he recognized that these ruins must once have formed a city as large as Athens at the height of its glory. Who had built so mighty a city? Was this the Tavium he'd come to find?

He walked on until he found two mighty gates in the wall. On one of them he beheld the figure of a man carved in relief. It was perhaps a king, for the figure was of super-human size, the carving done in a strange manner, like nothing he had ever seen before. The other gate was orna-mented with the statues of lions. He attempted to draw these and had his companions also make some sketches. But the draftsmen were children of their age, breathing the stolid middle-class spirit that prevailed in the France of Louis Philippe; they could admire monumentality, but they could not really grasp it. Consequently, the pictures they have left us are of highly conventional lions, with Biedermeier scowls and curly manes.

Texier promptly made a first stab at interpretation. "Wholly possessed by the idea of finding ancient Tavium, I was inclined to take these ruins for a Temple of Jupiter, with the sanctuary mentioned by Strabo. . . . But I later found myself compelled to abandon this opinion," he wrote. And then he confesses: ". . . No edifice of any Roman era could be fitted in here; the grandeur and the peculiar nature of the ruins perplexed me extraordinarily when I attempted to give the city its historical name. . . ."

Later on, preparing his account for the press, he had the opportunity to look through the notes made by a dis-tinguished antiquary who had visited Boghazköy the year after Texier himself. This was William Hamilton, who as a young man of twenty-five had helped Lord Elgin spirit the sculptures from the Parthenon to England. Hamilton also assumed that the ruins were those of Tavium. Texier, however, once more studied his source material on Ta-vium, came to the conclusion that the mysterious city could not possibly have been Tavium, and declared his conviction that it was Pteria, where Crœsus and Cyrus had fought their famous battle.

But other surprises were in store for Texier. A native led him away from Boghazköy along a difficult path that cut diagonally across a deeply incised river valley. They climbed a good two hours until they reached a plateau opposite the hill where he had seen the ruined city. And there he found the place that today is called Yazilikaya ("Inscribed Rock"). Precipitous cliffs mounted skyward here, and between them a broad cleft formed a natural chamber. Here, the stone of the cliff wall had been somewhat smoothed and on its surface were carved strange sculptures. Texier saw gods moving in stiff, solemn procession across these walls, their heads crowned with pointed caps, their garments girded at the waist. He followed the cleft around a gentle turn to the right and saw more sculptures, figures with different types of dress, wearing tiaras instead of pointed caps. Two of the figures were winged; others held unrecognizable objects in their hands, or stood upon the necks of still other figures, or were followed by animals.

Stunned by these strange processions in stone, Texier looked for the exit. Then he noticed on his left a narrow passage to a smaller cleft in the rock. At the entrance he paused—two winged demons cut into the stone on either side of the passage seemed to be warding off intruders. Nevertheless, he hesitantly went through—and beheld another procession on the steep west wall. Twelve warriors —or were they gods?—were marching stiff-legged one behind the other, going forward with deadly purposiveness; twelve men on parade, on their heads tall pointed caps and on their shoulders scimitars. Diagonally across, a tall figure held a smaller one in a protective embrace. Above its outstretched arm was a flowerlike shape composed of several signs resembling hieroglyphs. Obviously symbols —but for what? Texier looked around, then returned to the larger chamber. Here he observed still more of these

signs, some of them so worn by time they could scarcely
be made out. Were these marks merely ornament? Or
were they perhaps a script?

Texier made his way back to the entrance. Standing
there and gazing over the plateau that lay before him, he
perceived the remains of walls. Had there been buildings
here? Gateworks guarding the entrance to the cleft in the
rock? As he looked, it became for him a virtual certainty
that he stood in front of an ancient sanctuary, a highly unusual temple in the rocks. But built by whom, for the worship of what people?

He looked across the valley toward the ruins of Boghazköy, gazed at gullies and jagged ridges upon which
the sun blazed inexorably. God must have worked with
clenched fists when he molded this landscape. And then
some mighty nation had imposed its will here, had vented
its urge to build by piling blocks of stone atop all this natural rockiness, so that even now the ruined walls could still
be seen—walls that had linked these grim pinnacles into
powerful battlements. Such towering monuments could
only have been conceived by powerful kings, kings of a
wealthy and mighty nation.

In 1839 Texier published in Paris the several volumes
of his ambitious travel book, *Description of Asia Minor*,[1]
in which he confessed to being totally mystified. For as far
as historians of the nineteenth century knew, no such
mighty people had existed in Asia Minor.

As a matter of fact, the things Texier described were
only an embarrassment to archæology. Specialists were
naturally disconcerted at being confronted with so much
pictorial and descriptive material which they could not
make head or tail of. Moreover, archæology was still a

---

[1] *Description de l'Asie Mineure.*

young science, and in the decades after 1830 most specialists were chiefly interested in the fascinating excavations going on in Egypt and Mesopotamia. Lepsius and Mariette were discovering wonders in the land of the pharaohs; Botta and Layard were bringing to light the civilization of the Assyrians.

But in spite of having their attention centered elsewhere, the archæologists could not completely pass over the mysterious ruins in Turkish Anatolia. For now more and more fresh reports poured in.

William Hamilton had not only visited Boghazköy shortly after Texier; he had also discovered another area of ruins near by, at the village of Alaja Hüyük. Between 1859 and 1861 two German travelers, Barth and Mordtmann, provided more exact descriptions of Boghazköy and supplemented Texier's hasty sketches. The Frenchman Langlois tramped through the region around Tarsus in 1861. And starting in 1862 the French scientist Georges Perrot traveled through all of Anatolia, conscientiously exploring the country. He came upon a large number of fascinating new monuments. Among other things he found in the ruins of ancient Boghazköy a beveled rock covered with symbols. Some of these were already so badly eroded that they looked like nothing more than scratches in the stone, but their general character resembled the markings Texier had discovered in Yazilikaya. This rock, called Nishan Tash, was later to prove a highly significant discovery, but at the time it was submerged in the wealth of material Perrot, with the aid of his artist Edmond Guillaume, started publishing in 1872.

Just ten years later, in 1882, Karl Humann, the German archæologist, made casts of some of the Yazilikaya reliefs, and produced the first reliable plans of the Boghazköy ruins. He was peculiarly suited for this task because he had been a civil engineer before he succumbed to the enchantment of archæology and won fame as the excavator of the Pergamon altar.

Perrot recapitulated what had been discovered in Anatolia in his *History of Art in Antiquity,*[2] published in 1887. He even ventured certain conjectures about some of the sculptures and groups of symbols. Other specialists of his

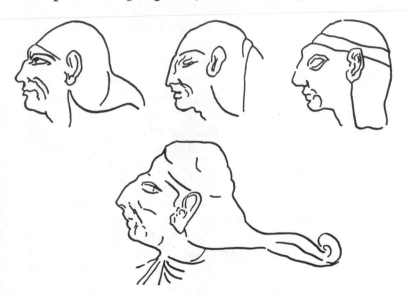

HITTITES AS PICTURED ON EGYPTIAN MONUMENTS.

time had come to accept the substance of these conjectures, convinced by the reports of two American travelers who had described certain slabs they had seen during a trip through Syria in 1870. These inscribed surfaces, called the Hamath Stones after the site of their discovery, were to introduce a new phase in the struggle to solve the enigma of the Anatolian ruins. As a matter of fact, the two Americans had not been the first explorers to see the

[2] *Histoire de l'Art dans l'Antiquité.*

Hamath Stones. These had actually been discovered fifty-eight years earlier by one of the most interesting travelers of the nineteenth century.

It was in the year 1809 that a bearded man in Oriental costume boarded a vessel sailing from the island of Malta to Syria. He called himself Sheik Ibrahim and identified himself as a merchant in the service of the East India Company. For three and a half years he remained in Syria —but he was the oddest merchant that had ever lived between Aleppo and Damascus. Instead of trading, he went to native scholars to be instructed in the languages, history, and geography of the area, with particular attention to the Koran. He interrupted his studies only in order to travel—southward into the Holy Land, eastward to the Euphrates, then through the valley of the Orontes. He climbed holy Mount Hor, where Aaron departed this life, was arrested in Nubia as a spy, was expelled from the country, and reached Egypt. A pasha, challenging his knowledge of Moslem laws, made him submit to an examination by two Arabian savants. He passed the examination so brilliantly that he was permitted to make a four-month pilgrimage to Mecca, the "forbidden city," and then to join eighty thousand other pilgrims to Mount Arafat. Thereafter he enjoyed the title of "Haji." When in 1817, at the age of thirty-three, he died suddenly in Cairo in the midst of plans for more travels, he was given a solemn funeral as a haji and was buried in a Mohammedan cemetery.

The real name of "Sheik Ibrahim" was Johann Ludwig Burckhardt, born in Basel in 1784, scion of an ancient family of Swiss patricians which has down to the present day produced many important diplomats and historians. His oriental manuscript collection of some three hundred and fifty volumes passed to Cambridge University after his death, and his journals proved to be a gold mine for geographers, ethnographers, philologists, and archæologists. Editors, working over these journals, published the books which he himself had had time only to plan.

In one of these books, *Travels in Syria and the Holy Land* (London, 1822), he described a stone he had seen embedded in the corner of a building in the bazaar at Hamath on the Orontes: "A stone with a number of small figures and signs which appears to be a kind of hieroglyphic writing, though it does not resemble that of Egypt."

In 1822, of course, seventeen years before the appearance of Texier's description of his travels, no one paid any attention to this casual mention, especially since it was obscured by tales of far more thrilling adventures. Fifty-eight years passed—and two Americans, J. A. Johnson and a Dr. Jessup, were strolling through the bazaar at Hamath. They were, apparently, as sharp-eyed as "Sheik Ibrahim" had been. For they spotted not only the stone that Burckhardt had discovered before them, but three others "with a number of small figures and signs." A year later Johnson reported his find to the American Palestine Exploration Society. But he was unable to present any on-the-spot sketches of the stones, let alone rubbings. As soon as he approached the stones, intending to touch them, the natives had raised a hue and cry, gesticulated frantically, and looked to be on the point of attacking him. Obviously these mysterious signs had been the object of superstitious reverence from time immemorial. This conjecture was corroborated shortly afterwards when another stone covered with "hieroglyphs" was discovered in Aleppo. The natives ascribed curative powers to the symbols; sufferers from the prevalent eye disease of the Orient came long distances to press their foreheads against the stone, whose surface had long since been worn smooth.

Another year passed before a scientist had the opportunity to examine the stones without hindrance. He was
William Wright, an Irish missionary who at the time was
stationed in Damascus. Chance, which has played so important a part in innumerable discoveries, came to his aid.
For in 1872 the governor of Syria, a narrowly orthodox
Moslem hostile to the Western passion for investigation,
was deposed. His successor, Subhi Pasha, proved to be an
enlightened liberal spirit. Hearing of the Hamath stones,
he permitted the Reverend William Wright to accompany
him on an inspection tour. Meanwhile two other groups of
travelers had been in Hamath and made vain attempts to
see the by now notorious stones. But Wright, unlike his
predecessors, had the support of the governor, and the
pasha evidenced his good will in the most effective possible fashion—by sending soldiers. With their assistance
Wright chiseled the stones out of the walls of the buildings—a difficult task repeatedly interrupted by demon-
strations on the part of the natives who were firmly convinced that these stones were their remedy against rheu-
matism—as the Aleppo stone was supposed to cure
ophthalmia.

With the stones temporarily deposited in the pasha's
guest house, one of the bearers reported that the streets
were swarming with angry mobs. Rumor had it that fa-
natics intended to storm the building and destroy the
stones sooner than have them be sent abroad. The police
were said to be on the side of the people of Hamath.

"I saw now that a crisis was reached," Wright wrote.
Accompanied by an armed guard, he went out into the
streets. All eyes were fixed on him, with hatred and menace. He addressed the mob, assuring them that the pasha
would pay them ample compensation for the stones. The
crowd flung back scornful replies; they knew, they said,
what such promises of money were worth. Seeing their

mood, Wright took a stronger line. They must disperse and go about their business. If there were any violence, he said, the pasha would mete out dreadful punishments.

He returned to the guest house in a state of intense uneasiness. "It was an anxious and sleepless night," he noted.

The night passed without incident. The following morning Subhi Pasha, to the speechless amazement of the inhabitants, paid the promised price. But the indignation which firm words had temporarily suppressed and money had placated flamed up once more. Wild dervishes rushed through the streets crying aloud that a fiery rain of stars had descended during the night. The meteor shower had, as a matter of fact, been unusually brilliant. The people sent a delegation to the pasha, for was this not a sign from Heaven that the stones should not be removed?

The pasha considered the question for a long time. Then he asked whether the falling stars had done any damage. Had any people or domestic animals been killed? The delegates admitted that nothing of the sort had happened. Whereupon the pasha asked a Solomon's question: what better sign of Heaven's consent could there have been than that splendid display in the sky?

That settled the question. The trouble subsided. The stones were shipped off to Constantinople. William Wright was given permission to take impressions of them, and these were sent to the British Museum.

Texier had seen ruins in Northern Anatolia and had not known what to make of them. Wright had casts of the Hamath inscriptions and did not know how to interpret them. At the time, of course, there was no reason to suppose any connection between the ruins in Anatolia and the stones in Syria; there was no evidence for any link.

At this point, however, W. H. Skeene and George

Smith of the British Museum discovered near Jerablus on the right bank of the Euphrates a tremendous mound of ruins. They investigated and correctly identified the city with Carchemish, known from Assyrian sources. A few casual turns of their spades quickly brought to light figures that were also covered with mysterious symbols. And

SOLDIER, FROM CARCHEMISH.

now these fascinating signs, these human heads, hands, feet, animal heads, mingled with circles, crescents, hooks, and obelisks—all obviously forming a coherent script— began turning up all over the place. The most astonishing part of it was that their range was not limited to Northern Syria. F. J. Davis found the symbols beside a monumental relief in Ivriz in Taurus. Seals turned up likewise bearing this script. Before long there could no longer remain the slightest doubt that the hieroglyphs Texier had discovered along with the figures of the gods at Yazilikaya were at least similar to those found in Syria. Ultimately the mysterious script was found in the vicinity of Smyrna!

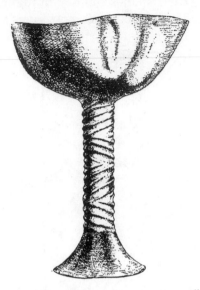

GOLDEN CHALICE, FROM ALAJA HÜYÜK.

Here was the most puzzling aspect of the whole situation. For if these symbols really did all belong to the same script—as seemed the case—then there must once have been a nation so powerful that its writing was used from the Ægean coast all the way through Anatolia and deep into Syria—a people with a unified script and therefore a unified culture. But aside from these symbols, and a few monuments that bore strong resemblances to one another, there was no evidence of the existence of such a nation. Nor were there any clues in the lore of other peoples.

Or was that quite the case? Were there, perhaps, certain citations which hitherto had not been understood?

In 1879—by which time it was clear that all the discussion had produced hardly any results—a British scholar examined the rock sculptures among the hills near Smyrna. A year later he delivered a lecture before the Society for Biblical Archæology in London. The talk was chock-full of references to the Bible, and presented a thesis that seemed, from the scientific point of view, utterly reckless.

The speaker, Archibald Henry Sayce, was only thirty-four at the time, but already one of the outstanding Orientalists of his day. Sayce stated his convictions that all the mysterious monuments and inscriptions which had been discovered during the preceding decades in such widely scattered spots in Asia Minor and Northern Syria must be ascribed to the *Hittites*—a nation mentioned in the Bible which had hitherto been dismissed as totally unimportant and had never become the subject of historical research.

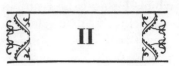

II

THE BIBLE AND NEW RESEARCH

FOUR YEARS BEFORE THIS, in 1876, Archibald Henry Sayce had already guessed the truth—purely in the course of his private Biblical studies. Writing about the Hamath stones the following year, he had boldly assumed that the strange symbols undoubtedly represented a script, and had even maintained that he could discern certain characteristic features of it. In 1879 he published an article unequivocally entitled "The Hittites in Asia Minor." But it was not until 1880, the year after his trip to Smyrna, that he delivered that epoch-making speech before the Society for Biblical Archæology. The lecture created such a stir that for some time he enjoyed the dubious notoriety of being the "inventor" of the Hittites.

Strictly speaking, the charge was mistaken on every count. Two years earlier Wright, the missionary, had already published a small article in the *British and Foreign Evangelical Review* attributing the recent finds in Asia Minor to the people known as the Hittites. But little attention was paid to his paper; its thesis was offered timidly, without the fire that such an announcement merited. It remained for Sayce to put the matter forcibly and in an arresting light, and this he certainly did.

The Sayce lecture stirred up lively debate which quickly moved out of scholarly circles into the forum of public opinion. A nation dead and gone for three thousand years suddenly made headlines in daily newspapers throughout England—for the British were, and are, fascinated by archæological questions as are no other people in Europe. Although fueled by little concrete evidence, the discussion raged with great heat. It reached a climax in 1884 when William Wright published a book that not only provided new material, but also bore the provocative title *The Empire of the Hittites, with Decipherment of the Hittite Inscriptions by Professor A. H. Sayce.* In the light of modern knowledge the contents of this book appear scanty indeed, but it may be said that its publication began the story of Hittitology. Its challenging thesis, that the Hittites had controlled a veritable *empire,* made it impossible for the Hittites to be ignored henceforth. From then on an incidental offshoot of Orientalogy slowly but surely developed into a special scientific discipline.

Wright's book was sensational because it described a discovery unique in archæology. Here was not knowledge gathered by systematic excavation, or confirmation of a theory already held. Instead, a whole nation had been rediscovered through accidental finds in the most scattered places. Wright was making the startling assertion that a third Great Power had been dominant in Asia Minor—a Power whose very existence had been forgotten even by Greeks and Romans who lived more than two thousand years ago.

What made Wright's bold statements particularly controversial was the extreme slimness of the evidence. For even when the evidence nearest at hand was taken for a starting-point, the path promptly led into the darkest regions. The Bible did, to be sure, mention the Hittites, but . . .

In the Hebrew Bible they were called *Hittim,* to which Luther gave the German form *Hethiter.* The English translators of the Bible rendered it as *Hittites,* the French as *Hétheens,* although they also later adopted the form *Hittites.* But the Book of Books mentioned them apparently only as one among a number of distinctly minor tribes. For example, in *Joshua* 3, 10: "Canaanites, *Hittites,* Hivites, Perizzites, Girgashites, Amorites and Jebusites." Abraham (*Genesis,* 23, 3–4) has a little more to say when he describes himself as a stranger before the *children of Heth* and asks them for a burying-place "that I may bury my dead out of my sight." Here is an indication that at some time the Hittites must have been the real rulers of the Promised Land. In still another passage, where the Bible goes into the geography of the various nations (*Numbers,* 13, 29), their name crops up again: "The Amelikites dwell in the land of the south: and the Hittites, and the Jebusites, and the Amorites, dwell in the mountains: and the Canaanites dwell by the sea, and by the coast of Jordan."

From these and a few other mentions in the Bible, the Hittite people would seem to have been a tribe inhabiting Syria, and of no particular distinction. There is one passage, however, which would have given historians pause long before Sayce if nineteenth-century science had not been so wary of the Bible as a source book for history. This was *Kings* II: 7, 6: "For the Lord had made the host of the Syrians to hear a noise of chariots, and a noise of horses, even the noise of a great host: and they said one to another, Lo, the King of Israel hath hired against us the kings of the Hittites, and the kings of the Egyptians, to come upon us." In contrast to all previous Biblical references, where the Hittites are coupled with tribes which never made any impression upon history, the Hittite kings are here named in one breath with the most powerful

monarchs of the ancient world, the Egyptian pharaohs—
are, in fact, even given precedence over the pharaohs.

But that was all the Bible had to offer on the subject.
Was this sufficient to support the thesis that the Hittites
had commanded an empire?

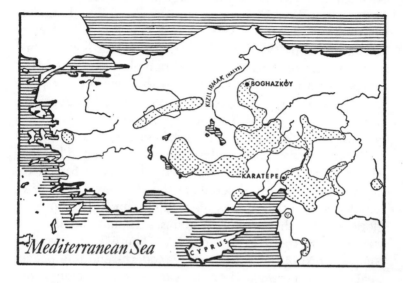

THE DOTTED AREAS INDICATE THE LOCATIONS OF HITTITE
RUINS, MONUMENTS AND INSCRIPTIONS. THERE ARE ABOUT 70
IN ALL. IT IS INTERESTING TO NOTE THAT THESE ARCHEOLOGI-
CAL FINDS OUTLINE THE POLITICAL EXTENT OF THE HITTITE
EMPIRE AS HISTORIANS HAVE RECONSTRUCTED IT AFTER THE
DECIPHERMENT OF THE CLAY TABLETS FROM BOGHAZKÖY
(HATTUSAS). COMPARE THE MAP PRECEDING THE TEXT.

Naturally Sayce and Wright did not rest their case on
this alone. They looked for other corroborative evidence—
and once the ice was broken the stream began to flow. Immediately after *The Empire of the Hittites* appeared, all

kinds of confirmations began pouring in, along with the
storm of argument. The obvious next step was to test the
new theory against all known ancient sources, especially
contemporary Egyptian and Assyrian information. But
these sources did not yield any overwhelming evidence.
Nevertheless, two facts did emerge which were arresting.
Did not the Assyrians repeatedly speak of the "Land of
Hatti" (or "Chatti")? And did not the Egyptians refer
constantly to battles with the "Heta"? (Heta is the arbitrary reading of the Egyptian hieroglyphic word *Ht*—the
Egyptian script used no vowels, so that our present pro-
nunciation of Egyptian words is not necessarily Egyptian;
rather it may be called "Egyptological"—that is, a pronun-
ciation based on our Egyptologists' assumptions.)

Egyptian sources disclosed evidence that Pharaoh
Thotmes III (fifteenth century B.C.) had been forced to
pay tribute to a certain people of the Hittites. There were
detailed accounts on the walls of Egyptian temples of the
glorious wars that the great Ramses II had fought and
won against the Hittites in Syria. There was also the
complete text of the unbelievably modern-sounding peace
treaty which terminated these wars—a pact crowned by
marriage between a Hittite princess and the pharaoh.

Certain details in the grandiloquent Egyptian battle
stories and, above all, the character of the peace treaty
should have given the archæologists and historians pause.
Other ancient records appeared to confirm the Egyptian
narrative. Assyrian King Tiglath-Pileser I (around 1100
B.C.) speaks of victorious battles in "Hatti Land." For a
span of some four hundred years mention of the Hittites
crops up again and again in Assyrian military annals, always as a nation organized in small city-kingdoms (especially in Carchemish, Samal, and Malatya in Northern
Syria) which never grew to be a really dangerous enemy
and which was consequently swallowed up by the Assyr-

ian Empire in 717 B.C., after the fall of Carchemish—an event which by no means seems to have shaken Asia Minor to its foundations.

Could such a nation, which appeared in contemporary accounts only as an enemy suffering continual defeats, have built up a civilization stretching from the Ægean throughout most of Anatolia? Knowing the facts as we do today, it is easy to say that merely the span of time during which references to a Hittite people occur in Egyptian and Assyrian records should have been a telling indication of the true power of these people. From Thotmes to the fall of Carchemish involves a period of no less than seven hundred years. A nation that was able to skirmish with those two superpowers of the Near East for so long a time must have been an empire to be reckoned with.

But the archæologists and historians of the eighties made vain attempts to explain this away. They disputed bitterly with Sayce, who month after month hurled fresh papers, enriched by new or different facts, into the fray. For years, however, no one contested the assumption, which we know today to have been totally wrong, that the Hittites were a nation of Northern Syria which for various reasons gradually expanded northward into Anatolia. Viewed in the light of this theory, the goals of Hittite military policy and cultural policy were diametrically opposed to one another. They supposedly fought their battles only in the south and apparently carried out cultural expansion to the north and northwest in a perfectly peaceful manner.

It was obvious that there was something peculiar about this. But what was it? Anyone who at that time had guessed and published the truth would have been ridiculed as an utter fool. In the 1880's the Hittite nation simply could not be fitted into any reasonable and meaningful historical picture. Once having made its great discovery, archæology seemed to have arrived at a blind alley.

In this situation, chance once more came to the rescue in 1887. As by a flash of lightning, much that was obscure was suddenly illuminated from a new quarter. The new light was the result of a ludicrous incident that happened hundreds of miles away, unexpectedly providing an important key to the Hittite mystery.

RELIEF FROM KARATEPE. MOTHER NURSING STANDING UP.

The story goes that the irate wife of an Egyptian farmer picked up some broken bits of clay to throw at a party of troublesome Europeans who were snooping around Tell el Amarna, about 225 miles downriver from Cairo, on the east bank of the Nile. The woman was trying to get rid of the foreigners; what she accomplished was the precise opposite. They began looking around the place for more of the same—and stumbled on the largest and most important clay-tablet archives that have ever been found, the records of the heretic king Amenophis IV.

We cannot be sure that this incident really took place, for no professional archæologist was on the spot when the first tablets from these precious archives were picked up. All we know for certain is that toward the end of the year 1887 some pieces were offered for sale in the markets of Egypt. They then turned up in the hands of antique-dealers at Cairo and were sold for ten piasters apiece. Since the Egyptian government had already passed strict laws regarding the disposition of antiques, the natives preferred to sell the tablets on the black market. That was ever so much more profitable than to turn their finds over to the government authorities for a token payment. In 1888 some two hundred tablets and fragments of tablets were on sale in Cairo. Sayce saw them there and reported them. Institutions and collectors promptly began buying, and the first specimens were sent to London and Berlin.

This traffic in clay tablets was not without its oddities. An Arab dealer named Abd-el-Haj of Gizeh showed some of his tablets to a museum official in Bulaq. The official declared that the tablets were obvious forgeries and refused to buy them. Whereupon the dealer, still representing them as genuine, hastily sold them to the Viennese collector Theodor Graf.

Today we know that these tablets from Amarna were genuine. After purchasing Graf's collection, the Berlin Museum found itself in possession of some 160 tablets, some of them of enormous size. A professional, the great British archæologist William Flinders Petrie, now took over. He started tracing the tablets back to their original source and on the basis of his investigations launched excavations at Tell el Amarna in November 1891. He dug there until the end of March 1892, making a succession of sensational finds. The archives yielded fascinating material about a particular segment of the middle of the second millennium B.C.

The Amarna tablets were readable, for the cuneiform script in which they were written had long since been deciphered. The language was Akkadian (Babylonian), in which international negotiations in the Ancient East were

AN ASSYRIAN REPRESENTATION OF THE CITADEL OF CARCHE-MISH (FOUND ON A BRONZE GATE AT BALAWAT). THIS DRAW-ING, THOUGH EXTREMELY PRIMITIVE, NEVERTHELESS CLEARLY SHOWS THE TOWERS AND BATTLEMENTS CHARACTERISTIC OF HITTITE ARCHITECTURE.

conducted. Among the finds were many letters supplying long-needed information on the importance of certain kings of other peoples—for example, of the Mitanni—who had hitherto been little more than names. Included were some royal missives which amounted to the most shameless kind of begging—sent by other kings who boldly called the pharaoh "brother," but who would be rudely turned down when they asked for a daughter of the pharaoh to add to their harem, although they had meekly to send their own daughters to the Egyptian king's harem. Dushratta, King of the Mitanni, wrote to Pharaoh Amenophis III: "You always maintained a very, very close friendship with my father. Now that we are friends, the friendship is ten times greater than with my father. Now, therefore, I say further to my brother: may my brother grant me ten times as much as to my father. Let my brother send me very much gold, immeasurably much gold; let my brother send me more gold than he did to my father!"

Nor is this letter a particularly flagrant example—it is a *typical* letter.

There were hundreds like it. But it was not this type of find, intriguing as it was, that excited the Egyptologists and Hittitologists. For them the archives were significant because they contained the diplomatic correspondence of one of the most interesting of the Egyptian pharaohs. Amarna was the new capital city which Amenophis IV (about 1370–1350 B.C.) had built for himself. Amenophis had been a starry-eyed intellectual on the throne of the pharaohs, a dreamer who did not see political realities because he did not want to see them. He had envisioned a new relationship between man and the gods, and had condemned the old Egyptian gods, the whole of the Egyptian pantheon. For him only one god mattered: the Sun God. He had his own name changed from Amenophis to Ikhnaton, "he in whom Aton [the Sun God] is satisfied." He also attempted to impose his private creed upon the whole Egyptian nation. No wonder the conservative Egyptian priesthood opposed him. It is hardly surprising that turbulence within Egypt was not the only result; the eternally combative peoples on the borders of Egypt would naturally seize the opportunity presented by a pharaoh more interested in religious thought than in military defense. They did not wait long to launch fresh attacks.

In those enormous Amarna archives, which could be read immediately, there were numerous reports of raids by bands of Hittite warriors across the far northern frontier of Egypt into Syria. But there were also actual Hittite letters indicating more amicable relations between the Hittites and the Egyptians. One tablet in particular had been sent by a "King of Hatti" with the mellifluous name of Suppiluliumas to Ikhnaton to congratulate the heretic Egyptian on his succession to the throne. This letter, since it was addressed to a pharaoh whose position in time had long since been established, provided scholars with the first definite date for a Hittite king. And the range of subjects in these Amarna letters for the first time proved unequivocally that Sayce and Wright had been correct: the Hittites had indeed been a Great Power, but they had not dwelt in Northern Syria, as had been assumed hitherto. It became clear that they must have infiltrated *into* Syria *from* Asia Minor, and that not before around 1400 B.C.

Two letters among the vast Amarna correspondence were in readable cuneiform script, but in an as yet unintelligible language. Labeled the "Arzawa letters" because they were addressed to a hitherto unknown king of Arzawa, these two were to prove of striking importance for Hittite research. Possibly these unrewarding clay tablets would have vanished into the vaults of some museum had not Ernest Chantre, a French archæologist, found in Boghazköy, in 1893, fragments of clay tablets which were undoubtedly written in the same unintelligible "Arzawa" language. This discovery gave rise to a new problem: had some one people speaking this same language been simultaneously dominant along the northern shore of the great bend of the Halys and along the Mediterranean coast of Asia Minor? The problem was so absorbing that a few years later one scientist whose specialty was actually Assyriology felt compelled to devote all his energies to solving it. And solve it he did.

But before we discuss his work we wish to give one example of how *excavations* were already being undertaken, even though ignorance and uncertainty dominated the proceedings. Without any conception of technique, out of sheer passion for exploration, men were already beginning to dig.

A small side trip provided the stimulus for the first excavations in the land of the Hittites.

While journeying in Southeastern Turkey three German archæologists, Otto Puchstein, Karl Humann, and Dr. Felix von Luschan, heard about a number of interesting reliefs at Zinjirli, in the foothills of the Taurus Mountains. Though they had little time at their disposal—the party was slated to leave Turkey in two days—Puchstein and von Luschan did not hesitate for a moment. They betook themselves to the spot to see what there was to be seen. They straightway found eight relief slabs *in situ,* which is archæologists' jargon for "at their original spots and in their original positions." Their pride in being the first to discover the plaques was quickly dampened, however. They learned that these reliefs had been dug up shortly before by Hamdy-Bey, general director of the Turkish museums, who might well be called both the first and foremost of Turkish excavators. It was clear, however, that the surface of the soil had barely been scratched and that it might very well conceal far richer finds.

Four years later, having received support from the Berlin Orient Committee, Humann was delegated by the Administration of the Royal Museums to go to Constantinople, request a concession for excavating at Zinjirli, and organize an expedition.

For the times, the preparations Humann made for his forthcoming expedition were exemplary. A few years earlier Schliemann had attacked the excavations at Troy with exuberant carelessness. At many excavation sites in those days the digging was little different from grave-robbing— a hunt for treasure rather than scientific research. But Humann got together an excellent archæological group. He provided for tents, army cots, kitchen equipment, overseers, masons, carpenters, blacksmith, and cook. He saw to it that all the necessary photographic apparatus and all sorts of special tools were at hand. Dr. Felix von Luschan of the Royal Museums in Berlin and his friend Franz Winter of the Archæological Institute in Athens were attached to his expedition.

Karl Humann and Felix von Luschan made a first-rate team. Humann, born in 1839 in Steele, in the Prussian Rhineland, threw into his work all the quick-witted liveliness of his breed. He was, moreover, already an experienced and famous man. A former civil engineer, he had for reasons of health been compelled to move to the milder climate of the South. (Forty years later similar considerations prompted the sportsman Lord Carnarvon to go to Egypt—where he and Howard Carter found the grave of Tutankhamen.) Digging as a young man on the island of Samos awakened his love for archæology. He did some work in cartography and from 1867 to 1873 directed road-building in the Near East. During all this time he never forgot archæology—and ultimately he became the discoverer and evcavator of the ancient city-kingdom of Pergamon. He began his work there in 1878 and finished it in 1886. The much-admired altar he uncovered was set up in a special museum in Berlin (to be destroyed during the Second World War).

Felix von Luschan was an Austrian, born in 1854 in Hollabrunn near Vienna, an anthropologist by choice, and a physician to boot—he had been a surgeon with the Austrian Army. This background was a great asset now that he was with an expedition working in the unsanitary conditions of the Near East.

The expedition's funds were limited, but generous by comparison with what modern expeditions must often get along on. Humann could in any case reckon on being able to stay in the field for three or four months and to employ about a hundred workers. It is of interest to note the equipment an expedition took with it in those days: twenty pickaxes, twelve mattocks (with a hundred extra handles), fifty-five shovels, twelve wheelbarrows, fifty-seven carrying-baskets, two windlasses, two crowbars, two sledge hammers, three ropes, one block and tackle, one heavy wagon with steel axles, one portable smithy, tools for all the various craftsmen, nails, cord, etc.

"I therefore had," Humann related, "tools for 170 or more men and could, moreover, easily replace broken articles." He does not add a single word about provisions for the comfort of members of the party. The time was as yet far in the future when expeditions would consider refrigerators and portable showers vital supplies for scientific work.

On April 5, 1888, the expedition set out from Alexandretta—following the old route of the crusaders, the same road on which some two thousand years earlier Cyrus the Younger and Alexander the Great had ridden through the dust. The road was still bad. It rained. It took them until seven o'clock in the evening to reach Islahié, a provincial capital which Humann called "a filthy, unhygienic hole containing some fifty hovels."

There was no better place for many a mile. And since Islahié was headquarters of the *kaimakam,* the provincial

magistrate, Humann could rally some official backing. He
was able to order wood for the barracks he planned to
build and to hire two more carpenters. Sunday, April 8,
they rode on; that is to say, the leaders rode on ahead.
Arriving in Zinjirli that evening, they suddenly discovered
that they numbered thirteen!

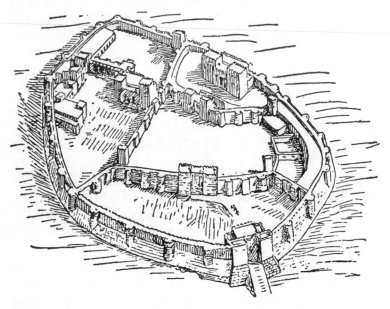

RECONSTRUCTION OF THE CITY AND CITADEL OF ZINJIRLI. THE
LAYOUT PROVIDED FOR SUCCESSIVE DEFENSE OF THE DIFFER-
ENT SECTORS. THE ROYAL PALACE WAS SITUATED AT THE
HIGHEST POINT.

Their first glimpse of the place on the following morning seemed to confirm the bad omen. Before them lay an
egg-shaped hill, against the western slope of which were
huddled the huts of the present dwellers, "frightfully dirty
inhabitants, Kurds and Anzarié." "The village was full of

filthy mud"; it was divided by a brook gone to swamp which wound its way among some eighty huts. And when Humann wanted to see the reliefs that Hamdy-Bey had excavated five years earlier, and which had been there for Luschan and Puchstein to see, he found that most of the plaques had been covered with earth again.

In spite of these inauspicious circumstances, they began excavating promptly on April 9. Word got around of the strange work these foreigners were engaged in. That extraordinarily high wages were being paid for plain ordinary digging in old rubble, and that there would even be a *baksheesh* for finding worked stones, generated such a vigorous word-of-mouth advertising campaign that by noon thirty-four and by the next day ninety-six workers were on the spot.

When the first day's work was done, the expedition had not only uncovered the five reliefs Hamdy-Bey had found, but had turned up four new ones. There was a warrior with shield, spear, and sword; there was a girl beside a wagon; there was a horse in the traces of a battle chariot. A courtyard, a gateway, then the gate itself, adorned with two lions, were brought to light. By the second evening the expedition had already accumulated twenty-six relief plaques. And the images of gods, men, and animals depicted upon them were different from anything known hitherto. There were, to be sure, resemblances to fragments that had been picked up here and there between the Euphrates and the Halys. But nowhere else had any such wealth of eloquent sculptures been turned up.

In the excitement that every archæologist before and after him has always felt when riddles begin cropping up out of rubble, Humann wrote: "So the first week came to an end, and our joyous excitement over these rich finds made us forget that the west wind was tearing our tents to shreds, that it was raining on our beds, in which we slept with an umbrella tucked under our arms, and that even inside these tents we were wading in filth."

What they uncovered was a fort. A round fort, staggering in size and stunning in ornamentation. Humann, who had read Sayce and Wright and was familiar with all the pros and cons in the argument, had not the slightest doubt that he was laying bare *Hittite* material. And he found such material not only within the fortified area itself. An Armenian schoolmaster led von Luschan and Winter to a distant village where there was an unmistakably Hittite relief: a woman sitting at a table, a man standing, facing her. And to the north of Zinjirli, about an hour's ride away, a Hittite inscription was found.

There were still many mysteries concealed in and around this hill. The temptation to deal in symbols when we plunge deep into the past is irresistible, and so we may report that a particular flower covered the hill with a rampant growth. The flower was asphodel, which grows wild in Asia Minor, and which the Greeks had called the "flower of the Nether World." What lay hidden beneath the earth which nourished its pale-yellow blossoms?

"This expedition can only be a preliminary," Humann wrote in his diary on May 4, 1888. He made a similar point in a letter to Berlin. "If I can only confirm the existence of an ancient palace, I shall probably have done all that can be accomplished this time and we can then think of starting a second campaign with greater certainty about our prospects."

But the weather hampered them. First it was cool and rainy; then, toward the middle of May, the hot and humid period usual to that climate descended upon them, and along with it snakes, scorpions, tarantulas, and myriads of mosquitoes. But then the expedition was once more given the kind of lift that only a good find provides. On May 3 a colossal lion was found. It had been buried tilted to one side, its head thrust upward, five yards below the fields of asphodel.

Humann approached the hill from the north and from the south, from east and west. But no matter how he attacked it, he could not arrive at any satisfactory picture of the layout. If he found one jamb of a gate, the expected counterpart was missing. If he found a sculpture which

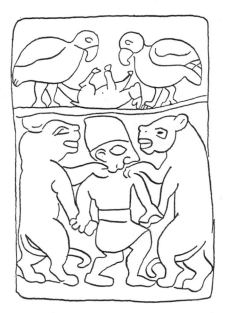

FROM THE NUMEROUS ANIMAL RELIEFS AT KARATEPE.

according to all archæological theories ought not to be an isolated piece, it turned out that this piece of sculpture actually had stood alone.

But dubious though his scientific results were at the time, Humann had to begin thinking about transportation for the material he had excavated. The experience of his predecessors stood him in good stead. The major problem

had always been the great weight of the various finds.
For—this was another oddity—the sculptors who had
been at work in this place had not carved their reliefs
on slabs of stone, but upon enormous blocks.

During the second week of May, Humann had the
eight reliefs chiseled off the gate of the great ring wall.
The backs were sliced off until the reliefs were only about
six inches thick, thus reducing the weight of the stone to
between five hundred and eight hundred pounds. The
Circassians of the neighborhood demanded ninety marks
for each wagonload, but the expedition's budget could
provide at most sixty-five marks. Humann sagely sent messengers a day's journey to Albistan. The first ten wagons
came from there, at a price of sixty-eight marks each.

But then the Orient took its revenge. On May 28 some
of the members of the expedition came down with fever.
Humann himself was flat on his back for five days. While
he was bedridden, a dispatch came from Hamdy-Bey, the
Turkish museum director, upon whose good will every expedition in those days was absolutely dependent. Hamdy-
Bey, in the friendliest fashion, asked Humann to meet him
on June 7 in Alexandretta. On the fifth, Humann, still very
ill, rode off, accompanied by Dr. von Luschan. He met
Hamdy-Bey on the appointed day and informed him of
the results of the excavations. With kindly insistence the
museum director urged him to go on at once to Constantinople and report there. There was no help for it; leaving
von Luschan to return to the site, the sick man boarded
ship for the Turkish capital. In Constantinople he succeeded in obtaining permission to send to Berlin twenty-
three reliefs, a stele, and all the smaller artifacts that had
been picked up. Immediately he sailed back to Alexandretta, where he arrived on June 11, and was back at
Zinjirli by the 13th. There he found only one healthy man

One of the "Hamath stones" that William Wright
pried out of the wall of a Syrian house in 1872.
It is meant to be read *bustrophedon* ("as the ox plows"):

ABOVE: How the reliefs of Yazilikaya looked to Texier in 1834—a good example of the way the artist's pencil is guided by the spirit and sensibility of his age. Compare these drawings with the photograph on opposite page. BELOW: View of the ruins of the temple at Boghazköy—drawing published by Charles Texier in his great travel book *Description de l'Asie Mineure.*

Modern photograph of detail of relief shown on opposite page. Compare with upper right corner. The Children's God, Sarruma, and two female goddesses.

Bronze male figurine, not pure Hittite; the extreme length of the legs indicates Syrian influence. From the end of the second millennium B.C. The apron is of silver. The eyeballs are oddly prominent, as in goiter, unlike the gods shown at right, whose eye formation is normal.

Man and woman—bronze statuettes a little over 12 inches tall. These probably represent household gods. The tiny crown on the headdress is not part of the design, but is the opening through which the bronze was poured.

Bronze stag.
A military standard from Alaja Hüyük.

A Hittite rouge pot of carved stone, 2 inches by 3½ inches.

Two plinths from the gate of the great temple of Boghaz-köy, cut from gigantic blocks of stone. The small picture suggests the accuracy with which the Hittite masons of more than three thousand years ago bored the hundreds of holes in which the pins of the huge doors turned. Their augers were rods of copper which they turned in wet sand.

left: Dr. von Luschan. All the rest of the European members of the expedition were down with fever.

Von Luschan had not been idle. Working from the south, he had penetrated into the "waste of burned rubble." The digging had been laborious and had yielded few results. But after a while four walls were uncovered, one of them no less than four yards across. The fever had wreaked such havoc with the orderly procedures and good

THE GOD TESHUB.

discipline of the expedition that soon only sixty laborers were showing up for work. Humann raised wages by a piaster (at that time worth about five cents); two days later 101 laborers were on the spot again.

The finds were of the most variegated types and origins. A Hellenistic coin would be found beside an Assyrian royal stele ten feet high; a Hittite bronze miniature would be lying next to a Roman bust; a Hellenistic elephant head alongside a Hittite inscription. A Kurd paid a call on the expedition's headquarters and related with flowery eloquence that he knew where "speaking pictures" could be seen. He led von Luschan and Winter to Oerdek-göl ("Duck Lake"). There they found a four-foot-high stele representing a banquet. The carving was done in the typical Hittite manner—but there was a nine-line *Phœnician* inscription.

All these finds were proof that here they stood upon soil drenched with the history of many peoples. This land was not going to tell its whole story clearly to the first digger who thrust a spade into it.

Now the fever began to rage in earnest, attacking even the natives. Some of the workmen had to be sent off to the more healthful climate of the mountains. Those who remained grew feebler with each passing day. The heat was growing more and more unbearable. "We called it a cool day if the temperature hovered around 100 in the afternoon." It was in such circumstances that transportation had to be organized.

On June 13 the first twelve oxcarts started off. On the road to Islahié, normally a journey of two hours, three of the wagons broke down. To heap insult upon injury, the other nine were confiscated by a Kurdish rural official swollen with his own importance. A letter of introduction from Hamdy-Bey did not sway the chieftain; only threats finally procured the release of the wagons.

The weak and feverish scientists were on the verge of despair. But next day one of the Circassians who had demanded such an outrageous price for transportation suddenly turned up with two strong horse-drawn wagons—which he was now willing to hire out for a reasonable sum. Other Circassians followed him, and soon wagon after wagon was rolling along the road to Alexandretta with the heavy slabs of stone. By June 30 eighty-two crates had been dispatched—to the natives just so many tons of chiseled stone, but to the scientist a picture book of an ancient, thrillingly unknown civilization.

One of the guards died of the fever. A saddened, dreary column of men and animals crept along dusty roads shimmering with heat waves, toward the coast. At last, toward noon of a fiery hot day, they saw the sea; they were four miles from Alexandretta. By the roadside was a small coffee house run by an industrious Negro; beside it was a well of icy water.

The next ship would not be sailing for another ten days anyway, would it?

They gave up in the face of those last four miles and pitched their tents. So, Humann wrote, they were able "to rest from our labors in sight of the blue sea." Perhaps this rest produced the optimism which led him to add: "The goal we had sought had been achieved; we had found the Hittite edifice we were seeking, and had not even had to dig very deep beneath the surface. Now we could approach a new campaign with courage, for the mound was no longer an unfathomable mass of rubbish. The curtain had been parted and it was now only a question of raising it entirely."

It should be said at the outset that Humann's estimate of his own work, and especially his hopes for the future, were vastly exaggerated. Just as exaggerated as the hopes of the first excavators of Carchemish, who had set to work in highly amateurish fashion in 1878. After their project was taken over by professionals like Ramsay, Hogarth, Lawrence, and Woolley, results of scientific importance were produced. But though interesting in their own right, the examples of the latest period of Hittite civilization which the excavations brought forth (belonging all to the first and not the second millennium B.C.) did not help to clarify the burning question of the day. For in this early stage of Hittitology the crucial problem was to establish whether the Hittites really had built an "empire" in the Near East.

It is very curious indeed that so well-conducted an expedition as Humann's yielded only incidental information, while an extremely ill-conducted undertaking some twenty years later brought to light really sensational finds which at last helped to solve the mystery about the role of the Hittites in the history of the Ancient World. An additional oddity is that the whole expedition—which was headed by Dr. Hugo Winckler (1863–1913), the German Assyriologist—took place only as the consequence of an accident of politics. For one of the best British archæologists had already received permission from the Turkish Government to dig at the city Texier had discovered, Boghazköy. At this time, however, the saber-rattling German Kaiser, Wilhelm II, was on better terms with Abdul-Hamid II, the Sultan of Turkey, than was the government of King Edward VII. This political amity rested on economic factors. In 1899 the Deutsche Bank had obtained the concession to build the Berlin-to-Bagdad Railway, one of the greatest railroad projects in the world. No wonder it was the German and not the Englishman who received the *ferman,* the official permit to dig at Boghazköy. In granting this concession the Sultan was making a gesture of friendliness toward the Kaiser, who liked to appear as a patron of archæologists—and here was a fine way to figure in this role.

As for the German scientist who left Berlin to tackle the mystery of the Hittites, he no more gave thought to these side issues of contemporary history which underlay his expedition than his British colleague would have done. In fact, he could not possibly have seen how these factors played a decisive part in his undertaking—only we, half a century later and viewing the whole picture—can see all this. It was this particular political combination that made Winckler the lucky man who took a decisive step toward the solution of the Hittite problem, a problem becoming more and more important to archæologists and historians. His method of approaching the task was thoroughly inadequate. But how can we carp at this, when his results, from the very first moment were so amazing?

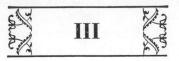

III

WINCKLER DIGS IN BOGHAZKÖY

THE PROBLEMS summed up by the very word "Hittites" were coming to a head. Now it is easy to apply hindsight and pick out the one coherent theme concealed amid the confusion of interpretations and misinterpretations advanced by the early investigators. But it was far from easy then. Let us see what the archæologist destined to make the next important discoveries had to say. In December 1907 Hugo Winckler wrote in the *Communications of the German Orient Society:*

"Along with the monuments of pure Asia Minor or Hittite civilization, occasional evidence had been turned up showing strong Babylonian influence upon these countries also. As chance would have it, at about the same time that the Tell el Amarna documents were discovered, clay tablets in cuneiform script came to light in Asia Minor. The site at which they were found proved to be a mound of ruins called Kültepe, near the village of Kara Hüyük about three hours journey to the east of Kayseri. Difficult to interpret and yielding little information, these tablets nevertheless proved the influence of the cuneiform script countries in Asia Minor, and so they added welcome evidence to the few letters from Asia Minor to the Egyptian Pharaoh which had been found at Tell el Amarna. Of these there were only a few items, meager in content, from Suppiluliumas, King of the Chatti, and two others which offered more enigmas than enlightenment. These were: 1) A letter to King Tarchundaraus of Arzawa from Amenophis III. That the land of Arzawa must have been situated somewhere in Asia Minor could be deduced; the precise location could not be determined. 2) A letter naming a certain Prince Lapawa who is elsewhere mentioned as a northern neighbor of the Kingdom of Jerusalem and whose seat must therefore have been somewhere in the vicinity of Carmel. How these isolated facts could be put together was a total puzzle. Nor could it be explained how a language which appeared to be that of the country of Arzawa came to be used in Palestine, in the area later occupied by Israel (Samaria)."

One possible solution had not as yet occurred to Winckler or the other archæologists of his day. Could the Arzawa letters have been written in the *Hittite* language?

Would that question be answered by the excavators' spades?

But first let us briefly sum up once more what the young science of Hittitology had accomplished up to the point where Winckler entered the picture. What, in other words, was the status of Hittite research at the beginning of the twentieth century?

First: Several travelers, Texier in particular, had reported monuments, reliefs, and inscriptions of a completely unfamiliar type in Central Anatolia and Northern Syria.

Second: A. H. Sayce had recognized that these monuments, scattered all the way from Smyrna to Northern Syria, must be relics of a single folk which he correctly identified with the Hittites mentioned in the Bible.

Third: From Egyptian and Assyrian sources, from certain clay tablets found in the area between Boghazköy

and Kayseri, and above all from the Egyptian-Hittite correspondence in the Amarna archives, it had been amply
demonstrated that Sayce's and Wright's hypothesis was
right: the Hittites had indeed been a Great Power. Moreover, the names of a few Hittite kings were now known.

Fourth: Scholars had determined that three principal
languages and scripts had been in use among the Hittites:
the Akkadian language in cuneiform script (readable and
intelligible); the Hittite language in cuneiform script
(readable but not intelligible); and hieroglyphic Hittite,
as found on the Hamath Stones (neither readable nor intelligible). In the next chapter we will deal with these
perplexing matters.

Fifth: On the basis of the Arzawa letters, a single
scholar, the Norwegian Knudtzon, had come to the conclusion that cuneiform Hittite was an Indo-European language. He had, however, retracted this assertion.

Sixth: Sayce and several others had deciphered the
first few symbols of hieroglyphic Hittite, in particular the
ideograms for "city," "country," and "king"; but they could
not prove that their readings were correct and were nowhere near being able to read the language.

Seventh: On the basis of all other documents which
at that time could be read, it had been assumed that the
center of Hittite power had lain in Central or Northern
Anatolia, not, as the Biblical texts suggested, in Northern
Syria. The finds at Zinjirli, where the first sizable excavations in a Hittite cultural area were undertaken, had been
recognized as Late Hittite, thus neither proving nor dis-
proving this important theory. Still, the reliefs and the outlines of the city uncovered there permitted some conclusions about the religion, architecture, and general cultural
influences in the life of the Late Hittites.

Such was the body of knowledge at Winckler's disposal
when he started out on his expedition. Actually, what was

known consisted largely of questions. But in science it is the framing of the right questions that leads to new discoveries.

Winckler's first expedition was rather amateurish even though there were great models which could have provided him with guidance. A few years before, Arthur Evans had begun his excavations at the palace of Knossos on the Island of Crete. Robert Koldewey had only recently started digging at Babylon. Both these expeditions were splendidly conducted.

It may be that the cloud which overhung the expedition from the start had something to do with Winckler's personality. Born in Graefenhainichen, a small town in Saxony, in 1863, Winckler became a prominent Assyriologist. He had already done some excavating at Sidon in 1903–4 before he went to Anatolia. Nevertheless, he affected everyone as he did Ludwig Curtius, who became his assistant the following year. Curtius, who had distinguished himself as an archæological annalist, wrote: "I had looked forward with great eagerness to working with an Orientalist whom I could not help imagining as a much-traveled man-of-the-world. I was consequently not a little surprised, upon meeting Winckler in Constantinople, to find an unimpressive looking fellow with a brown, unkempt beard, wearing a sports shirt with red silk trim, and conducting himself in a petty-bourgeois manner little suited to the real Orient. There was nothing at all of the man-of-the-world about him."

Moreover, Winckler was one of those unfortunates who always make enemies and seldom find friends, and he was "full of resentment against everyone who was more successful than himself." In addition he was utterly intolerant of scientific opponents. He was fanatically convinced that everything worthwhile in the world had origi-

nated in Babylon; any other view he took as a personal
affront and forthwith despised any humanist who dared to
speak up for the umbilical tie between Western and Greek
culture.

To top it all off, he was an anti-Semite—very odd indeed for a passionate Orientalist. It may be that the
protracted, ultimately fatal, illness that struck him in 1913

PRIESTESS, FROM CARCHEMISH.

was to blame for his irascibility and for his numerous inconsistencies. In spite of his anti-Semitism he was content
to have his first archæological explorations subsidized by
Jewish financiers. And far from transposing his profound
dislike for Jews into racial theories, Winckler was the man
who wrote a sentence that the jack-booted anti-Semites
and race theorists ought to have learned by heart: "Civilized peoples are never racially pure; rather they are always the product of a large number of strata formed by
more or less different races."

Funds for the exploratory probe were provided by
Baron Wilhelm von Landau, a disciple of Winckler's, who
had already financed the Sidon expedition. Companion,

collaborator, government official, and executive head of the expedition all rolled into one was Theodore Macridy-Bey, who had worked with Winckler at Sidon. A functionary of the Ottoman Museum in Constantinople, Macridy-Bey was the Oriental counterpart to Winckler. Curtius, who in all the five hundred-odd pages of his memoirs has hardly an unkind word to say for any person he describes, speaks of Macridy-Bey as a man "with impenetrable black eyes in a smooth-shaven face yellowed by malaria . . . Macridy-Bey," he continues, "was the most curious mixture of half-taught dilettante and passionate enthusiast; of secret dickerer and loyal official faithfully obeying the orders of his superior, Halil Bey. . . . He would without warning drop all interest in archæology and devote himself solely to his own pleasure. He might be full of noblesse and charm today, might be a cynical intriguer tomorrow . . . Sometimes he seemed to me like Iago in *Othello!*"

Although Winckler and his associates were by no means inexperienced, they set out on their first exploration like the rankest amateurs. They traveled by railroad as far as Angora; there they expected to stock up in short order on the things they most urgently needed. Aside from the fact that in the Orient you cannot buy anything at all if you attempt to do it in a hurry, Angora at that time was an insignificant group of mud huts surrounding the old castle hill. (Today, under the new name of Ankara it is the capital of Turkey, has 287,000 inhabitants, broad boulevards, modern bank buildings, and a man-made lake—all the creation of the dictator Kemal Atatürk.) The party took three days to make its purchases. Winckler, who could ill adapt to new situations, was driven to the point of madness by all the haggling. They could not even find good horses; nothing but worn-out mares were available. "For

saddles we had those painful Oriental devices which in
Europe would undoubtedly find a place of honor in the
torture chambers."

They set off at last on October 14, very late in the year
for Turkey. Winckler, the Orientalist, felt the Orient as
a hostile place. By day he suffered from the heat, by night
from the cold. He was upset by the most trivial incidents
and argued about everything and nothing.

The ride lasted five days. Nights the company camped
around a fire or put up at a *musafir-oda,* the shelter which
even tiny villages provide for wayfarers (the custom is for
each villager in turn to provide hospitality for a day).
Winckler preferred these to the *khans,* the old caravan-
series where he found too many *tacht-biti*—vermin. On
the other hand, in the *musafir-odas* he often had to share
his bed with cattle. "However," he remarked, "these beasts
are decidedly good-tempered and far less repugnant to
human nature than the rest of the inhabitants, whose im-
portunate servility toward outsiders is equaled only by
the Christian Syrians."

Conditions were different in Boghazköy, however.
Outwardly nothing had changed here since Texier's visit
seventy-one years before. But in the past two decades a
good many outlandish foreigners had come by and almost
immediately upon their arrival had asked with unseemly
haste whether any old walls were to be seen. And all these
foreigners had found the same cordial host, the landowner
Zia Bey. Endless tracts of land belonged to him, but he
was not allowed to cross the borders of his province—for
he was a member of the ancient Seljuk nobility still feared
by Sultan Abdul-Hamid, a hypochondriac perpetually ter-
rified of plots. Zia Bey had become a mixture of farmer
and aristocrat; he rode the noblest horses, always accompanied by his magnificently uniformed body-servant Is-
mail, but he himself preferred to dress in the collarless

peasant blouse, with slippers on his feet instead of riding boots. It was he who had sent a clay tablet, brought him by one of his peasants, to Constantinople where Macridy-Bey had seen it and called Winckler's attention to it.

Zia Bey, then, gave them a warm welcome. As prominent strangers they were entitled to silk mattresses. As Winckler tells the story, Macridy was the first to jump up and begin scratching himself. Winckler demanded a new

MEN OF CARCHEMISH PAY TRIBUTE TO SALMANASAR. FOUND IN TEMPLE RUINS AT RALAWAT.

bed. The servants were delighted; what an inexhaustible topic of conversation this would be: men who made a fuss about a few little bugs. With much to-do they brought new beds—which were no less alive.

On October 19 the work began. Winckler and Macridy examined the ruins and retraced the footsteps of Texier and all the other travelers after him. They themselves, however, were looking for something particular now: where was the spot where the tablets with the curious symbols had been found? When the natives of Boghazköy finally grasped what the strangers were after, they amiably brought fragments of tablets—as far as they were concerned there was nothing precious about these things. When they herded their sheep along the great old walls and one of the animals started off in the wrong direction, they thought nothing of throwing such fragments of clay at it—there were plenty of the broken tablets lying around. Winckler and Macridy were up and about from dawn till dusk; they narrowed a circle around the main source of the tablets and then discovered that at the spot where, according to the natives, especially large pieces of inscribed tablets were to be found, an excavator had already been at work. "This discovery, however, did not at all arouse any resentment in us," Winckler noted—most unusually for him. The reason was that the digging revealed itself as planless and casual in the extreme. Winckler was gratified to see that his predecessor had lost courage and given up far too soon. He already sensed that he was about to make a big find. For although after three days of incessant activity they had to stop their preliminary exploration—the rainy season had caught them by surprise and turned the plain into a sea of mud—they already had with them, carefully wrapped up, no less than thirty-four fragments of Hittite clay tablets. Since in the normal experience of excavators a *single* tablet may well constitute an important find, this was a tremendous, a sensational result of their efforts. But Winckler correctly guessed that still more and different treasures could be extracted from this soil. Describing the road back and the inn in Nefesköy, he, who usually grumbled and paid not the slightest attention to the wild beauty of the Anatolian landscape, records that he could not sleep and went to the door late at night to consider the future—and to look at the stars.

In less than a year Winckler had made a find such as no one had dared to hope for.

The expedition of 1906 was financed by the German Near Eastern Society and the Berlin Orient Committee, several private patrons providing funds for these groups. On July 17, 1906, Winckler and Macridy returned to Zia Bey's *konak*, as the "palace" was called. By now they were old friends. "We had kept up the best of relations with the Bey. He had made many requests—from a bottle of good cognac to helping him out of a 'temporary embarrassment.' By way of return he had repaid us after his fashion. A strike had been settled without any further fuss by an order from him. Little friendly services are worth their while in the Orient!"

At the fortress mound (*buyukkale*) they set up their headquarters tent. Winckler, feeble and ill, suffered from the heat and the bad food prepared by the Bulgarian cook whom they had hired because he spoke a little German. The archæologist huddled in a rude wattle hut, hat on his head, swathed in shawls, gloves on both hands. Often moaning with pain, he made copies of the clay tablets that were brought to him in a steady stream.

That Winckler, the excavator at the site, was able to draw immediate conclusions from his work was altogether unusual. It seldom happens that archæologists are also philologists, capable of using linguistic knowledge to exploit the results of their excavations. Moreover, here at Boghazköy the political correspondence of a nation virtually unknown until recently was readable the moment it was uncovered. The reason was that the Hittites of Boghazköy had composed their important documents and letters in Akkadian which was, as we have mentioned earlier, at one time the language of international communications in the Orient. Philologists had no trouble understanding Akkadian, especially when it was written, as it was here, in a script that had also long since been deciphered: Babylonian-Assyrian cuneiform writing.

It was a tablet of this sort that Winckler, sitting in his wattle hut, received into his gloved hands one day. As he deciphered it, this sick, embittered man became wild with excitement.

He recalled the Egyptian hieroglyphic inscriptions that had given archæologists their first hints of the existence of a nation known as the "Hatti" (or "Chatti"). Among these was an inscription on a temple wall at Karnak mentioning a treaty between Ramses the Great and Hattusilis III, King of the Hatti. (Those idiotic Egyptologists read the name as Chatasar, but he, Winckler, already knew it should be Chattusil, the "ch" representing the rough German aspirate!) Of course treaties in the ancient world were usually drawn up in several texts, just as they are today, and almost always in the languages of all the countries concerned. But was it not wildly fantastic for him to hope that after more than 3,100 years a full report on this treaty could be found, not chiseled into stone as it was in Egypt, but inscribed on a fragile clay tablet in the land of the other partner to the treaty, more than 1,200 miles from the temple wall at Karnak? Winckler had had such a dream and had put it out of his mind. Such a find would border on the miraculous; it would be comparable to such archæological wonders as Schliemann's discovery of Troy on the basis of the Homeric descriptions, or Layard's finding Nimrud. Comparable most of all, in fact, to George Smith's amazing triumph—in the eighteen-seventies Smith had traveled from London to Nineveh to find a few clay tablets that were needed to complete the Gilgamesh epic, and had found them!

And now a similar miracle had taken place. Winckler, the dry scientist and chronic invalid, kept shaking his head in awe as he wrote with feverish enthusiasm:

"On August 20, after some twenty days of digging, the breach into the gravel of the hillside had advanced as far

as a first sectional wall. Below this wall a beautifully preserved tablet was found, which even in outward appearance looked promising. I glanced at it—and all my previ-

A RELIEF FROM TELL HALAF. PERHAPS A REPRESENTATION OF
THE HITTITE-HURRIAN COSMOLOGY: BULL-MEN, DEMONS OF
THE ABYSS, UNITE THE EARTH WITH THE FIRMAMENT AND
SUPPORT THE STARS AND SUN.

ous experiences vanished into nothingness. Here it was,
the very thing I might perhaps jestingly have longed for
as a pious wish: a letter from Ramses to Chattusil on their
mutual treaty. True, in the past several days more and
more small fragments had been found in which there was

mention of the treaty between the two states, but here it was now confirmed; the famous treaty, known from the hieroglyphic inscription on the temple wall at Karnak, was now to have fresh light cast upon it by the other treaty-making side. Ramses, with his titles and descent given exactly as in the text of the treaty, was writing to Chattusil, who was also quoted, and the content of the letter was in places verbally identical with paragraphs of the treaty."

Then he went on to speak of his emotions:

"With what strange feelings I of all persons regarded this document. Eighteen years had passed since I encountered the Arzawa letter of el Amarna in what was then the museum of Bulaq, and since in Berlin I learned the Mitanni language. At that time, in the course of following up the facts disclosed by the find at el Amarna, I had expressed the supposition that the Ramses treaty might originally have been composed in cuneiform script —and now I was holding in my hands one of the letters exchanged in the course of discussion of the treaty—in the finest cuneiform script and in good Babylonian!"

It was time to be thinking of a more thorough and carefully prepared expedition for the following year, 1907. For already Winckler had become convinced that the object of his excavations was not just any Hittite city, but that he was actually standing on soil covering the *capital* of the Hittite Empire. There were, after all, so many important government documents lying around here. Would not the state archives normally be located at the king's residence? And was not the king's residence as a rule identical with the capital of the country? But if that were so, what was the name of this city? In the Ancient East the name of the country and the name of the capital were frequently one and the same. Winckler therefore deduced that the "Land of Chatti" must have had as its capital the

"City of Chatti." And as it turned out, his guess was right. Today we write the name of this city "Hattusas," but the principle stands; the name is only a more modern reading based upon greater philological knowledge.

It was really an incredible piece of good fortune. With his first efforts Winckler had laid bare the heart and brain of the Hittite Empire, the city which had briefly enjoyed the glory of being ranked equal to Babylon and Thebes. Recognizing the magnitude of his find, Winckler wrote in 1907: "These newly-revealed archives will keep more than one man busy far into the future." He himself went on working, and his second year proved more successful than the first—although some of the incidental circumstances were distinctly unpleasant. But Winckler was quite right —today, nearly fifty years later, profitable excavation is still going on at Boghazköy.

It is no wonder that Winckler now felt that he belonged to Boghazköy. But in this twentieth century, archæological undertakings are no longer a matter of pure enthusiasm. The days of excavations by adventurous amateurs—Layard in 1845 setting out with sixty pounds in his pocket and discovering Nineveh; Belzoni in 1817 opening Egyptian royal graves with battering rams—those days were long since gone. To go on working, Winckler had to raise more money.

Pressure of necessity forced him to ask help from his fellow classical scholars whom he, as a Pan-Babylonian, so thoroughly disliked. The Director of the German Archæological Institute in Berlin was Otto Puchstein, whose whole personality was the direct opposite of Winckler's. Puchstein was a man of the world, the leading cosmopolitan gentleman among the German archæologists—and at the same time a first-rate scientist. He also had a sense of irony, for after listening to Winckler's plans he expressed

regret that the Institute was in no position to finance such
an indubitably important expedition without outside assistance. But he offered to interest a well-known philanthropist—on condition that Winckler himself undertake to
discuss the financial question directly with the prospective
patron.

The memorable encounter took place promptly.
Winckler, the strong anti-Semite, found himself confronting James Simon, the Jewish banker. We owe our knowledge of the pithy conversation once more to Ludwig
Curtius, although this writer was not present and does not
name his source:

"James Simon asked him how much he needed to continue his excavating. Winckler replied: 'Thirty thousand
marks.' Whereupon James Simon took out his checkbook,
wrote a check for the sum, and with a smile handed it to
the petitioner. Puchstein, for his part of the expedition, received an equal amount from the private funds at the disposal of the Kaiser."

For his own sake and in the general interests of
archæology, Puchstein had insisted on one condition: the
work in Boghazköy must also direct attention to the architecture of the city. This was a perfectly logical request.
Since Texier's visit, after all, it had been known that Boghazköy contained the remains of temples, towers, and
fortifications. No one disputed the fact that further investigation of the inscriptions was important, but study of the
architecture was just as important. That would have been
obvious to anyone not so fanatically monomaniac as
Winckler in hunting down inscriptions. Winckler assented
to Puchstein's idea, but with great reluctance, and as
events proved, did not live up to the agreement very well.

As was by now customary, the new expedition of 1907
started out from Zia Bey's *konak*. This time a gargantuan

feast was given in the *selamlik*, the largest living room, whose walls were lined with silken tapestries. The foreigners sat upon precious rugs between their host and the *imam* (the priest-magistrate). Boys bearing bowls and napkins washed their hands and sprinkled them with fragrant perfumes. Dainties and lemonade were served first. Then the servants trundled into the room, a seven-foot-long copper platter loaded with delicacies. Curtius, who was with the expedition as an assistant, noted with the carefulness of a trained scientist that the platter was covered "with verses from the Koran in fifteenth-century Kufic script!"

The guests took up their spoons—there were neither knives nor forks—and ate the first course, a milk soup. Here is Curtius's account:

"The length of the menu filled us with anxiety. The laws of Oriental politeness require the guest to eat a great deal; no one may excuse himself on grounds of slender appetite or pretended weak digestion. The Bey served the guests with his own hands. Although the first morsel of all these courses tasted good, the extraordinary amount of fat employed in the cooking, the unfamiliar mixtures of spices, the mountainous portions heaped on our plates, and above all the use of the hands in eating—a custom which still obtained at the table of Louis XIV in elegant Versailles—all caused us the greatest difficulty. The last course consisted of a whole sheep roasted on a spit and brought in on a gigantic platter—one of that breed of fat-tailed sheep which are the pride of the region. How describe my horror when the Bey, with his right hand, ripped a large chunk of fat out of the tail and laid it on my plate as a sign of special honor.

"The cook standing at the Bey's side had to taste every course as it was served, to relieve us of fear of poisoning. While we dined, there stood humbly behind the Bey's chair, just back of his *kavasses* or bodyguards, a group of about a dozen persons. Throughout the meal they did not utter a word. These were his male relatives and the lower clergy, who were also guests, but invited as guests of the second rank and served after us.

"Dessert consisted of terribly sweet pastry. Afterwards the servants again went around with basins, ewers, and towels and washed everyone's hands. We then stood up and the magnificent table top was lifted and trundled out . . ." And Curtius, still an enthusiastic scientist in spite of the ordeal he had just gone through, adds: ". . . at which point I seized the opportunity to examine it more closely."

The question was: what, after this staggering send-off, did the expedition accomplish? Since we do not wish to falsify Winckler's results in the light of hindsight, it is best to let Curtius continue to report. He is an unbiased witness; aside from his natural integrity, he was a "classical" archæologist and therefore had a healthy detachment about the whole problem. Curtius writes:

"Winckler himself did not take the slightest part in the actual excavating. He sat in his study all day long and read the texts of the quantities of cuneiform clay tablets that were being turned up every day, in order to obtain a bird's-eye view of their contents. Macridy saw no reason to give us any information about the place or the manner in which these tablets had been discovered. His liaison man, who served as a kind of chief foreman of the laborers, was a handsome, lanky young Kurd by the name of Hassan dressed entirely in the brown of his native costume. One morning I noticed this man leaving our house, which had been built half way up the excavation site, with a basket and a pickaxe. He headed for the large temple in the plain below. I followed him to see what he intended doing there. And I saw in Room 11 of the big temple fully preserved clay tablets which were lying diagonally in neatly-stratified rows. The Kurd attacked them as casually as a peasant woman digs potatoes out of her field and broke off enough pieces to fill his basket. With this harvest he returned to our house and turned the tablets over to Macridy-Bey, who triumphantly delivered them to Winckler.

"It bothered me to see the digging at this extremely important site left in the hands of Hassan. But when I proposed assisting him in surveying the site and investigating the place for the presence of ceramics, I had a run-in with Macridy. According to our contract I had no business there, he replied. He himself would do all the reporting on the excavation of clay tablets. He never did so. But my clear memory of those tablets in orderly rows contradicts the explanation offered by Puchstein that they had come to lie where they were because they had been used as rubble fill. Their location can only be explained by assuming that they had been archives stored originally in a chamber above the cellar in which we found them and had slid down as the result of a disastrous fire. At the time Macridy would only permit me to look through the Kurd's daily yield for fragments of vases. But among these very clay tablets no shards at all were found. This, too, is an argument against the theory of rubble fill."

Such a method of excavation violated the most elementary rules of archæological research. Winckler and Macridy were working as crudely as Schliemann during his first excavations at Troy—but at least Schliemann had the professional scientist Dörpfeld to keep an eye on him. Horrified though he was, Curtius was far too young to intervene authoritatively. Important finds were being piled in heaps; the connection between individual pieces and their surroundings could no longer be determined; the

stratum depths of the finds were not being noted. Faced
with these unassorted heaps of clay tablets it was impossible any longer to say whether they had come from the
citadel or the temple. In all probability the workmen's
hands had sundered pieces that belonged together, and no
one had so much as told them to take care.

And yet—the site was so rich, so productive in spite of
all the bungling, that in the end everyone went wild with
enthusiasm. Winckler found a total of more than 10,000
fragments of clay tablets, including some that were
splendidly preserved. This was the greatest yield from an
archæological excavation since the finding of King Assurbanipal's clay-tablet library at Nineveh and the archives
at Tell el Amarna.

Even the archæologists who were there to study the
architecture were not entirely cheated. Living here within
sight of the kings, sphinxes, and lions, able to pace off the
miles of city walls, they were able to form some approximate picture of the extent of Hittite power. For the first
time also they recognized the independent and native element of Hittite culture— "self-taught, original, and savage." In Boghazköy "a bold, imaginative, but also crude
and rather barbarous, grandeur was a constant reminder
of the Mycenæan civilization of Greece." This was a
startling comparison to all those who had not seen Hittite
buildings and had scarcely even heard of them, for at that
time the Mycenæan ruins were considered to be absolutely the mightiest remains of the newly-discovered early
history of Europe.

At the foot of the paved rampart of the castle wall,
which was crowned with towers, the party discovered
what is called a *poterne,* a sally-port in the shape of a tunnel two hundred and twenty feet long, connecting the in-
terior of the city with the terrain outside the wall. They
attempted vainly to crawl through, but were blocked by

the mud and rubble of millennia. When these were at last cleared away and they were able to walk erect through the tunnel for the first time, they were so overwhelmed by emotion that Curtius, writing almost fifty years after the event, said:

"Af'er we had had it cleared, we celebrated a kind of second opening day for it, solemnly walking upright through the tunnel—the first persons to do so after perhaps more than three thousand years. We were honoring not ourselves, but the great and nameless architect who had conceived this impressive structure."

It was still 1907 when Winckler published his preliminary report [1] on the results of the excavations and his readings of the first clay tablets. Among other things this paper contained the first, and of course still incomplete, king list of the Hittites. The list covered the period from about 1350–1210 B.C., from Suppiluliumas to Arnuwandas IV, and it supplied phonetic readings of these kings' names based on evidence rather than on the mere assumptions of the Egyptologists. Thus, to give only two examples, Sapalulu was corrected to Suppiluliumas, and Maurasar to Mursilis.

"This unpretentious little work," a specialist in the field declared many years later, "will always have to be considered one of the most important productions of Orientalogy."

In that same year, 1907, a thirty-one-year-old English archæologist, John Garstang, was traveling through Syria and Anatolia. He dug at Sakje-gözü and called on Winckler at Boghazköy, where he looked around with eager interest. Three years later he published *The Land of the Hittites: An Account of Recent Explorations and Dis-*

[1] *Vorläufiger Bericht.*

*coveries in Asia Minor, with Descriptions of the Hittite
Monuments, with Maps and Plans, Ninety-nine Photo-
graphs and a Bibliography*. This fat volume was, after
Wright's and Sayce's largely theoretical treatises, the first
major attempt at drawing a comprehensive picture of the
Hittite Empire based upon documents and monuments.

FABULOUS BEAST, FROM CARCHEMISH.

For years Garstang's book remained the standard work
in Hittitology. This was inevitable, for the number of
readable texts (texts in the Akkadian language and Babylonian-Assyrian cuneiform script, that is) was limited; and
at that stage of Hittite research, archæologists, while finding more and more monuments, were not yet able to offer
an intelligible interpretation of them.

Winckler himself dug once more in Boghazköy, in
1911–12. He was already fatally ill. He had to have in
constant attendance upon him a nurse whom he gave out
to be his wife—to satisfy the austerely moralistic natives.
D. G. Hogarth, Leonard Woolley, and T. E. Lawrence dug

at Carchemish on the Syrian border from 1911–14. Winckler's clay tablets were deposited in the Berlin Museum; sculptures and hieroglyphic inscriptions from Carchemish were sent to the British Museum, and in later years to Ankara. But Hittitology had reached an impasse. Something had to be done, some new approach was needed. But was not this new approach ready at hand? It seemed obvious that the initiative would now have to pass from the excavators to the linguistic scientists.

Many of the clay tablets from the Boghazköy archives had been deciphered by Winckler, but there were a great many others still available—written in the unknown, incomprehensible "Arzawa language," that is, in Hittite. The next task would seem to be to look for missing information in the Hittite texts—in other words, to make the Hittites explain themselves.

When Winckler died in 1913, his will was found to contain references to years of work on the deciphering of "cuneiform Hittite." But no notes or manuscripts of his could be located. Then World War I descended upon Europe. Excavations were abruptly halted—only a few Turkish scientists continued to dig here and there, but they worked unsystematically and with little success. The long and fruitful co-operation between British and German specialists also came to a halt—between the Berlin Museum and the British Museum ran long lines of trenches and flaming artillery. Archæological research withdrew from the site of diggings to the quiet of the study. And there, in the study of one scholar, a discovery was made which opened new vistas for the young science of Hittitology. That discovery was the decipherment, or to put it more accurately, the linguistic exploration of cuneiform Hittite.

At a time when all of Europe was locked in deadly combat, a mere lieutenant in the Austrian Army made it possible for a scholar to spend the four war years investigating a dead language instead of firing a machine gun. For that service he achieved immortality in the history of philology. In his preface to his decisive book on the language of the Hittites,[2] the Czech scholar Hrozný acknowledges his gratitude to one Lieutenant A. Kammergruber for his "understanding consideration of the author's work." In his easygoing Viennese way, Kammergruber had exempted the young student of Hittite from all military duties.

[2] *Die Sprache der Hethiter, ihr Bau und ihre Zugehörigkeit zum Indogermanischen Sprachstamm.*

Part II

THE RIDDLE OF THE SCRIPTS

BAS RELIEF FROM ENINK.

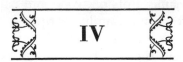

IV

ON THE ART OF DECIPHERING

Tᴀ HERE IS NOTHING about the study of ancient civilizations which appears more mysterious than the black art of reading inscriptions which have been buried under sand and rubble for thousands of years—inscriptions whose authors belonged to nations that had died out just as long ago, to whom we are linked by no ties of race and by only the slightest and most general ties of historical continuity. Yet this black art is being practiced with ever greater success today.

Problems of decipherment can be of many different sorts. The Latin script is still being written by everyone today, although the language is dead. Everybody can read an inscription two thousand years old on a Roman triumphal arch. A good many persons can not only read it, but understand it. Latin as a popular language did not long outlast the Roman Empire; but as a language of culture it has survived the centuries down to our own days. It is a dead language—but knowledge of it has never been lost.

This ideal situation did not exist for most of the languages and scripts of the ancient Orient. The archæologists of the last century salvaged from the earth innumerable literary monuments—inscriptions in stone, clay tablets, seals, manuscripts on wood and papyrus. Some of these were written in a familiar script—but the language was incomprehensible. In the case of others the language was known—but the symbols of the script were an enigma. Still others were composed in unknown languages and written with unknown symbols. To make matters still more complicated, some of these were the literary monuments of nations that were *unknown as nations*.

That was precisely the sort of threefold riddle confronting William Wright when he chiseled the Hamath stones out of the wall—covered with symbols never seen before, in an unknown language, written by an unknown people.

Commenting on just such a problem, Alice Kober, the brilliant young American philologist who has made important contributions to the decipherment of the Cretan inscriptions, remarked not so long ago: "Let us face the facts: An unknown language written in an unknown script cannot be deciphered!"

Yet we know today that William Wright's stone was written in a hieroglyphic script employed by the nation of the Hittites. Those hieroglyphs have been virtually deciphered, and the Hittite language is almost understandable.

To follow the process of the solution of the riddle, we must begin where Hittitology itself began—with the incomprehensible but readable *cuneiform* texts found at Boghazköy.

Behind the decipherment of ancient inscriptions lies a tradition of some one hundred and fifty years. The two momentous triumphs in this field are linked with the names of Georg Friedrich Grotefend, the brilliant German schoolmaster, and Jean-François Champollion, the child prodigy who at sixteen already knew eight languages. In both cases one element in the script was already known. For Grotefend, who deciphered the cuneiform script, this element was admittedly pure hypothesis at first (his assumption that certain signs represented three known names of Persian kings), but it proved to be correct at the very first test, and the way was then open for further deciphering. For Champollion, the unraveler of the Egyptian hieroglyphics, the known element was contained in a readable Greek text. On the trilingual Rosetta Stone, Champollion identified the name of Ptolemy, mentioned in the Greek text, with a group of hieroglyphic signs that were emphasized by being framed in a ring, and thus he determined the first few letters—the basis for further interpretation.

Both Grotefend and Champollion, then, had used for their starting point names which were known from other sources. In the course of the next century it developed that this method of searching for names was in principle the best way to attack a deciphering problem.

In very recent times a new approach was tried by the archæologist Ernst Sittig, based on his experiences as a code expert for the German army. After scholars had spent some fifty years in vain efforts to decipher ancient Cretan inscriptions, Sittig achieved some success by combining, for the first time, the method of comparative linguistics with the statistical approach used by intelligence services trying to crack enemy codes. Nevertheless, the method of clues from names proved its worth, since a still greater success in interpreting Cretan inscriptions was scored by a young Englishman named Michael Ventris who entered the field as an outsider (he had been an architect specializing in prefabricated school buildings) and patiently compared signs for names.

From Champollion's day on, however, a text in two languages—what archæologists call a bilingual—has re-

mained the dream of all philologists when confronted with
newly-discovered scripts. Rarely has such a dream been so
beautifully fulfilled as it had been for Champollion. On
the other hand, such staggering luck is no longer necessary
—techniques have been refined greatly in the past century. Insignificant hints which would have meant nothing
to the pioneers of deciphering now furnish vital informa-

BAS RELIEF FROM CARCHEMISH.

tion. And with each new decipherment has come a growth
in understanding of the network of interrelationships link-
ing the ancient languages with one another.

It is curious that the most important of these networks
among ancient languages was detected long before the
first decipherments, in the year 1786, to be precise. And it
was discovered not in the traditional centers of Near Eastern studies—England and Germany—but in India. The
man with phenomenal linguistic gifts who first perceived
this critical system of interrelationships, and thereby made
the most fruitful discovery in the history of philology, was

at the time Chief Justice of the Supreme Court of Judi-
cature in Calcutta. In his leisure hours he was concerned
not so much with comparing languages, as with collecting
and translating Hindu and Mohammedan legal lore.

His name was William Jones; he was born in London
in 1746. He studied ancient languages and history at Har-
row, and specialized in Persian, Arabic, and Hebrew. But
realizing that such a field was scarcely remunerative, he
abandoned it and, for purely financial reasons, turned to
law. It is indicative of the quality of his intellect that his
career in this new field was rapid and brilliant. Even more
indicative of his ability is the fact that he made a philological discovery which has had tremendous influence
upon virtually all the historical sciences. It has been an
extremely useful tool in the investigation of ancient history, has enormously extended our knowledge of eth-
nology (the great migrations and the intermingling of
races and cultures), of ancient geography, of sociology
(familial law, the formation and nature of early social
organization), and has even contributed to zoology and
botany (the distribution of animals and plants in early
times; the extent of early domestication of animals).

It was probably William Jones's transfer to India that
stimulated him to study Sanskrit, the Hindu language
of literature and scholarship. As he worked with Sanskrit,
he perceived in the languages he knew a concealed skele-
ton. Back of the individual features of numerous languages
he discerned their true face, their family resemblance.

The busy colonial magistrate had no time to work out
his discovery in detail. But there were others to build on
the basis of his ideas. Rasmus Christian Rask (1786–
1832), a Danish classical philologist and highly unprofes-
sorial cosmopolitan traveler, made a point of studying on
the spot the various subjects that interested him. For four

years he traveled through Persia and India investigating
the ancient languages of those countries. But it remained
for Franz Bopp, the German linguist (1791–1867), to
crown the insight of Jones with a book whose main section
alone was the fruit of sixteen years of incessant labors.
Bopp's *Comparative Grammar of the Sanskrit, Zend,
Greek, Latin, Lithuanian, Gothic, and German Languages* [1] introduced strict scientific method into comparative linguistics. He became the Winckelmann of
philology.

Bopp proved conclusively that there existed a group of
languages which, because they included the languages of
India, central and western Asia, and most of Europe,
could be called "Indo-European"—languages bearing astonishing resemblances to one another in vocabulary
and form, and which were therefore related. A favorite
and illuminating example is that of the English *father*,
German *Vater*, French *père*, Spanish *padre*, Latin *pater*,
Greek *patér*, Old Irish *athir*, Gothic *fadar*, Sanskrit *pitar*,
Tocharian *pacar*. The older the languages under investigation were, the closer were the agreements. The conclusion
was obvious: related languages, what the philologists call
cognate tongues, must have sprung from a common original language, no matter how different they may seem today.

A further crucial step was taken when it was discovered that changes of both sounds and inflections in languages were governed by regular laws. Once sufficient material for comparison had been gathered, therefore, it was
possible for scholars to reverse the natural process of
change. In other words, fragments of an ancient language
—once it was established as Indo-European—could be
systematically reconstructed because the laws governing

[1] *Vergleichende Grammatik des Sanscrit, Zend, Griechischen, Lateinischen, Litthauischen, Gothischen und Deutschen.*

the subsequent changes were understood. Still a further step was possible when finer relationships proving closer degrees of kinship were recognized within the large Indo-European linguistic group. Thereafter conclusions could be drawn, for example, solely from the geographical or tribal localization of these languages. Therein lay the value of such linguistic studies for the student of ancient civilizations. They did not directly lead to decipherment, but they were of inestimable value when it came to illuminating the structure and grammar of a language available only in bits and pieces.

Naturally the first reward of the early Indo-European philologists was mockery. It seemed on the face of it ridiculous to claim kinship between Afghan and Icelandic, Sanskrit and Russian, Frisian and the language of the Gypsies, or Latin and Old Prussian. After all, the geographic area supposedly covered by this linguistic group ranged from India over the Near East to the westernmost point of Europe. It was an area broken by deserts, mountains, and seas, populated by widely differing races.

The Indo-European philologist is still confronted by a great many problems. For example, the "original home" of this linguistic group has by no means been definitively established—it is now held to have been somewhere between Southern Russia and Central Europe. But the basic fact of its group existence, of close and more binding kinships among the members of the group as against other language groups of the white race (Hamito-Semitic, Caucasian, Dravidian, and the isolated Basque language), is no longer open to doubt.

In addition to the tried and tested methods which had led to the decipherment of dead languages and scripts throughout the nineteenth century, Indo-European philology now contributed a new key with which to unlock the enigma of the Hittite clay tablets from Boghazköy.

Oddly enough, the man who first used this key was not an Indo-European philologist. He was an Assyriologist—linguistically speaking, a student of the Semitic group of

VOTIVE STELE FROM MARASH.

languages, for Babylonian-Assyrian is reckoned among the East Semitic tongues.

What a patent application is to the inventor, the "preliminary report" is to the scientist. Priority to a new discovery is assured by the publication of such a report.

In December 1915 there appeared in a volume of the *Communications of the German Orient Society* an essay entitled: "The Solution of the Hittite Problem," [2] a "preliminary report" by Dr. Friedrich Hrozný.

In his first footnote the author explained his reasons for hasty publication:

"In consideration of the war, which may very well significantly delay the completion as well as the printing of my work, and in consideration also of the probability that publications on Hittite may be expected from other quarters, I have decided to publish the introduction to my paper right away in abbreviated form in these *Communications of the German Orient Society.*"

It was certainly surprising that anyone should have succeeded so quickly in cracking the secret of the Hittite cuneiform tablets. But what was far more of a surprise, what was in fact a sensation for the specialists in the subject, was the nature of the solution. For no one had dreamed what the result would be.

After Winckler's death, the German Orient Society of Berlin had handed over the collection of Hittite cuneiform material from Boghazköy to a group of young Assyriologists, in order that they might arrange and transcribe it. From the start there were two diametrically opposite personalities in this group: the rather ponderous, grave German Ernst F. Weidner, and the lively, gifted Czech Friedrich (or Bedrich) Hrozný—born in Poland in 1879.

When the First World War broke out, the Germans promptly put such useless creatures as students of ancient languages into uniform. Weidner, a great hulk of a man, was assigned to the Heavy Artillery. While he was slowly working his way up to the rank of corporal, his rival Hrozný fell into a featherbed. Drafted into the Austro-Hungarian Army, he found a tolerant superior in Lieutenant Kammergruber, an easygoing Viennese who took a

---

[2] "Die Lösung des hethitischen Problems," *Mitteilungen der Deutschen Orientgesellschaft.*

liking to the young professor and who, as far as lay within his powers, gave Hrozný the freedom to pursue his researches. Hrozný gratefully acknowledged:

"The present paper was only given its definitive form during the author's military service." In fact he tells us that his second paper was also completed during this period. When we consider that these articles were far from easy to write, that they represented scientific pioneering of the highest type, we can well imagine that the thirty-five-year-old scholar's military service was not especially burdensome. He was even given the opportunity to spend weeks in Constantinople examining cuneiform Hittite material which at that time was scarcely accessible to any other European scholar.

But we certainly do not want to imply that Weidner, sweating over his cannon, might have, but for that, outstripped the more fortunate Czech—especially since we know now that Weidner was on the wrong track. And it would be foolish to maintain that Hrozný deciphered the Hittite language solely because he had more time at his disposal than his rival. Hrozný was a man who had already done a great deal in his field; at the age of twenty-four he had participated in excavations in Northern Palestine and had published highly esteemed reports on cuneiform texts, while at the age of twenty-six he had been appointed to a professorship in Vienna.

So it is evident that Hrozný tackled his task equipped with phenomenal knowledge. He was also blessed with enormous scientific audacity. His approach was altogether unbiased; he did not want to let the suggestions of others predetermine his conclusions and was thoroughly prepared to be surprised himself. He would work directly from the evidence, even if his observations should contradict all the established views.

We know on his own testimony that at the beginning

of his labors he had not the faintest idea what kind of language would be revealed to him.

Again and again in the history of such discoveries as Hrozný's there comes a climax at which the innumerable false starts and fresh insights, the endless patient labor of formulating, comparing, and rejecting, culminate in a single idea which proves to be the crucial one. And this idea, the fruit of so much toil and searching, is as a rule strikingly simple.

The starting point of Hrozný's work was the usual determination of proper names. The second point was the perception that the Hittite texts contained what were called "ideograms."

The Babylonian-Assyrian cuneiform writing in the Boghazköy texts had in its earliest form (like all other scripts) been picture-writing which later developed into a syllabic script. A large number of the earlier pictures had been retained in this syllabic script. Such ideograms had been taken over by the Hittites and could be "read" by scholars of cuneiform writing—that is, they could be understood without knowledge of the language.

An example will make the matter clear. As readers of English alone, we can see the numeral "10" in an English, German, and French text and understand it immediately. The fact that a Frenchman may call this figure *dix* and a German *zehn* in no way affects our understanding.

In this fashion, with the aid of ideograms, Hrozný read the words "fish" and "father." And then, in the course of wearisome examination of the closest details, he groped his way forward from word to word, from form to form— until one day he discovered (simply by changes in the form of words and despite the fact that he could not yet arrive at the meaning of a single sentence) that Hittite displayed grammatical forms typical of the Indo-European linguistic group. In particular he recognized a participial form.

This discovery was extremely confusing. There already existed a large number of theories about the Hittite language. But with the exception of a single scholar, who afterwards recanted, it had occurred to no one that Hittite might be an Indo-European language. There was no objective basis for this idea, for to assume that Indo-Europeans had been dominant in Inner Anatolia in the middle of the second millennium B.C. was to contradict all that historians of the Near East had learned.

No wonder, then, that Hrozný was wary of this conclusion. It looked to him as though he was being deceived by accidents of language. But as he worked on, he was reluctantly forced to note more indications pointing to the membership of Hittite in the Indo-European family of languages.

But then came the day when Hrozný, sitting over a certain text, took a deep breath and, conscious of the boldness of his own thesis, dared to think: "If I am right about the interpretation of this line, there is going to be a scientific storm." But the sentence he was reading seemed clear and unambiguous. He had only one choice: to say what it was he saw—even if it overturned the views of all specialists in ancient history.

The text which led Hrozný to this resolve was the sentence: *nu ninda-an ezzatteni vâdar-ma ekutteni*

In this sentence there was only a single known word: *ninda*. It could be deduced from the Sumerian ideogram that this word meant "bread."

Hrozný said to himself: "A sentence in which the word bread is used may very well (though it need not necessarily, of course!) contain the word 'eat.'" Since at this point the indications that Hittite might be an Indo-European language were already becoming overwhelming, he drew up a list of various Indo-European words for "eat." Was it possible that he was dealing here with a Hittite cognate? English "eat" was in Latin *edo*, in Old High German . . . As soon as Hrozný wrote down the Old High German word he knew he was on the right track. *Ezzan* certainly bore a strong resemblance to the Hittite *ezzatteni*.

VOTIVE STELE FROM MARASH.

The next significant word, which seemed to cry out for such comparisons, was undoubtedly the Hittite *vâdar*. Since it occurred in the same line as "bread" and "eat," it might very well be related to food. Hrozný, a veritable bloodhound on the trail of an Indo-European language, saw a similarity to the English *water*, German *Wasser*, Old Saxon *watar*. We need not go into the complicated grammatical considerations which led him to an interpretation of the Hittite sentence, but at this point he ventured a translation: "Now you will eat bread, further you will drink water."

Such a reading of the sentence was an amazing confirmation of the idea which had been suggested as early as 1902 by the Norwegian Orientalist Knudtzon, whose theory, however, had been greeted with such universal scorn by the other experts that he had retracted it. Hittite after all was an Indo-European language!

Further conclusions followed. Since the archæologists were able to establish the period at which the Boghazköy texts originated as the fourteenth and thirteenth centuries B.C., and since there were indications that many texts were copies of much older documents, some of perhaps the eighteenth century B.C., Hrozný could lay claim to having deciphered possibly *the* oldest Indo-European language. His texts compared in age with the oldest parts of the Rig Veda, the Hindu scriptures, which had begun to take shape in India around the middle of the second millennium B.C.

On November 24, 1915, Hrozný delivered a lecture on his decipherment to the members of the Near Eastern Society of Berlin. The following month this lecture was printed. But his book on the actual decipherment itself was first published in Leipzig in 1917. It was entitled: *The Language of the Hittites; Its Structure and Its Membership in the Indo-European Linguistic Family*. The first sentences of the preface stated:

"The present work undertakes to establish the nature and structure of the hitherto mysterious language of the Hittites, and to decipher this language. . . . It will be shown that Hittite is in the main an Indo-European language."

In the 246 pages of his book, Hrozný presented the

most complete decipherment of a dead language that had ever been given to the public. Hardly any of his statements were hypothetical or provisional; he presented definitive conclusions.

At the same time, he took occasion to deal with his opponents. For shortly before he completed his own book, Hrozný had come across the latest book by his rival, Weidner. *Studies in Hittite Linguistics* [3] was its title. In an appendix to his work Hrozný noted that Weidner, "who seems to have changed his mind since the summer of 1915," now admitted "that a certain Aryan element in Hittite can no longer be denied." He attributes Weidner's revised views to acquaintanceship with his own article of 1915, the "Preliminary Report." Although he does not directly accuse Weidner of borrowing, he poses in a footnote some highly suggestive questions, hinting that Weidner brashly took over several of his ideas while "as far as possible avoiding mentioning my name."

Such squabbles may not be altogether edifying, but they are understandable. At the same time, Weidner's views were by no means without sense; we must remember that when he formulated them everybody was still groping in the dark. Hrozný admits that Hittite *also* contains many foreign elements, probably of Caucasian origin. On the one hand he comments: "Taken as a whole, Weidner's theory unfortunately must be termed inadequate from the point of view of Hittitology." But on the other hand he reluctantly adds that the work "is nevertheless not without value," and that "from the point of view of Assyriology" Weidner had "in some passages extended our knowledge of the vocabularies."

But there is no need to review the many points of dispute between the two researchers. Hrozný's work remains the sterling triumph that the old master of ancient history,

[3] *Studien zur hethitischen Sprachwissenschaft.*

Eduard Meyer, hailed in his introduction to Hrozný's book. Meyer said:

"Of all the rich fruits that have come of the excavations undertaken by the German Orient Society, discoveries which have widened and deepened our knowledge of the oldest history and culture of mankind in all directions, it may be said that nothing approaches in significance and range the discovery which Professor Hrozný is publishing in this volume."

The excavator who finds golden treasure and the mummies of long-dead kings is not the only one who experiences that moment of illumination when he seems to lay his hand on the very past. The same thrill can come to a man sitting bent over books in his study, pondering a single sentence, until suddenly he feels that shudder of awe which voices from immemorial tombs evoke. There is more to such a matter than dry philology. For does not "water," uttered as a cry in a desert landscape, mean parching thirst? *Vâdar, water, Wasser*—how staggering it is to realize that with three thousand years intervening, a Frisian living on the North Sea coast of Germany and a Pennsylvania Dutchman of Eastern North America would understand a Hittite's cry of thirst!

V

DID THE HITTITES SPEAK HITTITE?

O NCE HROZNÝ HAD DECIPHERED THE LANGUAGE, a second part of the national archives of Hattusas began to speak. Of the countless clay tablets unearthed at Boghazköy between 1906 and 1912 a part had been decipherable on the spot. Winckler had been able to handle this work because the Hittites had written their state documents in a borrowed language, Akkadian—by now the well-known language of international relations in the Near East—and in a borrowed script, Babylonian-Assyrian cuneiform writing.

Another part—the documents in which the Hittites also used the cuneiform script but wrote in their own language—had now been made accessible by Hrozný's brilliant work. The law, religion, and medicine, the morals and customs, the deeds of kings and tribes, were now revealed in the language of the Hittite people themselves. The history of this nation emerged from darkness at one bound. But where the historical sciences are concerned, there is never any final knowledge; there are only way-stations. Hrozný's decipherment had barely appeared when fresh problems sprang up, and with them fresh disputes.

In the first place the specialists in ancient history were extremely put out. The assumption that Indo-Europeans had been a dominant group in Asia Minor did not at all fit in with their preconceptions. With some scorn the historians demanded that the philologists kindly inform them where these Indo-Europeans were supposed to have come from. The question was an unfair one—the historians themselves should have been the ones to answer it.

The Indo-European specialists also threw themselves into the fray. They were up in arms against Hrozný, no Indo-European expert himself, because in the excitement of discovery he had in many cases ventured out on the slippery ice of scientifically dubious assertions. That was especially the case in questions of the specific family relationships of words. Naturally, the need for correction here and there in no way diminished the luster of his original achievement—but considerable touching up of details was necessary before further progress could be made.

The first set of corrections was supplied by the German philologist Ferdinand Sommer (born 1875 in Trier), who by 1920 had published a purely philological but extremely severe examination of all of Hrozný's arguments. Sommer's work was filled out and perfected in many details by Johannes Friedrich, who worked at the University of Leipzig and since 1950 has been at Berlin, and by Albrecht Götze, now of Yale University. The grammar of Hittite was elaborated by Louis-Joseph Delaporte, sections of whose *Manual of the Hittite Language* [1] appeared in Paris between 1929 and 1933, and by E. H. Sturtevant of Yale University (*A Comparative Grammar of the Hittite Language,* 1933). In 1940, Johannes Friedrich brought the grammar to a stage bordering on completion in his *Elements of Hittite.* [2] In 1946, a second part was added, con-

[1] *Manuel de la langue hittite.*
[2] *Hethitisches Elementarbuch.*

taining numerous reading selections in transcription, with explanations and vocabulary; and in 1952–54, his big *Hittite Dictionary* appeared.[3]

In a preface to the *Elements*, however, Friedrich confesses that knowledge of the Hittite vocabulary and the peculiarities of its grammar is as yet by no means complete. In the religious texts especially, he points out, there are "numerous technical expressions whose meaning is still obscure to us and may well remain obscure for a long time to come." He is extremely cautious and instead of defining nouns often prefers to give only their classification such as "a dress" or "baked goods"; he will even say: "Substantive of undetermined meaning."

But such reservations appear unnecessarily pedantic by contrast with one of the last sentences in his introduction in which the scholar remarks casually, as though it were the most natural observation in the world, that he has undertaken what is certainly one of the greatest triumphs of the art of deciphering:

"In a very few passages obvious *errors* of the old scribes—a few wrong or doubled terminations and similar oversights—have been *corrected* without comment."

The historical development we have just described was not so continuous as it appears when we run on from date to date. By 1919, for example, a Swiss philologist named Emil Forrer had completed a task which had theretofore been neglected because nobody wanted to introduce unnecessary complications so long as simpler problems still remained to be solved. Forrer plunged into the heart of the complications when he published an essay entitled *The Eight Languages of the Boghazköy Inscriptions.*[4]

Eight languages!

[3] *Hethitisches Wörterbuch.*
[4] *Die acht Sprachen der Boghazköi—Inschriften.*

The short but extremely meaty article began with the following direct statement:

"Examination of all the Boghazköy fragments has shown that no less than eight languages occur in them: in addition to SUMERIAN, AKKADIAN, and the language hitherto known as 'HITTITE,' which as we shall soon see should more correctly be named Kanisic, there are PROTO-INDIC, HURRIAN, PROTO-HATTIAN, LUVIAN, AND PALAIC.

It was not so much the number of the languages Forrer had named which produced surprise and consternation. His observations were correct, but it soon developed that two languages were predominant, the others present only in fragments. A polyglot population is an integral characteristic of every metropolis. Among the ruins of a long-dead London, future archæologists will some day find fragments of Chinese script—inscribed on shops in the Chinese quarter. They will not necessarily have to conclude that Chinese was one of the important languages spoken in London during the twentieth century A.D.

What was so confusing was Forrer's incidental contention that Hittite should really be called Kanisic. Two years after Hrozný had published his principal work, Forrer was raising doubts as to whether the decipherer had really deciphered Hittite. And although Forrer's argument was cogent, people refused to dispense with an established name, even if it were erroneous, only in order to adopt a new one which might some day prove to be equally erroneous.

Forrer started from the assumption, which no one contested, that the Hittites must have migrated into Asia Minor, since they were an Indo-European people. Immediately the question of the previous population arose, and since for a long time nothing could be found out about them, they were simply called "proto-Hattians."

Their *non*-Indo-European language appeared in several of the documents from Boghazköy, and was always preceded by the word *hattili* ("in Hattian"). This term was undoubtedly derived from *Hatti*, the name of the country. Hatti, then, where Hattian (Hittite) had been spoken, had existed as a kingdom before the Indo-European ruling class invaded Asia Minor. Evidence for this was contained in three inscriptions of King Anitta of Nesa in which a successful war against the "King of Hatti" is mentioned.

Hattians (Hittites) should then be the proper name for the original inhabitants, not for the Indo-European conquerors.

Unfortunately, however, the scholars found out about the speakers of Hattian only after the name Hittites had become attached to the conquerors—on the basis of the Biblical texts. This plain blunder can no longer be repaired. For a short time after the publication of Forrer's essay it was taken seriously, but it is no longer. O. R. Gurney, Oxford Professor of Assyriology, gives the question short shrift. The Kingdom and its official language have become known as Hittite, he remarks, and the name must now be accepted.

Forrer supported the use of the name "Kanisic" for the language Hrozný had deciphered by arguing that Hittite religious songs were often presented as recited by a "singer of the city of Kanes." This reason is no more and no less valid than others which have been used to support other names. None of the arguments are adequate. We have no way of knowing today what the "Hittites" called themselves when they invaded Asia Minor.

Although the rapid decipherment of Hittite—once it was recognized as belonging to the Indo-European family —contributed enormously to the scholars' ability to fill out in color the history of the nation, a number of problems

having to do with the script and with linguistic affinities
remain to this day. We will mention only three of these.

First: It is established that the Hittites migrated into
Asia Minor. The question is: Where did they come from?
Hrozný seemed to have solved this problem along with his
decipherment, for he had shown not only that Hittite *was*
Indo-European, but that it belonged to the "centum" or
western group, which includes Greek, Latin, Celtic, and
Germanic. (Indo-European is divided into two main
groups known, according to the form of the word "hundred," as the "centum" and the "satem" language groups;
included among the "satem" group are the eastern
branches, such as Slavic, Iranian, and Indic.)

It seemed an obvious conclusion, therefore, that the
Hittites had come from the West, penetrating Asia Minor
via the Balkans and the Bosporus. Today, when we know
somewhat more about the strange migrations undergone
by different Indo-European languages, this theory is by
no means universally accepted. Many scholars demonstrated by highly refined reasoning that the Hittites must
have come across the Caucasus Mountains. Ferdinand
Sommer, for example, points to the beginning of a prayer
selected from a ritual promulgated by Hittite King Muwatallis (around 1300 B.C.):

> *Sun God of Heaven, shepherd of man!*
> *You rise out of the sea, Sun of Heaven.*
> *Up to Heaven you move in your course.*
> *Sun God of Heaven, my Lord! To children of men,*
> *To dogs, to swine, to the wild beasts of the field,*
> *You give justice, O divine Sun, day after day!*

The second line, "You rise out of the sea," is worth re-
marking. Since in the time of Muwatallis the Hittites had
dwelt in Inner Anatolia for at least four hundred years,

this invocation could only be based upon a memory, for as far as Anatolians are concerned the sun does not rise out of the sea. But two possibilities remain: either the Black Sea or the Caspian Sea might have lain on the Hittites' left during their migration.

The second problem: The names of the kings of this Indo-European people are absolutely *non*-Indo-European. From the first they are proto-Hattian. The same may be said of the names of the Hittite gods—these are either proto-Hattian or Hurrian. The explanation offered is that elements of the proto-Hattian population mingled with the conquering Hittites; the masters supposedly tried to consolidate their power by assimilation. But this explanation is hardly satisfactory.

The third problem: At the time of the early Hittite kings there existed a number of flourishing Assyrian trading settlements in Anatolia. One of the most important of them was located at present-day Kültepe, near Kayseri. Many clay tablets bespeak a vigorous commercial life. Now it is very odd that the Hittites, who from the first wrote most of their documents and reports in Babylonian-Assyrian cuneiform, did not at all use the type of writing of these Assyrian colonists and merchants; they employed instead an entirely different style of the familiar Akkadian calligraphy which is found nowhere else, but which is probably of very great antiquity.

Now, whether the Hittites invaded Hatti Land from the Northeast or the Northwest, they could not have brought a cuneiform script with them. Cuneiform is an invention of southern Mesopotamia. But then, where did this Hittite cuneiform come from?

Such is, in broad outline, the story of the decipherment of the cuneiform Hittite clay tablets of Boghazköy—the writings of the Hittites in their own language, but in a bor-

AN INSCRIPTION FROM CARCHEMISH, WITH DISTINCTLY PIC-
TORIAL SYMBOLS.

rowed Assyrian script. But we must remember that it was
not the cuneiform tablets of Boghazköy which first at-
tracted attention to the Hittites. It was, rather, those
strange hieroglyphics which had been found principally in
Carchemish, less frequently in Central Syria and Central
Anatolia. These hieroglyphs, altogether unlike those of the
Egyptians, were what had once prompted Sayce and
Wright to assume the existence of a hitherto unknown
civilization to the north and south of the Taurus.

Once the Boghazköy tablets with their readable script
had been found, most scholars (especially the historians)
followed the path of least resistance and concentrated
their attention on these cuneiform texts. But a few scholars refused to give up trying to track down the mystery of
the hieroglyphs.

It was the darkest riddle of Orientalogy—for both language and script were unknown. But it was also the most
alluring problem—for the Hittites had apparently used
their very own hieroglyphs not for profane but for sacred
purposes, not to write down the commonplaces of life, but

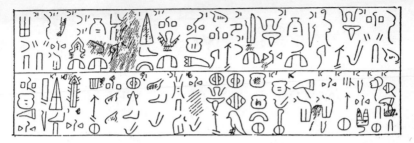

PART OF AN INSCRIPTION FROM BULGARMADEN. IN CONTRAST TO THE CARCHEMISH INSCRIPTION (PAGE 94) THE SCRIPT IS MUCH MORE CURSIVE; THE PICTORIAL QUALITIES ARE SUPPRESSED.

those things which are of greatest importance. Their hieroglyphs, it seemed, had been reserved for the deeds of gods and kings. Work on these had started with the discovery of the Hittites—about thirty years before the decipherment of cuneiform Hittite.

But only today, as these lines are being written, is the task nearing completion.

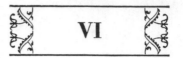

VI

"NOTHING CAN BE DECIPHERED OUT OF NOTHING!"

Remember that if you want to make discoveries you must be content to make mistakes." This salutary warning is taken from the memoirs of Archibald Henry Sayce, who devoted his entire life to the investigation of Oriental languages. Let us recall that he was the first to propose the bold thesis that the hieroglyphic monuments scattered from Hamath to Smyrna bore witness to a unified Hittite Empire, and he it was who made the first attempts to decipher this script. Throughout his life he turned again and again to this problem, and he constantly followed the efforts of younger scholars—some of whom were his pupils —giving encouragement and advice. In 1931, at the age of eighty-six, he wrote his last paper on the subject—he died two years later.

Modern Hittitologists, looking back upon the history of the decipherment, often speak deprecatingly of Sayce's early work. Friedrich declares that it would be "a waste of time" to quarrel with Sayce's "fantastic readings" which were, he says, "often actually amateurish." But in his memoirs, published in 1923, the wise old man freely admitted that he had often worked too hurriedly and roughly. His excuse is the sentence quoted above—and he is right. It is only too easy to reproach a pioneer for having strayed off the track—but the track did not exist when he began his work. In fact, A. H. Sayce was not only the first to recognize the Hittites as builders of a civilization; he was also the first to read some of the signs in their hieroglyphic script—a real feat.

From the start helpful clues had been gathered from general experience with certain peculiarities of ancient scripts. For example, in the scripts of almost all ancient peoples special emphasis was given to the names of kings; in Egyptian this was done by an oval frame now called a cartouche. Another peculiarity in ancient inscriptions is the constant addition of a particular sign to a pictured figure which is stressed as a royal figure in other ways—for example, by its size. Hence, this particular sign can be assumed to be a royal "determinative" when it appears in other connections. In a hieroglyphic passage the sign marks a pictograph as royal just as surely as does the golden crown when it appears upon the head of a figure in an Occidental fable. All ancient scripts use such determinatives; beside the names of kings, the names of cities and countries are usually treated in the same fashion.

For the scholar attempting to decipher a script, discovering such determinatives is of utmost importance because he then at least knows that a group of signs connected with the determinative must signify a king, a country, or a city. He can draw further conclusions from the length or brevity of the group of signs; he examines the writing in its historical relationships and looks for names already known to him from the contemporary history of neighboring nations.

On the other hand, for the decipherment of Cretan hieroglyphics—whose mysteries have only very recently begun to be conquered—the decisive factor was the recognition of a small diagonal line as a word divider. The significance of this comma-like sign had to be grasped, for without this mark how could hieroglyphic signs running continuously from line to line be broken up into their component words? How could the initial and final syllables of the Cretan script be systematically investigated by statistical methods—as has been done since 1950—if the little diagonal line had not told scholars where to look for the beginning and end of words?

What must be established first, of course, before decipherment can even begin, is how the script is meant to be read. That is, does it run from left to right or right to left, from top to bottom or from bottom to top? Only the peoples of the West take it as a matter of course that writing and reading proceed from left to right. A hundred and fifty years ago, when Grotefend was examining the first copies of cuneiform texts, the direction of the writing was his basic problem. Given a rectangular tablet, any one of the four sides may be the top.

Fortunately, this problem did not come up in connection with the Hittite hieroglyphic inscriptions because most of them appeared on monuments, on rock walls, or sculptures. It could hardly be assumed that the stone-mason expected people to stand on their heads in order to read the writing. Moreover, there were simple indications that the inscriptions were intended to be read "bustrophe-don"—"as the ox plows." (See plate VI and plate XVI.) Experience with other languages has shown, for example, that on the first line of an inscription this hieroglyph will in all probability be the beginning. Then, depending on which side the free space of the final line is found, the course of the lines can be determined. The fact that on alternate lines such pictorial signs as hands, feet, and heads point in opposite directions supports this conclusion.

Another trick the scholar uses to determine the character of an unknown script is—elementary though it sounds—to count the symbols. The logic behind this is simple enough: an unknown script containing less than thirty different signs cannot possibly be a syllabic script, for thirty syllables are not enough to reproduce a language. Such a script would have to be an alphabetic script. On the other hand, if there are around a hundred signs, it may be assumed at once that the script is syllabic. If there are still more signs, the script must be ideographic: separate signs for each word or idea.

"Nothing can be deciphered out of nothing," Friedrich declares, and as examples he mentions the Easter Island script and the Indus script of Mohenjo-Daro; for these there is at present no point of approach, and not the slightest connection with known scripts is even suspected. With the Hittite hieroglyphs, on the other hand, there did exist from the start chances for determining at least the character of the script in the ways we have indicated. And on the basis of the experience amassed by two generations of decipherers, at least a few signs could be established out of hand.

But fortune seemed to be with Sayce when he began his first attempts at interpretation (before 1880). At the start the friendly goddess tossed into his lap the dream of all decipherers—a bilingual, an inscription in two languages. He had his bilingual but . . .

Around 1860 a Constantinople coin collector named Jovanoff purchased in Smyrna a small silver disc on which was depicted a human figure surrounded by strange, unknown signs and rimmed with a cuneiform inscription. In the course of his research, Sayce came across a description of this disc—a Dr. Mordtmann had mentioned it briefly in 1862—and hearing of the cuneiform writing somehow sensed that the strange marks on the face of the disc were

Hittite hieroglyphs. He felt that the dream was about to come true: to find a bilingual during the first stages of decipherment!

His disappointment, however, was great when his efforts to locate the seal failed completely. It had been taken to England; there was no doubt about that. But there it had vanished without a trace. Sayce appealed to his colleagues, to museums, to the public; he wrote letters, requested anyone who knew anything about the seal to inform him at once.

THE TARKUMUWA (TARKONDEMOS) SEAL, WITH WHICH THE DECIPHERMENT OF HITTITE HIEROGLYPHS STARTED.

Finally an official of the British Museum responded. Oh yes, he declared, he well remembered that a curious seal of the kind Sayce sought had been offered to the museum in 1860.

And what had happened?

The museum had declined to buy it, the official said.

Why, in heaven's name?

Well, it seemed that the seal had presented such a strange appearance that the museum authorities suspected a forgery.

Sayce saw his hopes dashed.

But, the official reflected, if he remembered rightly, an electrotype of the seal had been made. That ought to be around somewhere.

Shortly thereafter Sayce had a copy of the seal. His guess was confirmed—this was a bilingual! But for all that he now had his inscription in two languages, there was one thing sadly wrong with it: the text was too short. There were far too few signs for him to make comparisons and establish unequivocal relationships between the hiero-glyphs and the cuneiform groups.

Reading of the cuneiform text gave the following re-sult:

"*Tar-rik-tim-me šar mat Er me-e*," Tarriktimme, Lord of the land of Er me-e. The disc was then known as the "Tarkondemos Seal"—the name has now been corrected to "Tarkumuwa." When Sayce compared the cuneiform inscription with the hieroglyphs, he intuitively decided

that the signs and must correspond to "king"

and "land" in the cuneiform texts. There is hardly any point in belittling this accomplishment by saying that he had only established word signs and not phonetic signs. These were in any case the first signs that had been read in Hittite hieroglyphic script, and as it turned out later they had been read correctly.

But unfortunately, these two signs were all that could be extracted from the Tarkumuwa seal. All attempts to establish further correspondences between the cuneiform script and the hieroglyphs led the scholars astray. More and more such attempts were made, and later with greater success when other seals, found by Kurt Bittel at Bo-ghazköy, could be compared. But the texts of these seals were always too brief.

Sayce had, however, attacked the other available material. He arranged, compared, discovered relationships. And as the result of his primary efforts at the decipherment of hieroglyphic Hittite there remained the correct interpretations of the following signs: = king, = city, = country, = God (this last sign he deduced from the Yazilikaya temple, where the inscriptions flanking the representations of divinities always began with this symbol), and the endings = "s" and = "n."

It is truly amazing that in the very year the Hittites were discovered no less than six symbols of their script, written in an unknown language, were correctly interpreted. Granted that Sayce's later interpretations were often highly fanciful. But his work, and perhaps the power of his imagination, inspired the scholars who came after him. Certainly his very blunders had a fruitful effect. Almost twenty years were to pass before another, younger man came along whose struggles to solve the riddle of Hittite hieroglyphs would prove as stimulating to further research as Sayce's had been.

But it was now high time for another kind of work to be done. After the period of discovery, with all its excitements, there must always follow a brief pause for reflection. And during that interval there is always some man who is quietly gathering and arranging materials, putting things into *order*. Such a man was already on the job.

When around the turn of the century Sir Arthur Evans discovered the "Palace of Minos" on Crete and in toilsome

years of digging brought it to light once more, he unearthed some 2000 clay tablets. Evans reserved publication of these tablets for himself—as was his right as the
discoverer. In 1909 he published part of the inscriptions
in his book *Scripta Minoa I,* promising that the second
volume would soon follow. This promise, however, was
not kept. The tablets, of the greatest significance for the
early history of Europe (and, as the work of Michael Ventris has demonstrated, containing some sensational revela-
tions) were virtually buried again in boxes piled up in
Cretan huts and in the cellars of the Athens Museum.
Scholars who for decades had been applying their minds
to the deciphering of Cretan script were denied access to
the original tablets. *Forty years* passed before John Myres,
a friend and disciple of Evans, published (in 1952, after
the latter's death) the second volume of the *Scripta Minoa.* As chance would have it, new tablets had recently
been discovered in Pylos by the American archæologist
Blegen, and these were published in 1951—twelve years
after their discovery. A few current finds had also been
published without delay—and with all this additional material it became possible virtually to solve within two years
the major mystery of Cretan script which had baffled
scholars for more than a generation.

This example from a related field indicates how a pau-
city of material can hold up everything when a certain
point in decipherment has been reached. But in addition
there are other, purely technical obstacles. In most cases,
for example, tablets are scattered throughout museums all
over the world, so that it is impossible for scholars to examine the originals. They are dependent upon reproductions. And it often turns out that copies prepared on the
spot are illegible, that the initial drawings or photographs
are for one reason or another unsatisfactory and grow
poorer with each successive reproduction.

In former days the men who copied inscriptions and drew pictures of ancient monuments gave currency to innumerable errors. They tended to introduce into their sketches their own personal conceptions, which might be artistically justified but which were a source of mischief for the scientist's purposes. Consequently, the archæological world breathed a sigh of relief when photography became available (dry plates and snapshot film, that is, for in deserts and jungles nothing could be done with daguerreotypes). Since "the camera doesn't lie," it was thought that now objective reproductions of the originals would be a certainty.

Such naïve faith in the dependability of photography has gone the way of other popular beliefs. A hieroglyphic seal could be photographed quite easily in the studio, it is true. But it was quite another matter when an archæologist hanging by a rope from a cliff wall tried to photograph an inscription chiseled into the rock. Clouds had a way of passing over the sun just at the strategic moment. How many days would the archæologist have needed to find the best point of suspension for himself and his camera? How many hours would he have had to spend dangling in mid-air before he determined which angle of sunlight was the proper one in order to bring out the three-dimensional quality of the weatherbeaten inscription?

It has happened that in the course of time half a dozen different photographs of a cliff inscription would be published, each picture taken at different times and under the most diverse conditions. On the basis of these photographs scholars drew important conclusions. Then along came a seventh or an eighth photograph on which, suddenly, symbols were visible which had been completely missing from all the previous pictures.

This brief digression will suggest how important it is in all deciphering work for someone to undertake, from

The sphinx gate at Alaja Hüyük.

The figure that adorned the east gate of the Hittite metropolis of Bo-ghazköy more than thirty-three centuries ago. This gate was called the "King's Gate"; we now know that the figure represents a god, not a king.

The "King's Gate" of Boghazköy. For reconstruction see drawing, page 148.

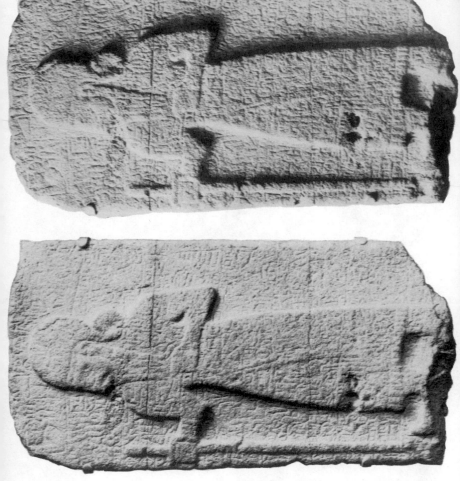

A Hittite stele found at Marash now in New York. In 1949 Charles K. Wilkinson (Curator of Near Eastern Archaeology at the Metropolitan Museum of Art) had four sets of photographs of this stele taken in different lighting for the decipherer, Professor Bossert. The two reproduced here indicate how much depends upon proper illumination. Bossert, busy with the Karatepe inscriptions, could not decipher this stele. Who is going to?

time to time, the thankless and wearisome task of assembling all the material within a certain field of study, arranging it, and then reproducing it with such exactitude that the closest possible approach to the original is achieved.

For the Hittite hieroglyphs this task was taken over by Leopold Messerschmidt in 1900, and carried out with German thoroughness. His *Corpus inscriptionum Hettiticarum,* followed by two appendices in 1902 and 1906, contained careful reproductions of all Hittite inscriptions available up to that time.

Investigation of the hieroglyphs had begun with the four inscriptions on the Hamath Stones. Messerschmidt's *Corpus* contained about a hundred inscriptions, long ones from monuments, short ones of a few symbols, undamaged ones and defaced ones, taken from stone and clay. When this collection was published it was realized for the first time that here was more material than had sufficed, in the case of other ancient languages, for scholars to arrive at real results. It now seemed certain that with a little more labor Hittite would yield its mysteries.

A few years earlier a scholar had come along whose work for the next forty years was to be tremendously influential in two directions at once: as a fertile source of ideas and of confusion. His first paper was published in 1894 and appeared four years later in a book entitled *Hittites and Armenians.* A good twenty-five years later so able a worker in the field as Friedrich could say of it: "The paper rather strains the understanding, and it is not easy to rethink all the intellectual labor that has been poured into this article."

The author of the paper, who had offered a series of new hypotheses inspired by extraordinary insight and intelligence, was the Assyriologist Peter Jensen (1861–

1936). His work is absolutely phenomenal—a brilliant intermingling of wild blunders with remarkable perceptions, so that all the scholars who came after him have necessarily had to begin their own work with a critical analysis of Jensen's. Some of his errors were supported by arguments so cogent that decades of study were necessary to overcome them. His ingenious reasoning was backed by such a wealth of philological learning that winnowing the chaff from the wheat was no easy affair.

The hieroglyph , for example, he correctly interpreted as "I am." This was a correction of Sayce, who had assumed it to be "I speak." But then Jensen introduced a note of confusion by misinterpreting one of Sayce's best correct insights: the ideograms "king," "city," and "country." He saw no difference between and , reading both signs as "king," and consequently interpreting as "double king," or in other words "great king." Then he contributed a great deal to further research by correctly deciphering the name of the city of Carchemish, , and finally, on the basis of many right and wrong interpretations, all equally well demonstrated, he arrived at the conclusion which represented the climax of his work: that Hieroglyphic Hittite was related to Armenian.

There were about a dozen good arguments against this contention. Probably the best of them is Friedrich's first—

Verständnis

1. = Gott'
2. = Königsnamen
3. = (Gross-)König"
4. = Königsschirm
5. ⁱᶜ = Gelenk, verbindet die Redeglieder
6. = „Sonne"
7. = „Sonnengott'
8. = „Göttin'
9. = „(Gross-)Königin'
10. = die nackte Göttin'
11. Übereinstimmung der Endungen bei Substantiv, Adjectiv und Apposition.
12. ` = Personennamenzeichen
13. und = Nominativ-Endung
14. = „dieser'
15. = „Siegel'
16. = „Stein'
17. = „Denkmal'
18. = „Säule'
19. = „Werk-, bearbeitet'
20. = „Schale'
21. = „Bild'
22. = „Schrift (?)'

23. = Tor(turm)
24. = „folgen"
25. = Personennamenzeichen
26. ⁱᶜ = „Kind'
27. ⁱᶜ = „Erbsohn'
28. ⁱᶜ = „Enkelkind'
29. ⁱᶜ = „Ur-Enkel'
30. ⁱᶜ = „Ur-ur-Enkel'
31. ⁱᶜ = „Ur-ur-ur- '
32. ⁱᶜ = „Ur-ur-ur-ur- '
33. = Possessiv-Suffix
34. = „Herzog', Heerführer'
35. = „Götter'
36. = Particip-Endung
37. = „lieben'
38. = „von' beim Passiv
39. = Ortsnamenzeichen
40. = „Land'
41. = „Herr'
42. = „ich heisse'(?), ich bin'(?)
43. = Gentil-Endung
44. und sind gleichwertige Casus-Endungen
45. = „und'

Lesung

1. = mu
2. = va
3. = ta
4. = li
5. = kal
6. = pa, pe
7. = Runda
8. = gar'
9. = ga
10. = mi, me
11. = is, es
12. = si
13. = gur - gu'
14. = gu
15. = ma
16. = tu
17. = na
18. = e (ä)
19. = hi
20. = la
21. = sa
22. = hu'
23. Abstrich = ' (aus r)
24. = kar' Var. = gar', = ga'
25. = as
26. = sur
27. = ai
28. = ti
29. = urar
30. = ra
31. = sanha, sana
32. = ha

PAGE 34 OF EMIL O. FORRER'S BOOK, DIE HETHITISCHE BILDER-SCHRIFT ("HITTITE PICTURE-WRITING"). THIS IS FORRER'S READING OF HITTITE HIEROGLYPHS IN 1932.

that "between the use of hieroglyphic Hittite and the literary fixation of Armenian (around 400 A.D.) there is an interval of from 1000–1200 years."

Jensen's temperament was such that he never revised his opinions. Any attack on his views made him more stubborn and more extreme, and he would defend his theories with violent polemics. It took many years of argument before he was prevailed upon to modify some of his older ideas—and then the results were tragicomical, for he now declared that his earliest *correct* readings had been wrong (for example, his reading of Carchemish).

For the reader who is interested in following up the various approaches to the problem of the decipherment, here are the names of the scholars who along with Jensen worked on it up to the end of the twenties. In the order in which they published their important papers, they are: C. J. Ball, J. Menant, J. Campbell, F. E. Peiser, J. Halévy, C. R. Conder, L. Messerschmidt, Fritz Hammel, A. Gleye, R. Rusch, R. C. Thompson, A. E. Cowley, G. Arthaud, Carl Frank.

It is indicative of the uncertainties in which they were floundering that none of them could agree on the reading of particular symbols. Sometimes their entire work was deprived of value because they had started off with a single false assumption. Peiser, for example, propounded extremely ingenious interpretations of a Carchemish inscription after having incorrectly arranged the order of the lines. Halévy clung to the idea that the Hittites had been a Semitic people; Gleye, a self-taught outsider, tried to interpret the hieroglyphs by finding etymological relationships with the Finno-Ugrian languages. Cowley favored Caucasian.

Nevertheless, by the end of the nineteen-twenties some *names* had been deciphered with a fair degree of certainty —among them Tyana, Hamath, and Gurgum—and thus a few additional symbols had been established on which future work could be based.

The violence of the disputes over matters which may seem trifles to the layman, and the manner in which such professional disagreements could degenerate into personal recriminations, may be illustrated by the controversy between Carl Frank and Jensen in 1923–24. Yet the very fanaticism which brings on such quarrels is a necessary motive force if scholars are to make discoveries.

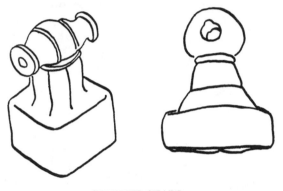

HITTITE SEALS.

Frank had published in the *Zeitschrift für Assyriologie* a new paper on decipherment entitled: "The So-called Hittite Hieroglyphic Inscriptions." [1] The paper discussed Jensen, and promptly the feathers flew. Jensen acidly pointed out that the "new" method of decipherment which Frank proposed had been applied by himself thirty years before. Then he went into detail, tearing Frank's work to bits, ending with: "One must lay down the pen, blushing with shame."

Frank immediately struck back in his article "Studies on the Hittite Hieroglyphic Inscriptions": [2] "It is psycholog-

[1] *Die sogenannten hethitischen Hieroglypheninschriften.*
[2] *Studien zu den hethitischen Hieroglypheninschriften.*

ically impossible for me to debate all these trivia. . . .
His work completely lacks any really profound penetra-
tion into an understanding of the inscriptions. . . . *Nowhere is there a significant step, nowhere an ingenious
speculation.*" This last sentence he printed in italics to
drive his insult home.

Naturally, both men were right and wrong—right
when they asserted that the other had made bad errors;
wrong when they maintained that they themselves had
made none. To feel that such a dispute among scholars is
mere impropriety is to forget that even purely intellectual
work, if a scholar's whole working life is devoted to it,
must also engage his heart and temperament.

After this violent disagreement, the problem of the
Hittite hieroglyphs seemed to most scholars such a hot
chestnut that they preferred not to touch it. A number of
years passed during which no one would make any positive statements, until in 1928 a young Italian linguist
named Meriggi came forward with some new interpretations. Then, from 1930, a whole new group of scholars of
a younger generation suddenly attacked the riddle and began a re-examination of it from the ground up. They were
Ignace J. Gelb, Emil O. Forrer, and Helmuth T. Bossert.

The significance of their work lay in the fact that for
the first time in the history of the decipherment these men
were in fundamental agreement on a considerable number
of readings. Meriggi and Bossert were the first to arrive at
the same results. Unexpectedly, their work was confirmed
by the dean of the Hittitologists, Friedrich Hrozný, who
after years of silence suddenly spoke up. On the basis of
comparisons with cuneiform Hittite, which he knew better
than any man living, Hrozný drew certain conclusions. At
this point a lucky accident suddenly illuminated aspects
of the problem which had remained obscure in spite of

long, laborious years of effort. In 1934 the German archæologist Kurt Bittel was digging at Boghazköy, the Hittite
capital, where Winckler had found so much precious material. Right at the start Bittel found some three hundred
clay seals of which *about a hundred were bilingual!*

After all the false readings of the early days, the interpretation of seals had been pretty much dropped. Now,
however, the scholars set to work with revived energy. In

THE INDILIMMA SEAL AND THE TABARNA SEAL.

1936 Bittel and Güterbock first obtained a reading of the
king's name, over which many arguments had hitherto
raged. This time there could be no question about it—it
was Suppiluliumas, who had lived from 1375 to 1335 B.C.
And the reading led to a further discovery, which followed logically from it.

At Nishan Tash, a rock cliff in Boghazköy, was a long
but badly weathered hieroglyphic inscription which had
been known for many years. It had been guessed that the
inscription ought to be attributed to Suppiluliumas, but
now it was possible to prove it. There stood his name in
hieroglyphs, capped by the curving "ædicula" which always dignified the names of Hittite rulers, as the car-

touche enclosed the names of pharaohs. Beside it were other "ædiculæ" indicating the names of other rulers. The conclusion, dictated by experience, was that this was a genealogical table extending to the third generation—all

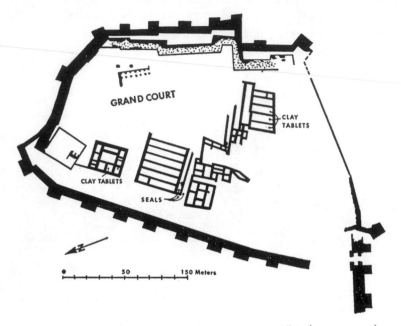

GROUND-PLAN OF THE CITADEL OF BOGHAZKÖY (HATTUSAS). IN THE NINE-FOOT WIDE CORRIDOR OF "BUILDING D" BITTEL FOUND NUMEROUS ROYAL SEALS WHICH ENABLED THE DECI-PHERERS TO PROVE WHAT THEY HAD HITHERTO ONLY BEEN ABLE TO ASSERT.

Oriental monarchs were fond of listing their ancestors in inscriptions.

The striking fact was that the hieroglyphs for the fa-ther and great-grandfather were the same, but that the name of the grandfather differed from these. The obvious question was: were there two kings among the predecessors of Suppiluliumas who bore the same name, between whose reigns a king of another name had ruled?

There were in fact, and their names had long been known because the succession of the Hittite kings was mentioned frequently in the already deciphered cuneiform documents found at Boghazköy. The father of

THE ÆDICULA, THE SIGN OF ROYALTY, IS INSCRIBED ABOVE THE NAME OF ALL KINGS. HERE THE KING IS TUDHALIYAS.

Suppiluliumas had been King Tudhaliyas III, his great-grandfather Tudhaliyas II, while his grandfather had borne the entirely different name of Hattusilis. These names fitted beautifully into the Nishan Tash inscription. Examination of more of the new seals confirmed this reading, and supplied a few further symbols.

Now at last the names of four Hittite kings, Suppiluliumas, Tudhaliyas, Hattusilis, and Urhi-Teshub had been read in hieroglyphs beyond a doubt. This was the

THE STATUE CALLED "GODS ON TWO BULLS" WAS THE FIRST GREAT DISCOVERY AT KARATEPE. ALL FOUR SIDES BORE PHOENICIAN INSCRIPTIONS. WHEN IT WAS KNOCKED OVER BY NOMADS SEEKING GOLD, THREE OF THE SIDES WERE SEVERELY DAMAGED. THIS IS THE ONLY UNDAMAGED SIDE.

first absolute proof that most of the signs which had hitherto been interpreted without the aid of bilingual texts
had been read correctly—a triumph of fifty years of often
heart-breaking scholarly labors in England, Germany,
Italy, and the United States.

But once again the hopes which had been nourished
by the discovery of the new seals were disappointed. The
texts of the seals were unfortunately too brief, and all too
frequently the discs were in fragments or badly defaced.
Güterbock, the German professor in Ankara who devoted
much effort to interpreting the seals, became distinctly
pessimistic about the possibilities for further decipherment. And Sayce wrote resignedly: "Of a decipherment in
the true sense of the word I had given up all hope unless
fortune brought us a bilingual of some length."

Then the improbable happened. What Sayce named as
the last way out of the impasse, the bilingual of which the
scholars had dreamed for some seventy years, was found
at last in 1946. Oddly enough, it was found by a man
who had been working on the seals like Güterbock, but
who had never been so pessimistic as his colleague. On
the contrary, he had confidently announced that some day
the Hittite hieroglyphic script would be deciphered even
without a lengthy bilingual.

This man was Professor Helmuth Theodor Bossert. He
found the bilingual inscription only because in 1933, at a
Turkish Government reception in Ankara, he had given a
casual answer to a casual question. The Turkish Minister
of Education had asked him whether he would like to
come to Istanbul to teach at the university for a while.
And without thinking twice about it, Bossert had replied:
"Oh sure! Why not?"

We shall see later what came of this reply.

Part III

THE SECRET OF THEIR POWER

THE GOD TESHUB.

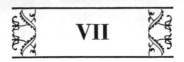

VII

THE KINGS OF HATTUSAS

I𝐹 WE ARE TO DISCUSS the history of the Hittites, we ought first to arrive at an understanding of the historian's task. This is a subject on which some confusion exists. By stressing the scientific character of their work, historians of the nineteenth and twentieth centuries have conveyed the impression that what they have written is strictly scientific and literally so.

Nothing could be farther from the truth. The one scientific branch of historical writing is source criticism, which was perfected in the nineteenth century. The source critic examines the existing sources with the manifold techniques of modern science. Chronicles, reports, deeds, charters, letters, traditions of all sorts are subjected to careful scrutiny. Scientific methods are used to determine the origin, genuineness, and value of the available material. But the *selection* of sources still rests upon the discretion of the individual historian. What he chooses as relevant depends upon his conception of the period he is studying. In this the historian is limited by his own temperament and guided by the spirit of his age.

Infatuated with their new "scientific approach," the early exponents of source criticism ignored this subjective side of the matter. The famous German historian, Leopold von Ranke, stated the conviction of many of his professional colleagues when he wrote:

"It has been said that the task of the historian is to judge the past so that his contemporaries may draw from it lessons for the future. This work boasts no such high ambitions; its aim is merely to show what actually happened."

". . . *What actually happened.*" These words reveal a point of view which was natural to an age when science was in the saddle. Implicit in them is the belief that the growth and decay of nations can be reconstructed out of separate items of data, the way chemical compounds can be put together out of separate elements. If we were to take that statement of Ranke's as a standard for historical writing, we would necessarily condemn all the great historians the world has ever known. Among those judged and found wanting would be Herodotus (traditionally nicknamed not only the "father of history" but also the "father of lies"), Thucydides, Tacitus, and Suetonius (who as an "anecdotalist" should be held in low esteem these days). Froissart and Gibbon would be demoted to the rank of writers of historical fiction—to say nothing of bolder spirits like Herder, Carlyle, Nietzsche, Spengler, and Toynbee. Yet we continue to prize the historical works of these men for all that they abound in obvious errors of detail.

On the opposite side of the fence stands Oswald Spengler who said in no uncertain terms:

"Historical writing is fiction!"

Again and again Spengler insisted upon the interpretative function of the historian. Johan Huizinga (1872–1945), the Dutch historian, expressed a similar view with great profundity when he wrote:

"History is the intellectual form in which a culture decides for itself the meaning of its past."

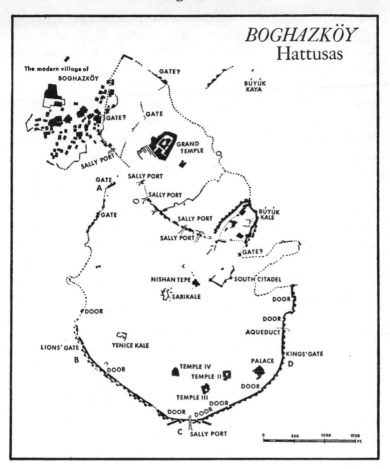

BOGHAZKÖY (HATTUSAS).

Neither Ranke's scientific method nor Spengler's interpretative approach will help us in our dealings with the
historical events of the second millennium B.C. in Asia
Minor. Our picture of the time is still too sketchy, our con-

ception too dim. The archæologists have found plenty of material, but the gaps are still enormous. With what the historian now has at his disposal he can at best piece together a history of the Hittite kings and their wars.

Kings and wars are all very well, but the nineteenth century taught us to look for something else: the way of life of a civilization, its cultural history. In this field the Hittites seem to have left us little to go by. Naturally, some conclusions about religion, law, art, and manners of the Hittite Empire can be drawn from clay-tablet texts dealing with special subjects. Every ancient culture tells us something about itself in this way. But Hittite culture remains a mystery in many respects because no organic development, no indisputably native style and character, has been discerned. As we shall see later, however, this very drawback affords tremendous opportunities to a bold and courageous historian.

In 1834 Texier stood before the ruins of Boghazköy, or Hattusas as we shall now call it, employing the historical name. In 1907 Winckler demonstrated that Hattusas had been the capital of the Hittite Empire. Nineteen centuries *after* the birth of Christ, research into Hittite history began. Once the clay tablets had been read, it turned out that the birth of the kingdom had taken place in Hattusas around nineteen centuries *before* Christ. It is fitting and proper that we begin our account of Hittite history with the story of Hattusas.

It started with a curse!

"I took it by storm during the night," the king declared grandiloquently, "and where it had been, I sowed weeds." And he continued: "Whosoever becomes king after me and again settles Hattusas, may the Weather-god of Heaven strike him!"

These words are part of a long temple inscription written in an ancient form of the Hittite language. They were spoken by King Anittas of Kussara who defeated the local princeling of the small fortress of Hattusas and leveled the town to the ground. His curse was disregarded. Some time around 1800 B.C. Hattusas was rebuilt by some other ruler, and made greater and more beautiful than it had been.

We know little about the ups and downs of the many tribes and nations that occupied Asia Minor, Syria, and Mesopotamia in those times. Sargon's Babylonian Empire (around 2300 B.C.) had long since decayed; the influence of the Assyrians in Asia Minor was steadily diminishing. City-states and petty kingdoms made war upon one another with varying success; alliances were formed; here and there shortlived *ententes cordiales* sprang up. But so far as we know there were no lasting concentrations of power.

This situation changed, however, when the Hittites descended from the north. Had they come from the northeast or the northwest? We do not know, any more than we know their real names (see Chapter 5). But in any case they were Indo-Europeans. Doubtless their army amounted to no more than a few thousand men. But obviously they were more intelligent and vigorous than the natives, the proto-Hattians. From the moment they appeared on the scene they displayed a rare combination of political shrewdness and military strength. They seem to have been so strong that no one put up any serious resistance against them. They took over the area and apparently had the wisdom not to enslave the peoples they conquered. Instead, they enlisted the loyalty of their new subjects.

Oddly enough, the first Hittite kings made a point of tracing their origins back to the House of Kussara, to the same King Anittas who had destroyed Hattusas and laid a curse upon anyone who should dare to build again in the "Narrow Gorge." We would know little today about these first Hittite kings had not one ruler, who lived some hundred and fifty years after the conquest, written a historical preface to his edicts—in order to justify his own innovations. This king, whose name was Telipinus, mentions three rulers as the fathers of the kingdom: Labarnas, Hattusilis I, and Mursilis I.

ROYAL STELE FOUND AT BIREDJIK.

The name Labarnas later came to mean "king"—so completely did its bearer become identified with greatness, just as, in a later era, the name Cæsar gave rise to the titles of Czar, Kaiser, and so on. If the slender information we have is accurate, Labarnas was really the founder of the first Hittite Empire. "And the land was small . . ." one of the texts tells us. "Wherever he took the field, his strong arm overcame the enemy," says another. He welded

the city-states and petty kingdoms into a new political
unit, extended his borders to the west and his sphere of
influence to the south and to the north perhaps as far as
the Black Sea and the Mediterranean. There are indications that he was the first to stabilize the institution of the
monarchy by providing for a degree of regularity in the
succession. He established, at any rate, the king's right to
name his successor.

His son, Hattusilis I (1650–1620 B.C.), built upon the
father's beginnings. He advanced southward toward
Aleppo in order to create a buffer state to protect his empire. But his most dangerous foes were behind his back.
Returning home ill from the Aleppo campaign, he set
down his testament, which was at the same time a personal lament. It is a document unique in the early literature of the world. The king's mournful dying words attain
the intensity of poetry:

*Thus the Great King, the Tabarna, speaks to the Assembly
        and to the dignitaries:*
*Behold, I have fallen sick. I had brought young Labarnas
        before you, saying:*
"He shall sit upon the throne."
I, the king, called him my son, embraced him, exalted him
And gave him the tenderest care. But lo! how the boy has
Behaved during my illness. It is indescribable!
He shed no tears, he showed no pity.
Cold he is, and heartless.
Therefore I, the king, summoned him to my couch.
*Well, then! Who henceforth will raise up his nephew like
        a son?*
*To the words of the king he has never hearkened. But to
        the words of his mother, the serpent, he hearkened.*
*Brothers and sisters brought evil counsels to him again and
        again.*

To their counsels he hearkened. I learned of this, I, the
*   king.*
So be it: Force shall be answered with force!
But enough! He is my son no longer! Then his mother
*   bellowed like a cow:*
"They have rent the womb in my living body. They have
*   ruined him*
And you will kill him!" But have I, the king, done him any
*   harm?*
Have I not made him a priest?
Always I raised him up before others; always I was
*   concerned for his welfare. But he has never*
Lovingly obeyed the king's wishes. How then could he,
If all went according to his wish,
Love Hattusas?

The dying king proposes a new successor to replace this disobedient nephew—his grandson Mursilis. He issues instructions for the punishment of his heartless heir, and his sister, reducing their income, banishing them to specific estates. He also makes some general remarks on the proper upbringing of princes and passes on some advice to the newly-chosen successor. Though the young man is to remain always within the court circle, he should nevertheless live modestly on water and bread. He should wait until old age before turning to wine. "Then drink to satiety."

This moving document, which was written around 1620 B.C., poses a peculiar problem. Could such dignified simplicity and power of language, such artful alternation of narration and dialogue, of lamentation and instruction, have sprung, as it were, out of the blue? If so, it would be something of a miracle. Experience suggests that this testament of Hattusilis must have been the culmination of a long literary development. But at present we possess no evidence of any such development within the Hittite Empire as a whole. One of the latest interpreters of Hittite culture, Dr. Margarete Riemschneider, believes that the testament was first and foremost meant to be a political document. This seems unlikely, in view of the exceedingly personal concluding sentences. But in any case, Dr. Riemschneider's thesis would explain only the content of the testament, not its polished *form*.

According to this testament, one of the last official acts of Hattusilis I was to pass over his unfortunate first-born son in order to make Mursilis heir to the throne. This grandson, Mursilis I (1620–1590 B.C.) forged the loose federation of city-states into the first Hittite *empire*, creating a third Great Power in the Orient, one that could vie with Egypt to the Southwest and Babylonia to the Southeast. He made the name of the Hatti feared throughout the Near East. Having conquered Aleppo, which his predecessor had failed to take, he threw all the resources of his empire into an attack on Babylon. The idea was as dramatic and senseless as Alexander the Great's invasion of India, or the attempts of Charles XII and Napoleon to conquer Russia. Mursilis did take Babylon, but of course he could not hold a city more than twelve hundred miles from his capital at Hattusas.

In 1590, shortly after his return from the war with Babylon, Mursilis was assassinated by his brother-in-law. This date is one of the few fixed points in Hittite history, for it corresponds to the well-established date of the fall of the first Babylonian dynasty.

Back of the roster of savage-sounding names—Hantilis, Zidantas, Ammunas, Huzziyas—are stories of palace intrigues and dynastic struggles for power among the kings, the nobles, and the priests. These are tragedies in the true Shakespearean manner—the Hittite Empire had its Hamlets, Macbeths, and Richard the Thirds three thousand years before the Bard of Avon wrote his first plays. Fratricide and parricide decided the succession to the throne; ambitious widows and power-hungry regents governed in place of helpless minors.

With the foundations of the monarchy so shaky, only the establishment of a legitimate royal line could restore order. Necessity forced upon the Hittites the idea of hereditary succession.

Telipinus appears to have been the one who put across this vital political concept. What he created was a kind of constitutional monarchy. Succession through the male heir was provided for by law, but the right to pass judgment upon the king himself was given to the *Pankus*, the council of nobles. This council could issue a warning if it suspected the king of intentions upon the life of any of his kinsmen. What is more, it could mete out the death penalty upon the king if there were proof that he had actually murdered any of his relatives.

The constitution marked a great step forward over the previous political situation. Since Telipinus had the power to enforce his royal authority, the functions of the *Pankus* were limited to intervention only in case a crime were committed by the king. On the other hand, since no claim was made that the Hittite kings were themselves divine or had been granted sovereignty by a god, the king's legal status derived ultimately from the *Pankus*. Political scientists should certainly look into this earliest form of constitutional monarchy.

It is not surprising that the first codification of Hittite laws took place in this period, most probably under the direction of Telipinus himself. These laws were surely based upon older collections. They also derived a good deal from Babylonian and Assyrian codes. But they were altogether different from all other Oriental codes of law

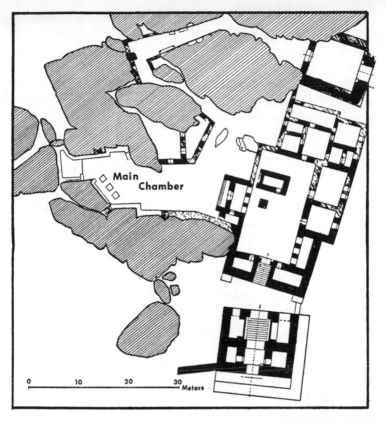

GROUND-PLAN OF THE ROCK-TEMPLE OF YAZILIKAYA NEAR BOGHAZKÖY (HATTUSAS). ONLY REMNANTS OF THE FOUNDATIONS OF THE BUILDINGS OUTSIDE (RIGHT) THE RECESS IN THE ROCK ARE LEFT. THE DRAWING IS A RECONSTRUCTION OF THE GROUND-PLAN AS IT EXISTED DURING THE FIRST HALF OF THE THIRTEENTH CENTURY B.C.

in the mildness of their penalties, and they contained a
great many legal innovations. In these respects they command our admiration.

Unfortunately we know little of how the new laws of
Telipinus worked out in practice. For decades scholars
constructed theories which turned out to have been based
on a misunderstanding. For this misunderstanding no one
is to blame. It is one of those errors which creep into the
texture of every new science. A question of chronology
was involved and chronology can be crucial to interpretation.

At one time the historians placed Telipinus in the era
1620–1600 B.C. The next set of texts had to be dated
around 1430 B.C. Hence historians were suddenly confronted with a gap of some two hundred years, a period
apparently an utter blank. Not a single document, not a
single inscription, not a single artifact could be found
which belonged to those years. Nowhere else in history
have two centuries disappeared so, leaving no trace of
themselves.

Kurt Bittel, Winckler's successor as excavator at Boghazköy, drew up a "Table of the Hittite Kings" in which
he simply left a blank for these two hundred years (from
about 1600–1400 B.C.). Albrecht Götze, one of the foremost living Hittitologists, was confounded by this same
gap, but promised that the riddle would soon be unlocked.
"For the present," he said, "I will only suggest that I see it
[the gap] as connected with a peak of Hurrian power, attained in the Mitanni Kingdom." Götze observed that scat-
terings of source material began to be present again
around 1430 B.C.—"after a period during which the Hittites relapsed into provincial insignificance."

Could that possibly have been the case? Could a great
and growing Power have "relapsed into provincial insignificance"—and have remained in that condition for two
hundred years?

Suppose, for example, that we blanked out a similar period in the history of the western world—let us say, the years from 1500 to 1700. In that case there would be no transition between the Middle Ages and modern times. Historians would find themselves surveying what appeared to be two entirely different cultures. The settlement of the New World would have been blanked out; the greatness of Spain; Portugal's era of glory; the entire Baroque Age; the Reformation with its deep effects upon every aspect of our civilization; the beginnings of modern science in the work of Giordano Bruno, Galileo, Tycho Brahe, and Johannes Kepler; the critical philosophies of Hobbes, Spinoza, and Leibniz; the rise of the modern theater in the dramas of Shakespeare, Molière, and Calderon.

What a task for historians to fill in by pure guesswork the possible happenings of those two hundred years—supposing that their latest data ended with Charles V and they were faced with a total void until the reign of Frederick the Great of Prussia! Yet such was the problem the Hittitologists thought they had to solve. There were those two hundred years during which darkest night appeared to have descended upon Asia Minor. Those missing pages, which seemed to have been torn out of history, prompted them to make the wildest conjectures.

All their theories were false.

Now that the enigma has been explained the solution seems simple enough. Yet it remains astonishing that no one thought of subjecting the established *chronology* of events in Asia Minor to a searching criticism. Surely someone should have guessed, even if he had not been able to prove it at once, that what had gone wrong was the whole system of dating. Surely it should have occurred to someone that a people's history cannot stop dead for two hundred years.

To understand how the weird confusion came about, we shall have to take a look into the field of chronology.

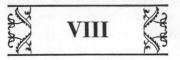

VIII

THE SCIENCE OF HISTORICAL DATING

Men's knowledge of their fathers, grandfathers, and great-grandfathers—the record of their own ancestry—is the simplest, the most natural, and at the same time the most elementary way of reckoning time. It is the type of reckoning that is still practiced by primitive peoples—supplemented by recollections of natural catastrophes. In rural areas to this day people will speak in terms of such memories: "When Grandpa was a boy. . . ." "In the year of the hurricane. . . ." "In the year of the big flood. . . ."

Usually, though not always, it is a sign of the beginnings of an advanced culture when a people develops more reliable methods of calculating time. Egon Friedell, the most brilliant cultural historian of our age, whose thoroughly unscientific books have been enormously suggestive to scientists, once remarked: "Man's most powerful longing, his eternal dream, is to bring *chronology* into the world. Once we have subjected time to a scheme of reckoning, once we made it comprehensible in terms of measurement, we have the illusion that we can control it, that it belongs to us."

Precise observation of the seasonal round of the year is usually the starting point for careful astronomical determination of time. In Egypt such observation arose because of the blessings brought by the river, in Babylonia out of fear of the destructive forces of the two rivers. In the Mayan civilization of Central America the establishment of great annual cycles degenerated into a calendar terrorism that bound the whole life of the people in the straitjacket of astronomical events.

Greek culture, which we customarily rank higher than any other culture of the ancient world, was distinctly peculiar in this respect, for it made no use of precise time-reckonings—aside from the Olympic Games. The Greeks in general possessed no historical sense; they ignored dates and carelessly massed together the events and personages of history until all was wild confusion—as we can see in Herodotus.

Oswald Spengler commented:

"In having a sense of history we heirs of Western European culture are exceptions rather than the rule. Universal history is *our* view of the world, not that of 'mankind.' " The truth of this is brought home to us when we consider the case of the ancient Babylonians who, for all their refined methods of calculating time, never utilized that technique for historical purposes.

Anyone approaching the study of ancient history for the first time must be impressed by the positive way modern historians date events which took place thousands of years ago. In the course of further study this wonder will, if anything, increase. For as we examine the sources of ancient history we see how scanty, inaccurate, or downright false, the records were even at the time they were first written. And poor as they originally were, they are poorer still as they have come down to us: half destroyed by the tooth of time or by the carelessness and rough usage of men.

As a matter of fact, the more we pursue our studies, the less are we impressed by the dates which initially filled us with respect. We begin to recognize the framework of chronological history for what it is—a purely hypothetical structure, and one which threatens to come apart at every joint. Crooked and tottering, it gives us a picture of a strangely arbitrary history, while at the same time our instinct tells us that the ancient civilizations must have had some sort of reasonable and organic growth. When we reach this point in our studies we begin to be doubtful of every single date!

To give an example of the untrustworthiness of chronology: investigators toiling for a century have had to shift the date for the unification of Egypt by King Menes, who established the first Egyptian dynasty, from 5867 B.C. to 2900 B.C. And even this latter date, which is considered the real beginning of Egyptian history, has not yet been determined with complete certainty.

When we learn of the two missing centuries in Hittite history, our confidence in chronological history is apt to be seriously shaken. But as we go even deeper into the subject, our respect for the achievements of historical detective work returns. We learn that the scholars have been careful to distinguish between "assured" and "assumed" dates. And we discover that the chronological framework of ancient history rests upon at least a few firm points. Certain key dates, around which other dates are mustered, can be determined almost without error. They are "assured."

Archæological research began by studying what lay in plain sight; only later did it seek the deeper cultural layers concealed beneath the chips and shards of the surface. Similarly, the historian started with clear written records and then slowly groped his way back to the more obscure chapters of the past. Wherever he found direct connections with Greek, Persian, or late Egyptian events, he was able to fit the new data into his time-scheme. By now the

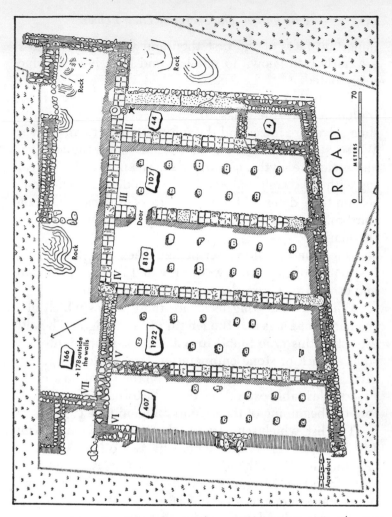

GROUND-PLAN OF "BUILDING A" OF THE BOGHAZKÖY (HAT-
TUSAS) CITADEL. HERE IN 1931 BITTEL FOUND NEW CLAY
TABLETS. THE NUMERALS WITHIN EACH OF THE SEVEN ROOMS
GIVE THE NUMBER OF TABLETS FOUND AND INDICATE THAT
ROOMS IV, V AND VI WERE USED FOR STORING ARCHIVES. THE
ASTERISK IN ROOM II INDICATES THE SPOT WHERE ONE OF
THE FEW GRAVES SO FAR LOCATED AT BOGHAZKÖY WAS
FOUND.

important facts of the first thousand years before Christ are fairly well known to scholars and have been satisfactorily dated.

The further we push back into the past, however, the frailer become the links to known events. The sources themselves are fewer and the information in them sparser. Worse still, they become more and more vague. Soon chronicles are myths, narratives sagas, kings gods. In dealing with the second millennium B.C. modern scholars must reckon their dates with possible errors of decades; by the third millennium their estimates may be centuries wide of the mark.

Once the cuneiform script had been deciphered, the first points of departure were provided by king lists, date and other lists, chronicles and royal inscriptions.

What we call "king lists" are those tables which give the names of kings and the length of their reigns. The oldest list of this type found in Asia Minor is an eight-inch-square block of stone enumerating the "proto-kings," the mythical rulers who reigned between the Creation and the Flood. This table extends as far as historic times—just before the beginning of the second millennium B.C.

This list, which scholars call the "Old Babylonian King List WB 444," is complemented by two others known as "A" and "B." With the aid of these, of the "Assyrian King List" found at Khorsabad in the winter of 1932–3, and of several fragmentary lists of later dynasties, chronology can be brought down to the first millennium B.C.—at which point there is sufficient information from other sources to make exact dating fairly easy.

When we hear of the existence of such relatively continuous lists of rulers, which give the length of each reign, and now and then even mention major events, we are apt to think that chronology should be no problem at all. But a mere glance at such a list quickly brings disillusionment. "WB 444," for example, begins with the kings before the Flood.

> *When the kingdom descended from Heaven*
> *the kingdom was in Eridu.*
> *In Eridu Alulim was king.*
> *28,800 years he reigned.*
> *Alalgar reigned 36,000 years.*
> *Two kings—*
> *64,800 years they reigned.*
> *Eridu was overthrown;*
> *the kingdom passed to Bad-tibira.*
> *In Bad-tibira En-men-lu-anna*
> *reigned 43,200 years.*
> *En-men-gal-anna*
> *reigned 28,800 years.*
> *God Dumuzi, the shepherd, reigned*
> *36,000 years.*

And so on.

This is the way "Babylonian King List B" begins:

Sumu-abi, King		*15 years*
Sumu-la-il		*35 years*
Sabu	*his son*	*14 years*
Apil-Sin	*his son*	*18 years*
Sin-muballit	*his son*	*30 years*
Hammurabi	*his son*	*55 years*
Samsu-iluna	*his son*	*35 years*

And so on.

We need not discuss the remarkable longevities of the kings before the Flood. It is obvious that for the present this aspect of the list has no historical value, though it is quite possible that archæology may some day verify the existence of these rulers. When that point is reached, it is likely that their reigns may turn out to have been a few years shorter than the list indicates.

These specimens suffice to show that the king lists provide historians with nothing more than a succession *without any fixed historical point of reference*. In other words, it is evident from "King List B" that Sumu-la-il reigned for thirty-five years after King Sumu-abi, who held his throne for only fifteen years. But *when* Sumu-la-il began his reign is not apparent.

But that is not the worst of it. Archæologists and historians would be delighted if they could at least depend on the order of succession. But that they cannot do. The Babylonian listers casually omitted kings whom they considered unimportant. Or else they copied wrongly. Or else they took dynasties which had reigned simultaneously and listed these one under another instead of side by side.

A document from the time of King Sargon I (about 2350 B.C.), for example, maintained that no less than 350 kings had ruled over the land of Assur before the said king —an utterly implausible statement which nevertheless gave rise to enormous confusion. Scholars finally discovered where the mistake lay: the copyist had simply added together several different, concurrent king lists.

Exploring the mazes of chronology, scholars are sometimes able to find help in the "date and eponym lists." From the time of Sargon I to the time of Hammurabi (almost 700 years) Babylonians were in the habit of giving names to the years and writing down catalogues of these names. This sounds simple enough—but the ancients made things hard for themselves and for us.

True dates, which cite a particular year, or a definite month or day within that year, are very rarely found. The Babylonian scribes would name the year for an important event which had taken place the previous year—to our minds an illogical procedure, but one which was long practiced in Egypt also, during the Old Empire. The event might be a military victory, the building of a temple, the appointment of a high official or general. The most important of all such events, of course, would be the accession of a new king.

Scholars soon recognized that these lists were tricky. The custom was for the beginning of a new reign to be counted officially from the time of the New Year Festival; the period from the actual change of government until the end of the year was included within the old king's reign. But there was no way of telling whether the customary method of reckoning had been followed. Moreover, the names of years were often changed—in obedience to the whims of kings, or in deliberate falsification of history, or for whatever reason. Finally, the scribes had a habit of abbreviating the names—often distorting them beyond recognition. Or else they cited from memory and made mistakes.

All this should make it clear that the establishment of a chronological framework for ancient history was no easy matter. There were still further complications. The "eponym lists," in which the year was named after a high official, general, or king, rather than after an event, were equally perplexing. (The same method, incidentally, was employed much later in Greece.) The Assyrians had long used this principle in naming years. But as with the date lists, there were irrational deviations from the norm.

In spite of these maddening inconsistencies, some progress could be made. By systematic comparison the scholars were able to recognize gaps, detect mistakes, and now and then establish a time-relationship between an event and a particular person. But still no historical fixed points could be obtained.

The situation began looking up when the "chronicles"

were deciphered and subjected to intensive study. These chronicles cannot be compared to those of our own Middle Ages. In our mediæval chronicles we meet with a slowly awakening sense of history. Those of the Near East (except for a few Hittite chronicles) were merely attempts to group significant events around eminent persons. The story was written long after the event; the ignorance of the narrator, the inadequacies of reports, and the fallacies of tradition found their way straight into the account. The chroniclers preserved what they knew; they made no effort to fill in what they did not know but might have found out. They arranged events in an order of their own making. A chronicler would copy from his predecessor, would smooth out thorny passages to suit his taste, would add anecdotes he had heard from his great-grandfather, and pass this garbled version of history on to the next chronicler who treated it in the same manner. The most important of the Babylonian chronicles has come down to us in such a "copy of copies" made during the age of Cyrus the Great (around 550 B.C.). The original version must have been exceedingly ancient—how old we do not know.

Curiously enough, a scholar living today can examine material which may have been inaccessible to a Babylonian chronicler living in the provinces. On the basis of this knowledge, the scholar is able to point out the shortcomings of a chronicler who died more than three thousand years ago. "We do not know where the author of 'Chronicle K' obtained his material," such a modern historian writes, "but he might have added greatly to his section on Sargon and his dynasty if he had made use of the inscriptions already assembled in the Temple Library at Nippur."

Supplementing and often confirming these chronicles are the "royal inscriptions," those accounts that rulers had chiseled in stone or baked into clay in order that posterity might know of all the great deeds which had been performed during their reigns. These inscriptions, however, must be evaluated with the greatest caution. Their contents are not only untrustworthy—they are often bare-

BRONZE STATUETTE.

faced lies. Oriental kings were usually tyrants, always despots. Since the dimmest beginnings of history such rulers have had the habit of deciding what the truth is to be. They do not even have to make their own boasts; because their very existence is felt to be superhuman, superhuman deeds are attributed to them. It is absurd to imagine that Oriental kings were the authors of their inscriptions, simply because their texts always begin with: "I, Great King. . . ." Despots do not need to compose their own eulogies. When Hitler was at the height of his power there were many clear-headed persons who realized that the end was already in sight, but there were still hundreds of thousands who went on singing the praises of the "greatest general in history," the "godsent Führer"—although nobody forced them to do so. Hitler no longer needed to order his panegyrics; his followers served them up of their own accord.

Nevertheless, even the royal inscriptions contribute something to chronology because they link particular events with particular persons. There is a high probability that the relationship at least is correct, even though the presentation may be false.

These then are the records from which we gather as best we can information on the history of the Near East. We have, in addition, a very modest text which was found during the nineteenth century in the famous clay tablet library of Assurbanipal at Nineveh. In clear and simple language this text treats of the wars between Assyria and Babylonia. It describes the kind of peace with which each war was concluded. In other words, the text synchronizes Assyrian and Babylonian history. A term has been coined for just this type of data: "synchronistic history." The text in question was of priceless value, since it gave scholars *fourteen* synchronizations to work with. "Synchronism" is the magic word, the "open Sesame," which in the end opened the doors to the dark, rich caverns of the past.

For a hundred years, with infinite patience and industry, scholars worked to establish these synchronisms. Like sailors on treacherous waters, they could see only a few beacon lights and did not know whether they dared trust these. Aided only by a handful of basic dates, these historians attempted to set up a system of coordinates covering more than two thousand years of ancient history. Thousands of papers were written around incredibly minor points. In general chronology, however, there are very few comprehensive studies; even chronological tables are exceedingly rare. No wonder, for anyone who published a table exposed himself to such unmerciful criticism that he thought better of it next time and kept rash suppositions to himself.

This painstaking comparison of dates would have led to nothing if the search had not eventually gone beyond the limits of Babylonian-Assyrian history. An obvious source of additional material was the Bible—which is a chronicle as well as a religious book. But it soon turned out that a far better comparative scale was available in the historical tables of the Egyptologists. In fact, Egyptian scholars were the first to provide the students of the Land of the Two Rivers with *fixed points*.

The Egyptologists had had a far easier time of it. The material at their disposal was incomparably richer. Archæological expeditions on Egyptian soil had yielded superabundant "loot"—for decades they had been finding above-ground material which their colleagues in Mesopotamia had had to sift laboriously out of the debris of millennia. In the great historical account by the Egyptian priest Manetho (*circa* 280 B.C.) the Egyptologists possessed a chronological survey extending from Menes, the founder of the Egyptian Empire, to the conquest of Egypt by Artaxerxes III, King of the Persians, in 343 B.C. For all its faults, this "history" gave them a sound chronological basis. Moreover, the Egyptian king lists were incomparably clearer and more extensive than those found in Mesopotamia. Their Egyptian royal inscriptions were almost too plentiful. But the unique boon which Egypt offered the historians of ancient times was the Egyptian calendar.

This calendar was priceless because it was relatively easy to understand and almost identical with the Julian calendar which continued in use in the West until the sixteenth century A.D. By means of this calendar the scholars arrived at their first fixed points in the ancient history of the Near East.

Since the rise of the Nile brought the annual blessing of fruitful alluvial muck to the land, the Egyptians naturally reckoned in terms of the "Nile year." Very early in the history of Egypt the priests noticed that this Nile year coincided with the annual revolution of the fixed star Sirius, which the Egyptians called Sothis and which they worshipped as the goddess Isis.

According to modern astronomical computations, a Sothis year corresponds almost exactly to a solar year. Egyptologists worked with astronomers and mathematicians, engaging in the most refined calculations to discover the precise margin of difference. It was found that 1461 Egyptian years were the equivalent of 1460 Julian solar years, and this discovery proved enormously fruitful for chronology. Archæologists could now employ the "Sothis Period" to establish their fixed points of reference with absolute certainty.

A Roman writer named Censorinus provided the first fixed point. He described the end of a Sothis Period with such precision that astronomers, by computing the ascension of Sirius, were able to establish the year as A.D. 137. From this date it was only necessary to subtract further Sothis Periods of 1460 Julian years in order to establish new fixed points. The mathematicians were willing to continue their calculations indefinitely, but the archæologists called a halt at the fourth period; their excavations showed no evidence of an advanced civilization at so early a date.

The next date established within this framework was

July 19, 237 B.C. (Old Style, that is, according to the Julian calendar). This was based upon an inscription, the "Decree of Canopus," in which the "emergence of Sothis" was mentioned. A papyrus named after Georg Ebers, novelist and Egyptologist, gave a date for the beginning of the eighteenth dynasty; from another papyrus, the astronomers were able to fix the start of the twelfth dynasty. Now the king lists, with their records of the duration of various reigns, suddenly took on meaning. More and more dates could be set down within the outlines already established. The Assyriologists also profited—letters, treaties, and reports of battles in which Egypt figured could henceforth be dated.

A splendid beginning had been made. With pride, the great German historian Eduard Meyer, in his *Egyptian Chronology* (1904–1908), calculated *"the oldest date in world history: July 19, 4241 B.C."* And then it was discovered that Sothis Period reckonings, though beautifully accurate as far as the second millennium B.C., were of doubtful value for more ancient times. In lengthy learned treatises the mathematicians explained why this was so, and most Egyptologists are now coming round to accepting their arguments.

This development dealt a particularly severe blow to the Assyriologists. All of Near Eastern chronology was once more thrown into a state of confusion.

We must now return to the question which led us to the subject of chronology. What had happened to those missing two hundred years?

Although the chronological framework of Babylonian-Assyrian history has been fairly well reconstructed, one great unsolved problem has persisted until very recent times. That is the dating of Hammurabi. The dates of minor kings of the second millennium B.C. had already been settled. Hammurabi alone remained at large in time. In spite of all their keenness and ingenuity the archæologists were unable to place the great lawgiver King, undoubtedly the most important of the monarchs who reigned between the Tigris and the Euphrates.

Scholars felt they could legitimately assume certain synchronisms. Again and again they calculated the regnal years from the king lists. They re-examined the archæological strata. They conferred with the experts in comparative art history, those connoisseurs who can read volumes in a piece of ceramic or a bit of sculpture. Again and again they arrived at the twentieth or the nineteenth centuries B.C. All the probabilities suggested this early date; there was no evidence indicating that Hammurabi might have lived later, closer in time to us.

Indeed there was a single scrap of data which nobody considered important. It was a legal document dated "in the tenth year of Hammurabi" in which an oath was taken in the name "of Marduk, Hammurabi and Shamshi-Adad."

Marduk was the supreme god, Hammurabi the Babylonian lawgiver. But Shamshi-Adad was an Assyrian king who according to all other other documents could not possibly have lived at the time of Hammurabi, but must have lived two centuries earlier. The wording of the oath was therefore assumed to have been a traditional formula; no one drew the conclusion that Hammurabi and Shamshi-Adad might in fact have been contemporaries. And because this possibility was overlooked, two hundred years were missing.

Within the chronologies of Ancient Egypt and Babylonia-Assyria the scholars were able to manipulate their data in such a way as to fit Hammurabi in somewhere—there were enough dynasties and enough kings to juggle. But since the Hittite documents were far fewer, and king lists were sadly lacking, there were no opportunities for such manipulations. The two centuries were just missing.

Gradually, therefore, it began to be apparent that the tried and tested chronology stood in need of revision. Weidner, the German Assyriologist, proposed assigning Hammurabi's reign to the years 1955–1913 B.C. In 1938 the American archæologist Albright suggested 1868–1826; in 1940 the German scholar Ungnad insisted upon 1801–1759. All these guesses were wrong. Evidence was needed in the form of some definite synchronism. This was supplied at last by excavation.

In the nineteen-thirties a French lieutenant was on duty near Tell Hariri, on the border of Syria and Iraq. He happened to observe a group of Bedouins gathering large stones. What did they want with the stones? he inquired. They explained that the stones were needed to protect the grave of a comrade from the nightly depredations of predatory animals. In the course of their chat with the lieutenant, the tribesmen mentioned that they had found a remarkably large stone shaped like a human being, though headless.

The lieutenant reported the find. The outcome was that in 1933 the First Curator of the Museums of France, Professor André Parrot, came to Tell Hariri to excavate. On January 23, 1933, at the very beginning of his work, he discovered from inscriptions on a statuette that he was on the site of the "Royal City of Mari," the "tenth after the Flood."

For some twenty years Parrot dug at Mari—"barring an annoying interruption during the Second World War," he remarks. He exposed ruins over which three thousand years of man's civilization had passed. The most interesting of his finds was the state archives of the kings of Mari, containing some *twenty thousand* clay-tablet inscriptions.

RECONSTRUCTION OF THE TWO FAÇADES OF THE "KING'S GATE" AT BOGHAZKÖY (HATTUSAS). SEE PLATE XXV.

There were letters and treaties, reports and deeds, chronicles and stories of daily life. Among the latter was the quaint tale of the "Lion on the Roof-balcony." To understand this tale we must realize that in those days lion-hunting was a privilege reserved to kings.

"So says Jakim-Addad, your servant: I wrote lately to my Lord in the following words: 'A lion was captured upon the roof-balcony of the house belonging to Akkara. If this lion should remain on the roof until the coming of my Lord, let my Lord write to me, and if he wishes me to send this lion to my Lord, let my Lord write this to me.' Now the reply of my Lord has been delayed, and the lion has remained upon the roof a full five days. A dog and a swine have been thrown to him, and he also eats bread. I said: 'This lion may cause a panic among the people.' Then I became afraid and closed the lion in a wooden cage. I shall load this cage upon a barge and have it taken to my Lord."

Anecdotes such as these, however, were of subsidiary interest to the scholars. For them the exciting finds in the Mari archives were documents which proved conclusively that Shamshi-Adad had been an elder contemporary of Hammurabi. The reign of Shamshi-Adad had been fixed with fair accuracy, on the basis of the Assyrian king list, at about 1780–1750 B.C. Therefore the reign of Hammurabi must have been "around 1700." In the twenty years since this discovery many more documents have been examined, and it may now be considered "relatively certain" that Hammurabi reigned from 1728 to 1686 B.C. (Or was until the final proofs of this book came to hand. For two other distinguished scientists, Albrecht Götze of Yale University and Benno Landsberger of the University of Chicago, have challenged the new dating. Götze has questioned the "short" chronology, and Landsberger in a long and brilliant article has calculated by reconstruction that Shamshi-Adad was alive in 1852 B.C. What, then, are Hammurabi's proper dates?)

One of the most vexing chronological problems of the Ancient World had been solved. All at once a whole chain of definite synchronisms followed. Scholars were able to plunge far deeper into the past and establish a date for the reign of Sargon I—who not long before had been dismissed as a legendary figure.

That date was 2350 B.C. It is now accepted as the earliest computed date in history which can be considered "very probably correct."

The spaces in the network of synchronisms which Assyriologists and Egyptologists had supplied were altogether too wide. Too few fixed dates had been caught in the mesh. The Hittitologists did not have neatly arranged king lists, and they did not know the duration of most reigns. Moreover, that troublesome gap of two hundred years had prompted them to divide Hittite history into an "Old Kingdom" and a "New Kingdom"—before and after the hiatus.

This division, of course, was entirely arbitrary. Once Hammurabi was accounted for, the history of the Hittite kingdom proved to have been continuous. But even today there are only two dates in the reconstructed king lists which are really certain. These are the years 1590 and 1335 B.C., which have been confirmed by Babylonian synchronisms. 1590 B.C. marks the death of Mursilis I. This took place shortly after his conquest of Babylon. The death of Suppiluliumas occurred in 1335 B.C.—we know from Egyptian sources that he died four years after Tutankhamen.

If, however, we do not insist on exact dates, we fare a little better. Synchronisms between events a decade or so apart are far more numerous. And since where three millennia have elapsed an error of a decade more or less may be considered minor, we may say that we are amazingly well informed about Hittite chronology—as a glance at the chronological table in the back of this book will show.

That most modern branch of science, atomic physics, has provided archæology with a remarkable tool for chronological research. The new method is dependent upon a characteristic of the isotope known as Carbon 14. Isotope is the name chemists give to varieties of the same chemical elements which differ in atomic weights. Nowadays there exist both natural and artificial isotopes. Carbon 14 is a natural isotope of carbon which is created in the highest layers of our atmosphere by cosmic ray bombardment of nitrogen. Although it occurs in very tiny quantities, Carbon 14 is absorbed by plants in the course of their life-cycle and subsequently passes into animals that feed on plants. The significant characteristic of the isotope for our purposes is that it is radioactive, and that the period of its disintegration is known.

Since at the death of a plant or animal the excretion of Carbon 14 ceases, its disappearance thereafter proceeds at the known rate of radioactive disintegration. Once-living organic matter, be it only a fiber or a chip of bone, will contain Carbon 14 in varying quantities. Determination of the quantity will reveal the *age* of the matter in question.

The foremost specialist in this field is Dr. Willard Libby of the University of Chicago. Born in Colorado in 1908, he planned originally to become an engineer, but turned to the field of chemistry where he specialized in radioactivity. He was one of the leading figures in the development of the atom bomb.

On January 9, 1948–a red-letter day for archæology—representatives of all the sciences concerned with chronology held a conference under the chairmanship of Dr. Libby. They discussed the potentialities of this new method by which the age of long-dead organic matter could be traced. The outcome was that Libby was deluged with an assemblage of antiques which must have made his laboratory look more like a witch's kitchen than the workroom of a modern chemist. There were splinters of bone, bits of plants, shreds of cloth, chips of wood, and pieces of excreta. These relics had come out of graves, funeral urns, pyramids, and temples, in the lands of the East and the Near East.

Since then Dr. Libby has had his hands full. The first step was to determine the age of an object by radioactive analysis. He then checked his conclusion against the best judgment of the archæologists. They in turn were soon correcting some of their opinions on the basis of his readings. During the last few years his methods have been greatly refined and the possible error reduced. Carbon 14 dating now holds out distinct promise for the whole science of historical chronology.

Furthermore, some organic objects can now be dated with reasonable accuracy even when wrenched from their cultural context. This marks an entirely new departure for the study of antiquity. The technique should prove especially valuable in the study of *pre*-history, for beyond the margins of history, time grows vague, unfathomable, and treacherous.

The sort of scholarship we have been discussing, however, the devising of chronologies by interpolation and interpretation, has not been superseded. It is as important as it ever was. The king lists and the chronicles continue to be studied. True, the goal of modern historians is not simply the history of kings, but the general cultural history of peoples; not the rise and fall of august personages, but the lives and sufferings of all. However, the early cultures tell us of little more than the deeds of their rulers. At that there are plenty of rulers who have left their names behind and nothing else. We know of their bare existence at some time in the past, but like their commoner contemporaries they have disappeared without a trace. There is not the slightest substance of their beings which can be placed in a chemical retort.

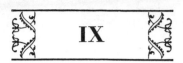

IX

THE BATTLE OF KADESH

Wɪᴛʜ ᴛʜᴇ ᴄʜʀᴏɴᴏʟᴏɢʏ straightened out, those vexing two hundred years between 1600 and 1400 ʙ.ᴄ. fell into line. There was no longer any need for far-fetched theories to explain why Hittite culture went underground for two centuries, for it had never done so. The kingdom of Tudhaliyas II (1460–1444 ʙ.ᴄ.) stemmed directly from that of Telipinus the lawgiver. Between these two important monarchs lay a few brief reigns of other kings of whom we know little at present.

The interim period contained one of the significant events of Near Eastern history. For some time the way of life of the peoples inhabiting the region had been undergoing alterations. So gradual were the changes that they are difficult to fix in space and time. By the middle centuries of the second millennium ʙ.ᴄ. their cumulative effect suddenly produced great upheavals.

The consolidation of the Hurrians was one of the dominant political factors of this era. These Hurrians were tribesmen who had long occupied the area to the east of the Hittites, as far south as Syria. Led by kings of Indo-Iranian origin, some of whom bore Indian names, they now formed the powerful and highly civilized kingdom of Mitanni. Profiting by the weakness of the Hittite kings after the death of Mursilis I, they became a serious threat to the Land of the Hatti.

In all probability there is a connection between the rise
of Mitanni and the sudden, fierce onslaught of the Hyksos
upon Egypt. As it emerges from our sparse sources, there
is something ghostly and freakish about that invasion. Out
of the mists of history there appears a fierce tribe, known

THE LION OF KALABA.

variously as "shepherd kings" or "foreign chieftains."
These Hyksos advance from the northeast deep into the
Nile delta, expel the pharaohs, take power in Egypt, and
reign for a hundred years. Then they are overthrown by
the Egyptian Amosis, are driven out of the land of the Nile
—and vanish into the darkness from which they had come.

The rise of the Hurrians, the mighty migration of the
Hyksos (in which Hurrians may have participated), the
invasion of the Kassites from Iran, who captured Babylon
in the wake of the Hittites and seized power in all of Babylonia—such appear to be the dramatic events of this tur-
bulent period in the history of the Near East. But behind
all these political developments lies a greater and more
lasting change. Similar sudden waves of migration had
taken place many times before. Now, within all the

ferment of nations, something utterly new had come into being—something that alone explains the irresistible force of the Hyksos' onrush. The future of civilization in the Near East, and therefore the future of the world, had been revolutionized by a new invention.

At some time during this period, in some place among the Hittites, Hurrians, Kassites, and the barbarian Hyksos, horse-training, the art of riding, and a special form of two-wheeled chariot had been perfected. The *light battle-chariot* had become a new weapon of war.

In the course of the excavations in the soil of ancient Hattusas, archæologists turned up a text of some thousand lines containing instructions on the breeding and training of horses. Certainly it is the oldest "handbook of equestrianism" that has come down to us—it goes back at least 3400 years. The language of the text is Hittite, and the place where it was found had, of course, once been the capital of the Hittite Kingdom. But the man who wrote the book identifies himself as a certain "Kikkuli of the land of Mitanni"—that is, a Hurrian. And he uses as technical terms words that are unquestionably of Sanskrit derivation. We will recall that some of the Hurrian kings bore Indian names.

These facts lead us to conclude that a Hittite king hired a Hurrian breeder and trainer from the land of Mitanni to run the royal stables "on the most modern principles." Apparently the Hurrians were considered the foremost horse-breeders of their day. Kikkuli's rules for the training of horses are marked by extreme pedantry, which suggests that he was working within an ancient tradition. He stipulated a seven-month period for training a horse properly.

It is evident that the Hittites cannot be considered the "inventors" of horse-training. But neither were the Hurrians. Neither of these peoples produced the first riders.

There is every indication that the equestrian arts were developed further to the East, in the depths of Asia. And since the smashing effectiveness of the war-chariot was dependent upon carefully trained horses, it is also fairly certain that the Hittites did not invent this new weapon.

The significant thing was not who discovered the chariot but who used it to best advantage. Amid the hurly-burly of stirring nations in the middle of the second millennium B.C., while Hurrians, Kassites, and savage Hyksos were ranging far and wide (though never seriously threatening the Hittite heartland in the great bend of the Halys), the Hittites absorbed all there was to be learned from their neighbors with regard to horses and chariots. They made improvements, added the fruits of their own intelligence and experience, and evolved the new engine of war with which they later won the greatest battle of antiquity, the weapon whose thunder, as the Bible tells us, made the Syrians tremble. The full development and exploitation of the light battle-chariot was the work of the Hittites.

The newly-domesticated horse was harnessed to a war-chariot long before it was ever used as cavalry. To us, for whom the chariot is an antique curiosity, this is cause for wonder. It is equally strange that cavalry, though ultimately invented by the peoples of the Near East, was lost again: the Greeks and the Romans, although they had riding horses, had no conception of mounted troops.

The light battle-chariot which the Hittites had perfected must have been so new in its day that we are justified in calling it an invention. Assyriologists may argue that the Sumerians used a type of war-chariot. But that is beside the point. The so-called chariots of that most ancient people were clumsy carts with four solid wooden wheels—they are clearly depicted on the so-called "mosaic standard of Ur" which Woolley dug up. Supposing that these carts were ever used in battle, they would only have provided moral support for the infantryman, like the ponderous vehicles of our Middle Ages—elephantine wagons that lumbered into combat at a foot-soldier's pace. It is far more likely, however, that these early Sumerian carts were merely a part of the supply train.

The wheels of the light Hittite chariot were not solid discs. They were six-spoked wheels which gave the vehicle the smart look of a nineteenth-century English dog-cart. Their great advantage lay in their speed and their mobility. Massed in formation these war-chariots revolutionized military strategy.

Each Hittite war-chariot carried three men—the driver with a warrior to either side of him. And with this fantastic thing galloping wildly toward them, this unnatural horror compounded of whinnying beasts, shouting men, and glistening weapons, the firmest infantry front broke asunder. Even if the foot-soldiers withstood the first charge, they soon found to their dismay that they had been surrounded, ringed in by the furious rush of the chariots. Showered with arrows, trampled by black hoofs, an infantry regiment could be transformed within a few minutes into a mass of frantic, fleeing men. True, some of the chariots might be shattered, but the flying splinters would also inflict wounds. Horses could be pierced by spears, but in their death struggles they crushed warriors beneath their bodies.

Sweat, the odor of horses and of blood, the biting desert dust, the screech of vultures, those scavengers of battle —such was and ever has been the panorama of the battlefield. And from the study of history we cannot help but take away the conviction that—all our hopes aside—this sort of scene will be repeated as long as there are men upon earth.

The most important battle of ancient history was of the nature we have just described. Its savagery was the more intense because both sides possessed such chariot troops. But we must now become acquainted with a few additional facts in order to see how the epoch-making conflict came about.

Most recent research seems to show that after the death of Telipinus the kingdom of Mitanni was the dominant power in the Near East. Nevertheless, four Hittite kings—Tudhaliyas II, Hattusilis II, Tudhaliyas III, and finally Arnuwandas II—managed to preserve their kingdom against fundamental changes, although the government underwent severe crises during the reign of Tudhaliyas III when the pressure from outside seems to have been at its heaviest.

Though we know little about the era between 1500 and 1375 B.C., we must not brush it aside as of small importance. A hundred and twenty-five years play a big part in the life of a nation. It is only too easy, in dealing with ancient history, to let the intoxication with millennia make us careless about centuries. But we must not yield to this temptation. It is worth while reminding ourselves that every *hundred* years is shaped by more than three generations of human beings.

After Arnuwandas, the Hittite people brought forth the greatest king in their history, the "king of kings," the new founder of a true empire, who might well be called the Charlemagne of the Near East. He was Suppiluliumas I (1375–1355 B.C.). He must have been a magnificent monarch, bold in the face of great decisions, armed with that courage and audacity which enables a man to master difficult situations in spite of the most adverse prospects. But if he was reckless, he also possessed the political wisdom to deal moderately with his foes. On the one hand he practiced religious tolerance; on the other hand he was earnestly concerned with preserving good morals and pure justice. These traits are clearly reflected in the numerous treaties he concluded during his forty-year reign.

Documents give us glimpses of his personal life. We know that he married his sister to the king of the land of Hayasa, and sent along the bride, her half sisters, and some ladies of the court for retinue. In Hayasa, however, certain customs obtained which by Hittite morality were barbarian. Among these were sibling marriage and distinct freedom of sexual relations among kinsfolk. Suppiluliumas abominated such practices. He wrote a letter to the king, his brother-in-law, informing him: "These are not the customs in Hattusas. . . . In Hattusas anyone who commits such an act does not keep his life; he is killed!" As a dreadful example he tells the story of a certain Marijas who caught his father in the act of incest and had him killed. And he adds: "Be greatly on your guard, therefore, against a thing for which a man has died!"

Suppiluliumas emerges as a highly ambivalent personality. Whatever he undertook was on the grand scale. He improved the fortifications of Hattusas; it was under his rule that the mighty southern wall of the city was built. He marched to war against powerful Mitanni, crossed the Euphrates, and conquered the Hurrian capital. But although he plundered the city, he did not enslave the people. By marrying his daughter to Prince Mattiwaza of Mitanni, he formed dynastic ties between that country and the kingdom of Hatti.

He conquered Syria, overwhelmed Aleppo and Carchemish—which had been troublesome to the Hittites for hundreds of years—and appointed his sons kings of these petty border kingdoms. To his success in warfare was added political good fortune. In Syria, for example, the

one adversary who might have been dangerous to him—
Egypt—did not seriously oppose him. Pharaoh Amenophis IV, the heretic king, was busy combatting Egyptian
polytheism and trying to persuade his people to worship
the Sun God alone. His successor, Tutankhamen, died at
the age of eighteen. With Egypt thus taken up with domestic affairs, Suppiluliumas was able not only to conquer,

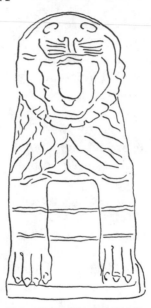

THE LION OF MARASH.

but also to consolidate his gains. He was in a position to
plan and execute long-range imperial policies.

After his long succession of triumphs he adopted the
forms of Oriental ostentation, emphasizing his greatness
by grandiloquent new titles. His predecessors had been
content with the simple "king"; Suppiluliumas styled himself: "Labarnas, the great king, King of the Hatti Land,
the hero, the favorite of the Weather-god." And in treaties
he referred to himself as "My Sunship."

That his might was recognized far beyond the borders of his kingdom is apparent from an exchange of letters which not only give us vital political information, but bring Suppiluliumas to life as a human being. We are indebted for our knowledge of this correspondence to his son, Mursilis II, who described in detailed narratives both his own deeds and those of his father.

The letters concerned a request from the Egyptian Queen Anches-en-Amen, childless widow of young Tutankhamen, that Suppiluliumas give her one of his sons for a husband.

This offer to set a Hittite prince upon the throne of the mightiest kingdom of antiquity was so extraordinary that even Suppiluliumas was taken aback by it. He happened at the time to be campaigning against Carchemish and was advancing triumphantly upon Amka, between Lebanon and Anti-Lebanon. Our text reads:

"Now when the Egyptians heard of the conquest of Amka, they were indeed afraid. And because their ruler had died, the Queen of Egypt, the widow, sent a messenger to my father, writing to him as follows:

" 'My husband has died, and not one son do I have. But of you it is said that you have many sons. If you will give me a son of yours, he could be my husband. For how may I take one of my slaves and make him a husband and honor him?' "

Suppiluliumas was thunderstruck. His son recounts: "Now when my father heard this, he called upon the great men of Hatti for consultation." Obviously the king did not trust this unprecedented offer; as a father he hesitated to expose one of his sons to so uncertain an adventure. He therefore sent a special envoy to determine the true state of affairs in Egypt.

"Go, and bring back to me reliable tidings. Perhaps they wish only to deride me; perhaps they already have a successor to the throne. Well, bring back to me reliable tidings!"

Meanwhile he did not remain idle. He besieged Carchemish and on the eighth day captured the city by a bold assault. His booty was enormous; the accounts mention quantities of gold, innumerable bronze tools, and 3300 prisoners.

An Egyptian ambassador arrived. Suppiluliumas remained skeptical; the narrative reiterates his doubts in exactly the same phrases. Meanwhile the Queen, slightly offended but still holding to her offer, communicated with him again:

"Why have you spoken these words: 'They wish only to deride me'? I have not written to any other country. To you alone have I written. It is said that you have many sons. Give me a son of yours; he shall be my husband and king over Egypt!"

Mursilis continues his tale: "Now because my father was friendly he granted the woman's wish according to her word and took action in the matter of that son."

Unfortunately, the king's doubts were justified. Suppiluliumas sent his son to Egypt, but the prince was assassinated before he arrived, probably at the instigation of some powerful group of Egyptian courtiers who had other plans for the succession. But how the pulse-beat of history throbs through these letters written 3300 years ago! And what fantastic possibilities open up when we imagine a Hittite actually inheriting the throne of the pharaohs!

With the death of its founder, an empire such as Suppiluliumas had forged is necessarily exposed to the greatest dangers. Hereditary succession does not assure the competence and greatness of a line. But by good fortune rare in the history of nations, the complicated federal structure the great king had created survived his death.

His sickly successor, Arnuwandas III, died of the plague after only a single year of rule (1335–1334 B.C.), and Suppiluliumas's second son came to the throne. Mursilis II (1334–1306) proved to be a worthy successor to his father.

We know Mursilis II quite well from his annals—narratives arranged in exemplary order, written in clear language without exaggerations. We know him also from his treaties, charters, and above all from a moving literary document, his *Prayers in Time of Plague.* In character he was utterly different from Suppiluliumas. In his father greatness was joined with boldness and magnificence; the greatness of Mursilis was compounded of austerity and a tendency toward painful introspection.

Immediately upon his accession he had to take up arms to defend what his father had built. In a two-year war he destroyed the power of the land of Arzawa in the west— a country of which we know little. He fought in the east also, and in the north held in check the Hittites' hereditary enemy, the barbarian Kaska tribes. He also fought wars with the people of Ahhiyawa, whom some scholars identify with the Mycenæan Achæans.

He was also compelled to fight against his own nature. It appears that he was not physically strong, and we have reason to assume that he suffered from a speech impediment. Religion concerned him deeply, and to this side of his character we owe the *Prayers in Time of Plague,* which must be considered a beginning of literature. The work has been compared with the Book of Job. By absolute critical standards the comparison may be unfounded, but in their presentation of a soul in agony these *Prayers* do have some of the qualities of Job. Here is a sample:

*Hattian Weather-god, my Lord, and you gods who are my
     Lords, it is so:
We all sin.*

*And my father also sinned and overstepped the command
of the Hattian Weather-god, my Lord.*
In nought, however, have I sinned.
*It is so: The sin of the father shall fall upon the head of the
son. Upon my head also the sin of my father has
fallen.*
*Now therefore I have confessed it to the Hattian Weather-
god, my Lord, and to the gods.*
It is so; we have done it.
And because I now have confessed my father's sin
*Let the Hattian Weather-god, my Lord, and the gods who
are my Lords*
Be no longer wroth.
Be once more well disposed toward me
And drive the plague out of the Land of Hatti.

---

*You gods who are my Lords, you who would avenge the
blood of Tudhaliyas,*
*Know that those who killed Tudhaliyas have paid the
blood-debt,*
*And this blood-debt has also brought down to destruction
the Land of Hatti,*
So that the Land of Hatti also has already paid.
But because the debt has now come upon my head also
*I and my family will also pay it by offerings and atone-
ment.*
*Let the minds of the gods who are my Lords be set at rest
once more.*
*You gods who are my Lords, be once more kindly disposed
toward me. And I will appear before you.*
*And because I pray to you, hearken to me. Because I have
done no evil*
*And because of those who once were at fault and did evil
none remain, since they are long since dead,*
Because my father's doings came upon my head also,

Behold, because of the plague which is upon the land I will give to you, O gods who are my Lords, atonement gifts.

———————

From my heart drive out the pain, O Lord, and from my soul lift fear!

Muwatallis (1306–1282), the son of Mursilis II, was bequeathed a stable kingdom which he only had to hold. But "holding" was a complex and difficult task because of fundamental changes in the situation in Egypt. After decades of internal dissension and consequent political weakness, a strong ruler had come to the throne of the pharaohs: Ramses II. With extraordinary vigor he set about regaining Egyptian dominance in the Near East. No sooner did he come to power than he disputed the existing Syrian frontier. Muwatallis resolved to fight—and defeated Ramses, the mightiest ruler of antiquity, in the Battle of Kadesh.

There are "famous battles" (those of one's own country, which are taught in school), "classical battles" (which are refought in sand boxes at military academies), "decisive battles" (which historians use to end their chapters on wars), but there are few "world-historic" battles—that is, battles which represent a culminating point in the history of the world.

The concept is relative, of course, for by "world" we mean the known world. For Hekataios, who drew a map of the earth in 500 B.C., the known world was *the* world. By the time of the Roman emperor Trajan (A.D. 98–117), when Roman hegemony was at its greatest, people knew that the world was a larger place than Hekataios had thought. In our sense they were still wide of the mark—

but in the historical sense their map was right because it coincided with their picture of the world.

We, to be sure, live in an age when Mr. Smith of Oklahoma City and Herr Schmidt of Frankfurt know from personal experience that the earth is round—because they can fly around the globe in two hundred hours. But we must not forget that our view is just as relative as that of the ancients. There is a good likelihood that before long the "world" will include the nearer planets and that geog-

LATERAL VIEW OF THE LION THRONE, BOGHAZKÖY.

raphy will be taught in our schools only as a part of cosmography.

We must keep this concept of relativity clearly in mind when judging historical events. Battles of "world-historic" importance may mean encounters between a thousand men on either side armed with bows and arrows. The famous battles are not necessarily the crucial ones. The struggle for Troy did not affect in any essential way the course of history in Greece or the Near East. Cannæ, cherished by military theoreticians as the classic example of a battle, did not change the "world" of the third century B.C. On the other hand, the Battle of the Catalaunian Fields was probably of historic moment for the entire world; the defeat of Attila may very well have decided the fate of Christianity. In more recent times, Waterloo merely confirmed on the field of battle the downfall of a system already toppled. But Napoleon's battle before the gates of Moscow truly changed world history; for that Pyrrhic victory decided the future shaping of Europe. Similarly, not Verdun but the Battle of the Marne deserves to be called "world-historical." Stalingrad, too, was a culminating point in the fate of Europe. And perhaps some day we shall term Dienbienphu world-historical, for there the bell tolled loudest to mark the end of the European's brief hour in Asia.

The Battle of Kadesh, fought in the year 1296 B.C. between Pharaoh Ramses II and the Hittite King Muwatallis truly belongs among these battles of first importance to the world. It decided the fate of Syria and Palestine as well as the balance of power between Egypt and Hatti. And what happened to the countries between the Nile and the Tigris was, in those times, world history.

There is another fascinating aspect to this battle on the Orontes River. It is the first battle in history which we are able to reconstruct. And in its wake came the first detailed peace treaty we have knowledge of, a pact surpassing in political wisdom many of the peace treaties that have been produced by the nations of the twentieth century A.D.

As we have seen, the battle was the inevitable outcome of years of aggression, years during which the initiative passed back and forth between the Egyptians and the Hittites or their allies. These prolonged conflicts were always bloody and cruel. They deserve far more attention than the Egyptologists have accorded them. For these scholars, thinking always in terms of the tremendous power of the

Land of the Pharaohs, have dismissed as "border skirm-
ishes" a struggle that in reality was more like a "Thirty
Years' War."

Again and again Syria and Palestine were devastated,
cities and fortresses razed to the ground, the inhabitants
slaughtered or expelled. Not just borders, but control of
the entire eastern coast of the Mediterranean was at stake.
In the letters found at Tell el Amarna we may read the
lamentations of the local princelings in Syria and Palestine. There are despairing cries that the outer forts can no
longer be held against the attacks from the north; there are
pleas to Pharaoh to send help quickly. Ikhnaton did nothing; in his fairy castle at Amarna he went on dreaming
while the conquests of his predecessors were gradually being lost. The general who ascended the Egyptian throne
under the name of Haremhab (1345–1318 B.C.) made an
effort to save what could still be saved. He accomplished
little. But his successor, Sethos I (1317–1301 B.C.) once
more penetrated deep into Palestine, drove out the desert
tribes, and secured the whole region as far as the ridge of
land extending from Tyre to Damascus. There he was
stopped by Muwatallis.

The inheritance of Ramses II (1301–1234 B.C.) was
therefore by no means secure. Almost as soon as he succeeded to the throne, the borders were once more in flame.
He took to the field in order to preserve what his father
Sethos had won back with such toil. In the fifth year of
his rule the Hittites invaded Palestine. Ramses rallied his
army and marched on the route Haremhab had chosen
before him—northward along the Phœnician coast. Possession of the ports guaranteed supplies for his expeditionary
force and the assurance that he could bring up reserves.
As he approached the Orontes River scouts reported that
the main body of the Hittites, under Muwatallis, lay directly in his path. They were encamped at the fortress of

Rows of reliefs at Karatepe. The subjects follow one another in arbitrary order, without meaningful connection; the script symbols are heedlessly scattered among the figures, wherever there happened to be room. In the background it is possible to make out the depth of the excavation that was needed to expose the reliefs.

The left side of the group relief "The Feast of Asitawandas," showing servants bringing food and drink and musicians performing. OPPOSITE, ABOVE: Asitawandas feasting. He resided in Karatepe around 720 B.C. Fruit and wine are being served to him; he is being fanned; an ox is being driven forward. The king is sitting in comfort and enjoying himself—more of a patriarch than a despotic ruler.

BELOW: Concert of animals. From Tell Halaf.

The Lion Gate at Karatepe. Phœnician inscriptions on the body of the lion are followed by reliefs, then by more Phœnician inscriptions. Note that in this last group there

was not room for the third orthostat in proper position, so
it was turned sidewise and inscribed on the thin side. Note
also how the lion's tail is cut into the relief.

Several layers of damp paper are carefully brushed onto the stone one by one. After the paper has dried in the sun, the impression, a faithful copy of the original, is removed. A superior modern method of securing an impression involves spraying liquid rubber; it is, however, relatively expensive. Madame Alkim is the wife of Dr. Bahadir Alkim, the Turkish head of the Karatepe expedition under Professor Bossert. The contours of the impression are outlined with India ink on the spot. Every little detail matters.

Kadesh. Ramses felt strong enough to meet them head-on. He decided to attack.

In Karnak and Luxor, in Abydos and Abu-Simbel, writers prepared odes and painters commemorative friezes lauding their leader, Ramses. An authoritarian state does not permit free and accurate reporting; three thousand years ago such "objectivism" was frowned upon just as it is in such countries today. And so they hailed *Setepenre,* the Chosen of Re, in language wildly effusive even for ancient Egypt. Ramses loved and fostered this cult of himself. No epithet was too extravagant for him—in fact, none seemed to him strong enough. He was "Horus, the mighty bull, who is loved by Truth . . . the bull of rulers . . . the fearless one, great in the regard of all lands, who made the land of Ethiopia cease to exist and put an end to the boastfulness of the land of Hatti." He attained "the ends of the earth" and "made the wide mouths of the foreign princes shrink." He was "the son of Re who trampled the land of Hatti underfoot. . . . He was like a bull with sharp horns . . . the mighty lion . . . the jackal who in a moment traverses the circuit of the earth . . . the divine, splendid falcon."

These examples tell us more about the character of his sycophants than the character of the Pharaoh. The course of the battle is described in similar language. The epithets cited above are taken from steles at the cliff temple of Abu-Simbel. Ramses's tremendous victory is also described in a long poem preserved both in temple inscriptions (five of them on three temples) and in a papyrus. The author is unknown. He was long thought to be a certain Pentowere who, however, finally proved to be a mere copyist—and a poor one at that, for the many spelling mistakes must be ascribed to him.

When this poem was first discovered, a number of enthusiastic Egyptologists hailed the author as the Egyptian Homer and compared his work to the Iliad. Amid all the excitement they suspended judgment on the outrageous exaggerations and glorifications with which the text was studded. Otherwise they certainly would have noticed not only the overstatements, but the contradictions, the obvious errors.

Today it is known that these reports inspired by Ramses were shameless falsifications of history. They are the first examples we have of such rewriting of history. It must be said to Ramses's credit that with no assistance from tradition he and his "propaganda minister" produced a masterpiece. Their version was believed for more than three thousand years. Modern scholars also fell for the story, the more easily because up to seventy years ago the Pharaoh's opponents had been looked upon merely as a rebellious border tribe. Nobody suspected that at Kadesh, Ramses had fought against a Great Power.

Even today, unfortunately, the whole story of Kadesh eludes us. Critical scholars have had to reconstruct the battle from scattered hints. The resulting picture, though incomplete, is clear enough. There can no longer be any doubt about the actual outcome.

At Kadesh two of the largest armies of antiquity confronted one another. Aware that he was facing a decisive trial of strength, Ramses had raised an enormous levy from among his subjects. In addition he had persuaded Bentesina, Prince of Amurru, an ally of the Hittites, to change sides at the last moment. Muwatallis had also gathered around himself all the auxiliaries he could rely upon. He had swelled his troops by hiring mercenaries and even a contingent of the feared pirates of Lycia. He had twenty thousand men—the biggest army any Pharaoh had ever met. The Egyptian poet does not attempt to conceal this

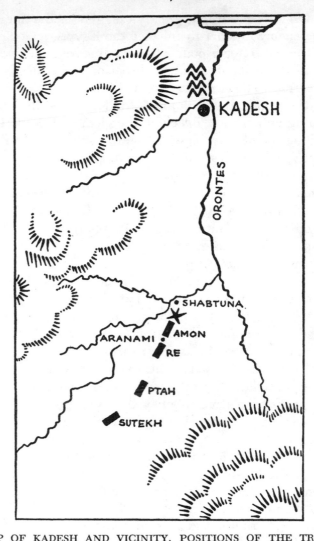

MAP OF KADESH AND VICINITY. POSITIONS OF THE TROOPS DURING THE NIGHT AND ON THE MORNING OF THE GREAT BATTLE.

M *Hittites* ▬ *Egyptians* ★ *Rameses*

fact. On the contrary, he greatly exaggerates the numbers of the enemy in order to enhance the Egyptian victory.

From a strategic point of view, Ramses's advance to Kadesh was a highly amateurish performance, planless in the extreme. His army was divided into four corps which bore the names Amon, Re, Ptah, and Sutekh—the names of the Egyptian gods. Reaching the vicinity of Kadesh toward the end of May, he set up camp on the heights above the city, which was faintly discernible from a distance through the haze. But there was no trace of the enemy, whom he had expected to encounter somewhere near here. While Ramses was discussing the situation with his puzzled officers, the Hittite king had already begun to take action. Unlike Ramses, he proceeded according to a definite plan. As a tactical preamble he dispatched two Bedouins to Ramses's camp. They pretended to be deserters, told of the composition of the Hittite army, and alleged that the Hittite king, stunned by the power and fame of Ramses, son of the gods, had already retreated in terror toward the north and was now near Aleppo.

Ramses, ill-informed by his own spies and apparently having so inflated an opinion of himself that he was a ready mark for flatterers, believed these self-styled deserters. He promptly placed himself at the head of his first corps and "His Majesty led the way like his father Month, the Lord of Thebes, crossing the ford of the Orontes with the first lord of Amon . . ." In other words, relying on the statements of the two deserters he split up his army, moving one corps some six miles ahead of the main body into unscouted territory. And as if this were not sufficient folly, he put himself at the head of these forward troops, instead of sending out an advance guard and staying with his main army.

Muwatallis immediately seized the initiative. Calmly he watched Ramses's approach and must have felt the thrill of satisfaction of the hunter who sees his quarry walk into the trap. Marching to the northwest of the city, he in his turn crossed the Orontes. Ramses, searching for the enemy, marched toward the north, passing Kadesh on the west, still at the head of a single corps. Corps Re followed

THE "FIRST ARMY OF AMON" ENCAMPS.

slowly; Ptah and Sutekh remained on the southern bank of the Orontes. Meanwhile Muwatallis kept to the east of the city, moving southward, with the city itself shielding him from the enemy.

This maneuver continued until the afternoon. Arriving at the place to the northwest of the city where Muwatallis had been encamped, Ramses raised his tent and permitted his weary troops to rest and prepare their meal. Corps Re was meanwhile slowly following, and by a lucky chance the Egyptians now captured two Hittite spies. Ramses wrung the truth from the pair by lashings: they confessed that Muwatallis had not fled from Pharaoh, but was on the other side of the city, with his entire army.

At this point his peril slowly dawned on Ramses. He railed at his officers, who earlier in the day had warned him against his reckless advance, and sent out messengers ordering Corps Ptah to join him as fast as possible. His one hope now was that Corps Re would come within hailing distance. But meanwhile Muwatallis had recrossed the river to the south of Kadesh. His swift charioteers hurtled into the marching corps. As we have mentioned, the Hittite chariots carried two warriors; there was only one fighting man beside the driver on each Egyptian chariot.

"They attacked the army of Re in its center while it was marching unsuspecting and not ready for battle. The army and the charioteers of His Majesty became faint before them."

The entire corps was scattered and almost annihilated. The Hittite chariots, newest, swiftest, and most beautifully manageable of offensive weapons, pursued the fleeing soldiers. The remnants of the Egyptian army corps fled before them panic-stricken. They came rushing headlong into the camp of the Amon Corps, throwing the ranks of their own people into confusion and carrying them along in headlong flight.

That was the climax of the Battle of Kadesh. The light chariots had introduced a new element of strategy into warfare: the art of swift encirclement. After such a rout, the defeat of the Egyptians was sealed; we cannot give the slightest credence to their claims to victory. The two armies had been approximately equal in strength, about 20,000 men on each side. By shattering Corps Re, Muwatallis had destroyed a good quarter of the Pharaoh's forces. He also cut off the Amon Corps (including the Pharaoh himself) from the main body. Corps Ptah was still on the march, unaware of the disaster; Corps Sutekh was still waiting on the southern bank of the Orontes. Taking instant advantage of the situation, Muwatallis used his charioteers to cut straight through the ranks of the fleeing Egyptians, wheeled the chariotry—and had the king hemmed in on all sides!

It was as plain as day that the greatest battle of antiquity would have to end with a catastrophic defeat of the Egyptian army. Muwatallis, his own forces intact, could now take each corps in turn and grind it to bits. Only a miracle could avert total annihilation of the Egyptians. In fact only a miracle could save Pharaoh himself and the shattered remnant of his army.

That miracle took place. The Egyptian chroniclers later ascribed it to the divine courage of Ramses. They were again embroidering the truth. For all we know, the Pharaoh may indeed have fought heroically. But his escape was due solely to two events which he could not possibly have influenced.

The discipline which held together the various tribes that made up the Hittite army was loose. With certain victory in their grasp, drunk with the lust of battle and the greed for booty, the Hittite shock troops broke off their pursuit when they arrived at Ramses's camp. The abandoned tents, the wagons filled with provisions, the tools and weapons, proved too much for them. These men who a moment before had been a fearsome army became an unruly horde deaf to the shouts of their commanders. At this point any vigorous attacker could have routed them.

Among Ramses's troops, still fleeing in panic, there was no such attacker. But a *deus ex machina* produced one from the direction of the coast. It was a small, firmly disciplined regiment of Egyptian soldiers who arrived on the battle-field, quickly took in the situation, and in a single vigorous

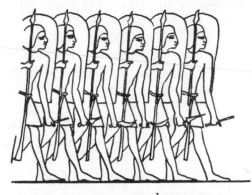

RAMSES THE SECOND'S INFANTRY
(AFTER AN EGYPTIAN RELIEF).

assault overwhelmed the bands of Hittite plunderers. We do not know where these troops came from; it has been as-sumed that they may have been a unit of cadets who had been landed at one of the coastal ports with no orders but to make contact with the Egyptian army. Whatever they were, this regiment saved Pharaoh's liberty and life. Had not these soldiers happened along in the nick of time, he would never have become "Ramses the Great."

The court poet has given a full description of how Ramses escaped the encirclement. If we can disregard the overblown language, we will find much that is stirring in his tale. The form of the narrative is also distinctly dra-matic, mingling chronicle with vivid pictures of the king in the midst of the battle. He is shown appealing to his god and complaining bitterly that his disloyal companions have abandoned him in his hour of peril.

"His Majesty was all alone with his bodyguards," the poet begins his description of the decisive phase of the battle. "The wretched prince of Hatti, however,"—here the enemy is being called a coward for showing ordinary good sense—"stood in the center of his own army, and for fear of His Majesty he did not come forth into the fighting."

When the Hittite charioteers broke through and shattered Corps Re, two of Pharaoh's own sons were among the Egyptians who came flying into Pharaoh's camp and involved his own troops in their panic. Then His Majesty "stepped forth like his father Month, after he had taken up his battle dress and laid on his armor; he was like to Baal in the hour of his wrath. The great team of horses that carried His Majesty was called Victory in Thebes and came from the great stables of Ramses. His Majesty drove rapidly forward, thrusting into the enemy army of the Hatti; he was all alone and no man was with him."

This charge, which is described as a piece of magnificent heroism, may well have been an act of sheer despair or terror. At this point, however, the poet gives free rein to his imagination. He goes beyond mere exaggeration and glorifies the king's action, whatever it actually was, into a symbol of the solitude of royalty.

"Now when the king looked behind him, he saw that he was blocked off by 2500 chariots. All the various warriors of the wretched king of Hatti encircled him, and of the numerous lands that were his allies—warriors from Aradus, Mese, Pedes, Keshkesh, Irun, Kizwadna, Chereb, Ekeret, Kadesh and Reke. They stood three to a chariot and had united against him."

Now the king raised his lament. There is greatness in this part of the poem, as the narrative alternates with Pharaoh's direct speech:

"No prince is beside me and no chariot driver, no of-

ficer of the infantry and none of the charioteers. My foot-
soldiers and my charioteers have abandoned me to the
enemy, and none of them held fast to fight against him."
And he invokes his god:

"His Majesty said: 'What is this now, my Father
Amon? Has a father already forgotten his son? Have I ever
done anything without you? Whatever I did or did not do,
was it not after your saying? And never did I stray from
the law which you had commanded. . . . What are these
Asiatics to you, Amon? These wretches who know nothing
of God? Have I not made very many monuments for you?
And filled your temple with prisoners? . . . I call to you,
my Father Amon. I am in the midst of strangers whom I
do not know. All lands have united against me and I am
all alone and no other is with me. My soldiers have left
me and not one of my charioteers has looked about to see
where I may be. . . . But I call to you and know that
Amon is more to me than millions of foot-soldiers and hundreds of thousands of chariot soldiers, than ten thousand
men who are brothers and children that cling together and
are of one mind. The works of many men are as nothing.
Amon is greater than they. . . . Amon hearkens to me
and comes when I invoke him. . . . He holds out his hand
to me and I rejoice; he stands back of me, calling: "Forward! Forward! I am with you, I your Father. My hand is
with you and I am better than a hundred thousand men, I
the lord of victory, who love strength."' "

By invoking the god the man makes himself godlike.
Ramses becomes a compound of Gilgamesh and Hercules.

"I have found my heart again; my heart bursts with
joy; whatever I will, is done. I am like Month; I let fly my
arrows to the right and fight to the left. I am like Baal in
the hour of his wrath. Behold, 2500 chariots surrounded
me, and now they lie hacked to pieces before my steeds.

Not one of the foe could lift his hand to fight. Their hearts in their bodies grew faint for fear, and their arms sag with weakness. They cannot shoot their arrows and have not the heart to take up their spears. I make them fall into the

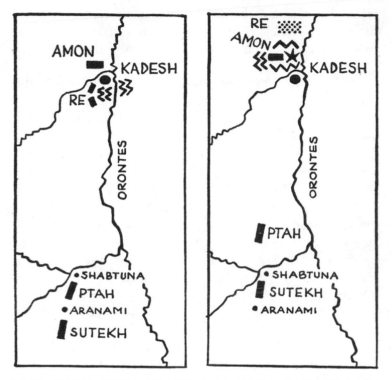

LEFT: UNDER COVER OF THE CITY WALLS OF KADESH THE HITTITES CROSS THE RIVER TWICE AND ATTACK. THE EGYPTIAN RE CORPS IS ROUTED.

RIGHT: CORPS RE IS IN FULL FLIGHT. CORPS AMON, LED BY RAMSES, IS STILL HOLDING, BUT IS ENCIRCLED BY THE HITTITES.

⪼ *Hittites* ▬ *Egyptians* ★ *Ramses* ::: *Fleeing Egyptians* water like crocodiles. They crash into one another and I go among them killing at will."

If the poem is telling the truth, Ramses had at last hit on an intelligent tactical maneuver: he attacked the Hittite front where it was weakest, along the river, in order to secure his rear and then attempt to break out of the encirclement. The inscriptions on the walls of Egyptian temples describe the enemy as driven into the river and drowning.

The "wretched prince of Hatti," who according to the Egyptian account had turned away in dismay from the wholesale slaughter, realized what was happening to his men. He assembled his nobles around himself and rallied the troops. "They were all together a thousand chariots who rushed straight toward the fire"—that is, toward Pharaoh, whose diadem of snakes spewed fire.

"I fell upon them. I was like Month; in a moment I let them feel the might of my hand. I slaughtered them, I killed them wherever they were, and one called to the other: 'This is no man who is among us; this is Sutekh the Mighty; Baal is in his limbs. His deeds are not the deeds of a man. Never before has one man alone, without footsoldiers and chariots, defeated hundreds of thousands. Come quickly, that we may flee before him, that we may save our lives and still breathe the air. Behold, whoever dares to approach him feels numb in hand and limb; whoever sees him charging forward can hold neither bow nor spear.'"

Let us assume that Pharaoh's bold attempt to break out succeeded. We can then understand his taking new heart and remembering that he can also count on his officers, his retinue, and his soldiers. He attempts to rally them not by dreary orders, but by appeals and encouragement.

"Take heart, take heart, my soldiers! You see my victory, though I am alone. But Amon is my protector and his hand is with me. How craven you are, my chariot fighters; it is indeed of no use to trust you. There is not one among you to whom I have not been a benefactor in my land. Did I not stand as your master, and you were humble folk? But then I made you great and daily you received your nourishment from me. I gave to the son the possessions of his father. All evil that was in this land has been banished. I lightened your taxes and I replaced for you what had been taken from you. . . . Whoever of you came with a petition, to him I said daily: 'Yes, that will I do.' Never has a lord done so much for his soldiers as have I, according to your wishes, for I allowed you to live in

HITTITE SPIES BEING BEATEN.

your houses and your cities even when you did not perform for me your duties as officers. And I did likewise for my chariot men, to whom I opened the way to many cities . . . and I thought I would witness a like boldness on their part in this hour, when we are going into battle. But behold! All of you together have done wretchedly; no one of you is holding firm and extending a hand to aid me as I fight. . . . As truly as the Ka of my Father Amon endures! If only I were in Egypt like my fathers who never saw the Syrians . . . !"

These are not the words of a victorious king, but of one in sore need.

"The crime which my soldiers and my chariot fighters have committed is greater than can be said. But behold, Amon has given me his victory even though soldiers and charioteers were not with me. I have made every distant land behold my victory and my strength while I was alone, without any noble following me and without a chariot driver. . . .

"For when Menna, my driver, saw that a great number of chariots had surrounded me, he grew weak and his heart was without courage and great fear was in all his limbs. He said to His Majesty: 'My good lord, mighty ruler, great protector of Egypt in the day of battle, we stand alone in the midst of enemies. See, the army and the charioteers have abandoned us. Why will you remain still until they rob us of breath. Let us be unharmed, save us, O Ramses!'

"His Majesty said to his chariot driver: 'Take heart, my driver. I shall break in among them like the darting of a falcon. I shall kill, I shall slaughter, I shall throw them to the ground. What are these cowards to you? My face has not paled before a million of them.' His Majesty hastened forward. He broke into the ranks of the enemy, he broke in among them a good six times. 'I pursue them like Baal in the hour of his wrath; I kill among them and grow not weary.'

"Now when my soldiers and my driver saw that I was like to Month in valor and strength, they came up one by one, stealing into the camp toward evening, and they found that all the peoples I had attacked lay slaughtered in their blood, with all the best warriors of Hatti and with the children and brothers of their princes. I had made the field of Kadesh white [with the white clothing of the corpses], and so many were the dead that there was no place to walk.

"My soldiers came to honor my name when they saw what I had done. My nobles came to glorify my strength, and likewise my chariot men, who praised my name thus: 'Hail, splendid warrior, who encourages our hearts; you have saved your soldiers and your charioteers. Son of

RECONSTRUCTION OF A WAR-CHARIOT. THE SICKLE-SHAPED ORNAMENT ON THE SHAFT IS A STANDARD MADE OF EMBOSSED SHEET COPPER, PROVIDING SYMBOLIC PROTECTION FOR THE DRIVER, DAZZLING AND FRIGHTENING THE ENEMY.

Amon, great warrior, you have destroyed the land of Hatti with your strong army. You are a fighter splendid beyond compare, a king who fights for his soldiers on the day of combat. You have a brave heart and are first in the turmoil of battle. All lands gathered together in one place have not withstood you; you won the victory before the army and in the face of the whole world. Here is no boasting. . . . You have broken the back of the Hatti forever.'

"His Majesty said to his soldiers, to his nobles and his charioteers: 'What crime is this you have committed, you my nobles, my soldiers and my charioteers who have not fought at all. . . . Leaving me alone in the midst of the foe—how glorious that is of you. . . . It will be told that you abandoned me. . . . I fought and defeated millions of countries, I alone. I was with my great steeds Victory of Thebes and Mut Is Satisfied; they only aided me when I was all alone in the midst of many nations. I shall continue to have them fed daily before myself, when I am back in my palace again, for they alone stood by me, they and also Menna, my chariot driver . . . !'"

The facts that emerge from this recital are as follows:

The king must have succeeded in rallying parts of his army—perhaps inspiring them by personal bravery—and pushing south on the following morning. The court poet avoids mentioning the regiment which by great good luck arrived from the coast and rendered really effective aid. Other sources declare that Ramses with the remnants of his corps retreated rapidly to the south until he reached the height of land near Damascus. These sources are convincing because they are consistent with the logic of the battle itself. There can be no doubt that Ramses, suffering heavy losses, barely succeeded in saving his own life, and that he marched home with a decimated army. What the court poet next tells is not in the least borne out by the treaty which was the outcome of the battle:

"The wretchedly fallen prince of Hatti sent a message honoring the great name of His Majesty: 'You are Re-Harachti, you are Sutekh the Mighty, the son of Nut; Baal is in your limbs and fear is in the land of Hatti. You have broken the back of the prince of Hatti forever.' He sent a messenger with a letter addressed to the great name of my Majesty . . . and saying as follows: 'You are the Son of Re who sprang from his limbs, and he has given to you all lands. The land of Egypt and the land of Hatti, yes, they are your servants and all lie at your feet. Your glorious father Re has given them to you.

" 'Be not terrible among us!

" 'Behold, your power is great and your strength weighs heavily upon the land of Hatti. Is it good that you should kill your servants? Yesterday you killed hundreds of servants, and today you come and will leave no heirs unto us. Be not strict in your demands, O powerful king. Mildness is better than warfare. Give us breath.' "

According to the Egyptian court poet, the king received this message during his retreat—which of course is not called by that name.

The most absurd phrase in this utterly fantastic message is: "The land of Egypt and the land of Hatti . . . lie at your feet." After a single great battle on the border of the two countries, after which the Egyptians made haste to pull out without having so much as glimpsed the kingdom of Hatti proper, Muwatallis allegedly laid his country at Pharaoh's feet! It must be remembered that the Hittite capital was a good 375 miles to the north.

But the poet does not bother to patch up the holes in his story. The king who charged forward like the war god himself to annihilate the enemy, whose warlike virtues are sung in the most extravagant language, who singlehanded kills hundreds of thousands of men in his royal rage, suddenly becomes the personification of generosity. His character changes with bewildering speed. When he gathers his generals around him and informs them of the message from Muwatallis (which must in fact have been of a very different nature from the poet's version), they tell him:

"Mildness is the greatest glory, O king, our master. Never shall anyone be reproached for desiring peace. *Who will honor you on days when you are wrathful?*" The quality which the poet has a moment before been lauding, now

comes into disrepute. His Majesty ordains that the words
of the Hittite may be heard, and he "held out his hand in
peace on the march to the south."

What else could a beaten man do but accept the offer
of peace—while at the same time cautiously continuing
his flight?

Ramses the Great signed a treaty of friendship with
Muwatallis, King of the Hittites.

Muwatallis's achievement was a remarkable one, as
must have been apparent at the time. As a direct result of

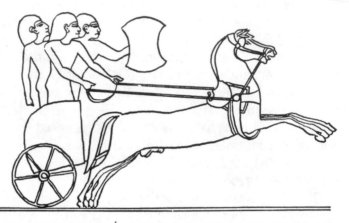

HITTITE CHARIOTEERS (AFTER AN EGYPTIAN RELIEF OF THE
NINETEENTH DYNASTY).

the Battle of Kadesh, Bentesina, ruler of the land of
Amurru, who had cast his lot with the Egyptians, returned
to the Hittite fold. Here, by the way, is further proof that
the Hittites had carried the field; for when has an ally of
a victor been known to change sides and join forces with
the vanquished? In addition Muwatallis had improved his
position vis-à-vis his hostile brother, Hattusilis. This
brother, a powerful personality whose victories over the
perennially rebellious Kaskas had won him the office of

viceroy, had had a secret alliance with Bentesina of Amurru. Now, however, he schemed no more against Muwatallis.

On the other hand, Syrian and Palestinian tribes on the border continued to make trouble—for the Egyptians, this time. The treaty of friendship seems to have averted any further major conflicts. We have no precise reports on any big battle between the Egyptians and the Hittites, nor even mention of any army under Hittite leadership. Ramses fought against tribes and small nations, but he never overstepped the newly established Hittite frontier which followed the course of the Nahr el Kelb, the "River of Dogs," in Phœnicia. The situation in those regions was much like what it is today—a constant alternation between hot and cold war. Since the struggle drained the economic resources of both parties, there was great pressure for a new decision. The issue was finally decided by peaceful means, due to the wisdom of the most important Hittite king after Suppiluliumas, Hattusilis III.

The death of Muwatallis brought to the throne his son, Urhi-Teshub, who proved to be a weak ruler. He made the fatal mistake of challenging his uncle Hattusilis's position as viceroy, which the latter had won by the sword. Hattusilis retaliated by the full unleashing of his power. He seized the kingship and felt himself sufficiently secure to send the foolish Urhi-Teshub into exile, rather than take his life. As a ruler the usurper proved to be wise rather than cunning, tolerant rather than oppressive—in these respects again following the example of Suppiluliumas. Although he had won the throne by force of arms, he showed himself a statesman as well as a successful general. To posterity he bequeathed a document which is the earliest of its kind surviving from antiquity. We find it particularly impressive as an expression of the Indo-European character of the Hittites. Anton Moortgat comments:

"We may call it the oldest autobiography on record. At the same time it is Hattusilis's defense for having usurped the throne. It belongs to a uniquely Hittite category of literary monuments. Here, for the first time in the ancient Orient, a man reveals a capacity for regarding his own life and the life of the nation in a meaningful relationship, for interpreting from a particular viewpoint a series of important events and of actions, his own as well as others— in other words, the capacity for thinking historically. Historical thinking is undoubtedly one of the most important differences between the world-view and the evolution of the Indo-Germanic Occident and of the Near East—even today."

Telipinus and Mursilis II had indeed left narratives possessing some of the characteristics of historical thinking. But Hattusilis went much further. What a contrast there is between his story and the vauntings of the pharaohs and all other Oriental rulers! Although Hattusilis was not writing a "confession" in the Western sense, he did attempt a genuine autobiography. Instead of heaping praises on himself, he tried to explain himself; instead of trumpeting forth the legitimacy of his rule, he often virtually apologized for his usurpation. This king did not make haste to claim his descent from a god as soon as he had taken power, although that was the customary procedure in the Orient. Instead he expressly emphasized that he was the *servant* of a god. "And my father took me up as a child and gave me into the service of the god." With an almost Christian humility he called himself the instrument of Ishtar of Samuha, guided by her in all things:

"Once when I was ill, I clearly saw in my sickness the will of the Divinity. The goddess, my mistress, led me by the hand always and upon every occasion. Because she cared so well for me, because in all my works I obeyed the will of the gods, I never behaved after the evil manner of mankind. . . ."

His secret conspiracy with Bentesina when his brother was marching toward Kadesh seems to contravene this claim to perfect virtue. But perhaps this conspiracy was only a rumor. Otherwise why should Muwatallis, after an investigation of all the charges against his brother, have appointed Hattusilis supreme commander of the army camp and of the chariot troops—certainly a key position if Hattusilis were meditating treason? In addition, after his brother's death Hattusilis observed the law and helped place the legitimate heir upon the throne. Only when his nephew threatened his hard-won rights did he issue the call to battle.

"But when I broke with him, I did not do this in ignoble wise by rebelling against him on the chariot or rebelling against him within the walls of the house. For I told him of my enmity, saying: you began the quarrel against me. And you are the Great King; but one single stronghold you left to me, and of this stronghold I alone am king. Up! The Ishtar of Samuha and the Weather-god of Nerik will decide between us . . . !"

The talent the Hittite rulers had for perceiving the causal relationships between their own acts and historical events must have strengthened their diplomatic position enormously, for their opponents were singularly lacking in this kind of intelligence. A grasp of causality is, after all, the mark of legal thinking, the basis of genuine jurisprudence, and obvious equipment for the diplomat who hopes to negotiate an advantageous treaty. In the Hittite agreements we find the only examples of that kind of thinking in the ancient Orient. The treaty which Hattusilis III concluded with Ramses II after decades of frontier warfare is *the earliest example of a major political treaty in the history of mankind.* It is the oldest written document of its kind, and its significance is even greater because it exists in a dual text. For this is the very treaty which Winckler knew in its Egyptian version and which to his utter amazement turned up at Boghazköy on a Hittite clay tablet on which it had been recorded three thousand years before.

The treaty was concluded some time between 1280 and 1269 B.C.—the exact date is the subject of dispute between Egyptologists and Hittitologists. On the basis of the latest chronology, that would place it around the twentieth year of Ramses's reign. The original official copy of the treaty was engraved upon a plaque of silver which has not been recovered. As we have already mentioned, the Egyptian text in hieroglyphs was found upon the walls of the Rameseum, the mortuary temple of Ramses, and in Karnak. Curiously enough, the treaty exists not only in two languages, but in two versions, each being a revised translation of the paragraphs concerning the enemy's obligations, and in each case the phraseology has been altered to suit the wishes of the revisers. The cuneiform version has not been preserved complete; it runs only as far as Paragraph 14, which corresponds to Paragraph 17 of the Egyptian version. The Egyptian text has thirty paragraphs in all and ends with a description of the original silver plaque.

Hattusilis's messengers came to Egypt with a draft of the treaty. The Egyptian text, as usual giving a slanted picture of the political situation, declares that in the twenty-first year (of Ramses's reign) on the twenty-first day of the month of Tybi, while Pharaoh was in the city known as House of Ramses (the newly-founded city in the Nile delta), the Hittite ambassadors Tarteshub and Ramose appeared "in order to ask peace of the Majesty of Ramses, that bull among princes, who establishes the borders of his land wheresoever he will." Which was precisely what he had singularly failed to do in the Land of the Hittites.

The treaty proper began with the grandiloquence cus-

tomary in the Orient. But this time there lay back of the
big words an impressive fact: the balance of power.

"The treaty which the Great Prince of Hatti, the mighty
Hattusilis, son of Mursilis, the Great and Mighty Prince of
Hatti, and grandson of Suppiluliumas, the Great and
Mighty Prince of Hatti, made upon a silver tablet for
Ramses II, the Great and Mighty Ruler of Egypt, son of

FALLEN HORSES, FELLED SOLDIERS—THE HITTITE CHARIOT
TROOPS OVERRUN RAMSES' ENCAMPMENT (AN EGYPTIAN REP-
RESENTATION).

Sethos I, the Great and Mighty Ruler of Egypt and grandson of Ramses I, the Great and Mighty Ruler of Egypt, the
good treaty of peace and brotherhood which shall create
peace between them for all time."

It is scarcely necessary to quote all the involved language. The two most important provisions were these:
Both parties agreed to refrain from offensive operations

against one another; and both parties entered into a defensive alliance. But we moderns will be most struck by a clause at the very end which obviously deals with the status of political refugees. There is an uncanny ring of contemporaneity to these words written more than three thousand years ago.

"If a man—or even two or three—should flee from the Land of Egypt and come to the Great Prince of Hatti, let the Great Prince of Hatti take him captive and have him sent back to Ramses, the Great Lord of Egypt. But if any man is sent back to Ramses II, the Great Lord of Egypt, let him not be charged with his crime, nor shall his house and his wives and his children be harmed, nor shall he be killed or injured in any way, neither his eyes nor his ears nor his tongue nor his feet, nor shall he be charged with any crime."

A similar clause applied to fugitive Hittites who had deserted to Ramses and were to be sent back.

The concluding sentence was of a portentousness appropriate to the importance of the treaty:

"And as for these words which are written upon these silver tablets for the Land of Hatti and the Land of Egypt —whosoever does not obey them, may the thousand gods of the Land of Hatti and the thousand gods of the Land of Egypt destroy his house, his land and his servants!"

Not the magic power of these words, undoubtedly, but the unfailing Hittite grasp of practical politics saved this agreement from becoming a "scrap of paper." The pact gave to the peoples of the Near East seventy years of peace! The history of the world holds few peaceful eras that long.

Even the best of treaties can survive only when the parties to it are honest in their intentions. Ten years after the conclusion of the pact, amicable relationships were sealed by a union unusual in Egyptian history. Ramses married a daughter of Hattusilis. It might be expected that she would have been taken into the royal harem as one woman among many. Instead the princess was made the chief wife of Pharaoh. The wedding was a splendid occasion for an ostentatious renewal of the great peace treaty before the peoples of both countries. It was also an occasion for two of the "Big Three" of antiquity to meet personally. There are reasons for believing that the Hittites took the initiative in proposing this marriage. It was, in other words, a deliberate act of statesmanship. Like the

THE FETTERED KING OF THE HITTITES
(AFTER AN EGYPTIAN RELIEF).

Hapsburgs several millennia later, the Hittites were on the lookout for profitable dynastic alliances.

The entrance of the Hittite princess into Egypt was immortalized on a stele found near Abu-Simbel. The bride, who assumed the name Ma'atnefrure ("Truth is the Beauty of Re"), is shown beside Ramses and her father, Hattusilis III. One of the accompanying inscriptions has recently been translated by Siegfried Schott. In his introduction, however, this scholar uncritically accepts the Egyptian claims. "After the victory of Ramses II over the Land of Hatti," he writes, "the latter is living in wretchedness and fear. The Great Prince sends his daughter to Ramses."

Is it likely that a pharaoh would provide such a magnificent reception for a princess of a ruined, abject nation? He sent forth a whole army and many of his noblemen to meet her.

It was reported to His Majesty:
Behold what the Great Prince of Hatti does.
He is bringing his eldest daughter, with innumerable gifts;
They cover the place where they are with their treasures.
The prince's daughter and the princes of Hatti bear them.
They are crossing many mountains and harsh passes
And will soon reach the borders of Your Majesty.
Send out an army and noblemen to receive them.

The king appears to be taken by surprise. It is, of course, highly unlikely that the king of the Hatti would set out with his daughter without having paved the way. But these lines do seem to imply that the marriage took place on Hittite initiative.

His Majesty was overjoyed. The Lord of the palace was
          glad
When he heard of this extraordinary event
Whose like was not known before in Egypt.
He sent an army and nobles to receive them at once.

What is more, Ramses prayed to the god of the foreigners, "Father Seth," petitioning good weather for the wedding guests:

> *Cease making rain and storms and snow. . . .*
> *And his Father Seth granted all he asked.*

The account now describes the procession and its arrival as an unexampled marvel:

There were troops of the Hatti, archers and riders,
All men from the Land of Hatti,

Mingling with those of Egypt.
They ate and drank together.
They were as harmonious as brethren
Between whom there are no grudges.
Peace and friendship reigned among them
As is wont only among Egyptians themselves.
The Great Princes of all lands through which they passed
Were stunned, unbelieving and helpless
When they saw all the men from Hatti
Who had joined with the army of our king.
One of these princes said to the other:
"What His Majesty has said is true;
How vast is this host that we see with our very own
*   eyes. . . ."*

Obviously, the border peoples considered the wedding procession a *political* wonder.

At last the grand host arrived in Ramses's own city:

The daughter of the Great Prince of Hatti,
She who had come to Egypt,
Was led before His Majesty,
And after her were brought the many, the countless
*   gifts. . . .*
Then His Majesty saw that her face was fair as a god-
*   dess'. . . .*
And it was a great and rare happening,
A magnificent marvel,
Like nothing heretofore known,
Like nothing any man has heard spoken from the mouths
*   of others,*
Like nothing that is set forth in the writings of our fore-
*   fathers.*

The last words of this narrative clearly indicate the political consequences of these nuptials. The final clause,

of course, is the Egyptian writer's genuflection before
Pharaoh:

*Henceforth, when a man or a woman in the course of their
affairs traveled through Syria and came to the Land of
Hatti, there was no fear in their hearts
because the might of His Majesty was so great.*

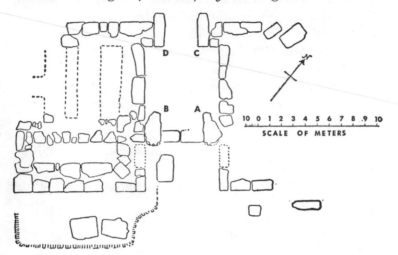

GROUND PLAN OF THE SPHINX GATE OF ALAJA HÜYÜK. A, B, C
AND D FORM THE BASES OF THE TWO GATES (SEE PLATE XX).

With this peace treaty the Hittites reached and passed
the peak of their power. The treaty was effective—but
with security, greatness was lost. Avaricious Assyrian
kings assailed the frontiers. Madduwattas, one of the most
dependable of the Hittites' vassals to the west, suddenly
defected. The Land of Arzawa acquired surprising
strength; and to the west the Ahhiyawa, who may have
been early Greeks, became a threat.

The empire which Suppiluliumas had forged and
which had lasted for a century melted away in the course
of two generations—under the weak direction of Tudhaliyas IV (1250–1220 B.C.) and the still feebler rule of Arnu-

wandas IV (1220–1190 B.C.). These kings were unable either to maintain Hattusilis's constructive peace policy or to win back by the sword what they lost by poor diplomacy.

There has been a great deal of speculation about this rapid distintegration of a great empire. The underlying cause is really simple: a new migration of peoples was beginning. It may be objected that such migrations cannot explain the speed of the collapse. There is one answer to that. In the past hundred and fifty years in our western civilization, or ever since Kant, there has been a great deal of philosophizing about space and time; but the relativity of the concepts "historical space" and "historical time" have not yet been thoroughly appreciated. History is full of leaps. We contemporaries of Winston Churchill see him as one of the most important, perhaps the most important, political figure of the twentieth century A.D. Perhaps posterity will remember him chiefly as the person in whose single lifetime the British Empire passed from the height of its glory into rapid decline.

However that may be—after Arnuwandas there appears to have been a brief reign of another Suppiluliumas, and perhaps of another Tudhaliyas. What we know for a fact, however, is this:

Around 1190 B.C. the city of Hattusas was put to the torch. Another migration, this time from the west, overran the weakened Hittite kingdom. The first of these invaders may have been Mysians and Phrygians; they are spoken of as "the sea peoples" in an Egyptian inscription on the walls of the temple of Medinet Habu:

". . . *And no land held fast before them—from Hatti down!*"

The conflagration which destroyed Hattusas—no doubt after the city had been thoroughly plundered— must have been of colossal proportions. Excavation reveals evidence that the walls of the citadel, the temples, and the houses must have been searing hot for days, perhaps for weeks, afterwards.

The capital never recovered from that disaster. From then on, for 3,245 years, it remained at best a small town, but most of the time a village. Along with the capital the other great cities near present-day Kültepe and Alaja Hüyük were smashed. At one blow the entire Hittite Empire was wiped out.

Since we are dealing here with the story of the *discovery* of the Hittites, we see their fate through the eyes of

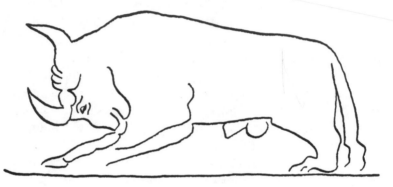

BAS RELIEF FROM ENINK.

the archæologist! Sir Leonard Woolley, the great British archæologist, gives the professional viewpoint perfectly, although his remarks may at first strike us as somewhat cynical. He says: "If the field archæologist had his will, every ancient capital would have been overwhelmed by the ashes of a conveniently adjacent volcano. Failing a volcano, the best thing that can happen to a city, archæologically speaking, is that it should be sacked and very thoroughly burnt by an enemy."

These words are not so unfeeling as they sound. Again and again the field archæologist is confronted by traces of fire, plundering, destruction, and killing—by the residue of all the horrors that make up the story of mankind. The archæologist can only accept this. He is merely stating a fact when he says that a swift and violent death, such as overwhelmed Pompeii and Herculaneum when they were buried under lava and pumice, preserves more for eternity than the slow, creeping rot by which a city also may be erased. Swift destruction mummifies a civilization, which otherwise might pass and leave nothing behind.

It may at first seem paradoxical that a fire should preserve and not destroy. But we must remember that even the worst conflagration never totally levels a large city. Edifices of stone, fortification walls, and foundations survive a fire, and at least the outlines of brick buildings remain recognizable. When, on the other hand, a city, abandoned as so many once-great cities have been, is left to disintegrate slowly, wind and weather and scouring sand eventually wear it down to the ground and it returns to what it rose out of: dust.

Because Hattusas was destroyed by fire, and went down, forming as it were a time-capsule about its own past, there were years of work at Boghazköy for the German archæologist Kurt Bittel. Hugo Winckler had dug mainly in order to find inscribed tablets. Bittel also found tablets, but his chief interest was the city itself. He studied its layout, its extent, the architecture of the fortress, the temples, and the library. As it happened, he also probed deeper, into the prehistoric layers of a settlement still more ancient than that of the Hittites. But this aspect of his work lies outside our province, for we are dealing with history, not prehistory.

The death of the empire did not put an end to the historic influence of the Hittite people. But before we discuss this, let us take time out to look over Kurt Bittel's shoulder while he digs.

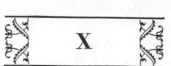

CITY AND LAND—PEOPLE AND CUSTOMS

KURT BITTEL'S EXCAVATIONS were not carried out in the romantic spirit of so many of his predecessors. Vastly productive from a scientific point of view, they followed the wearisome, routinized lines which are typical of modern archæology.

The technique of excavation has nowadays been standardized—it looks the same from Anatolia to Mesopotamia. In withering heat native workmen move at a deliberate pace, carrying baskets, pushing carts. Men in straw hats or tropical helmets, armed with measuring tapes and cameras, go about among a few visible remnants of walls laid bare in strange geometrical figures that mean nothing to the layman. The discoveries made are often sensational, but they take place in the minds of the specialists and cannot be seen.

For all that, Bittel's first excavation had its comical as well as its tense moments.

Kurt Bittel was born in 1907 in the town of Heidenheim in South Germany. He studied archæology, prehistory, and ancient history at the universities of Heidelberg, Marburg, Vienna, and Berlin. In 1930 he was awarded a traveling fellowship by the German Archæological Institute and set out to visit Egypt and Turkey. In Istanbul in April 1931 he met the director of the Turkish branch of the German Archæological Institute, Martin Schede, who invited him to join a field trip to Boghazköy which was to make plans for the coming excavations there. Bittel was twenty-three and enterprising; he agreed to go—and found his life's task. For nine years, until the outbreak of the war, he dug at Boghazköy; and at present he is again spending many weeks out of every year among the ruins of the ancient Hittite capital.

The work was initially intended to be only a scientific "control" excavation. In the course of years the flaws in Winckler's and Macridy's haphazard procedures had become all too evident. Bittel later reported a few of his corrections—though he was too gentlemanly to cast aspersions on the methods of his predecessors. But there is no point in suppressing the truth: from a scientific point of view the Winckler-Macridy excavation had made a fearful mess of it. Here are just two examples: in the so-called "house on the slope" Macridy—probably in 1911, but the date was not noted—had probed into rows of walls. The excavation was never finished and no notes whatsoever were taken. To the east of these walls he had found—as we happen to know from a letter of his—"remnants of ironwork"—certainly the most fascinating of finds. But on this he left no notes at all.

The new excavation was financed by a trust fund established in honor of eighty-year-old James Simon, the Jewish philanthropist who twenty-four years earlier had made it possible for the anti-Semitic Winckler to undertake the first excavations at Hattusas. And when Bittel and Schede arrived at Boghazköy on September 1, 1931, they were entertained by the very same person who had already opened his house to Winckler, Macridy, Puchstein, and Curtius—Zia Bey.

This worthy scion of the Dulgadiroghlu family had in

the meantime reached the age of sixty. He still resided in his *konak,* consisting of three two-story houses: the *haremlik* for the family and relations; the *selamlik* with its guest rooms; the servants' house with the kitchen. He refused to recognize that the world had changed in the past quarter-century; he went on playing the great feudal lord he had once been, master over the lives and properties of eight hundred villagers. In the meanwhile Turkey had become a republic. Bittel was soon to run into complications that resulted from these changed conditions.

It was not difficult for Zia Bey to round up the necessary workmen. The crew assembled, Bittel went out to make their acquaintance. Only then did it occur to him that he did not speak a word of Turkish. There was the crowd of staring, curious workmen, and there he stood, the ambitious archæologist, and fumbled in vain for some word or even some gesture by which he could communicate with these men on whose labor he was dependent. Suddenly a workman stepped forward, stood at attention, and in a blaring military voice shouted out in purest German: *"Morgen, Herr Hauptmann!"* ("Good morning, captain!") It turned out that the man had fought with a German regiment in Romania during the First World War.

The architect and the photographer came three days later, and on the fifth day after Bittel's arrival the digging began at the citadel of Hattusas. On the first payday there was an uprising among the workers.

What was it all about?

Zia Bey had not only supplied the workmen; he had also generously taken on the duties of paymaster. Too generously, for he had pocketed a good part of each man's daily wage of thirty kuruş (about ten cents)—pocketed it with a feudal lord's clear conscience, for did not everything that belonged to his people belong to him?

But news of the political upheavals and the reformed social order in Turkey had penetrated even to the hundred-odd houses of Boghazköy. The workmen armed themselves with stones and headed for the tents where Bittel and his party were camping. Ignorant of the language and therefore unaware of the cause of this revolu-

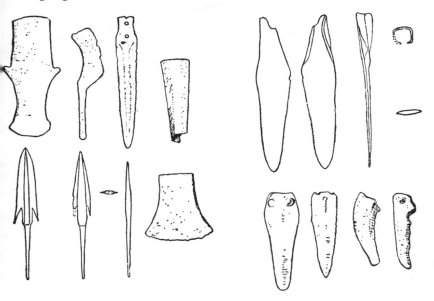

LEFT: HITTITE BRONZE UTENSILS FROM BOGHAZKÖY (HAT-TUSAS), 14–13 CENTURY B.C. SIZE OF LARGEST, 6.8 INCHES; OF SMALLEST, 3.3 INCHES.
RIGHT: HITTITE DAGGERS OF 18–16 CENTURIES B.C. SIZES: 3.8 TO 2.8 INCHES.

tion, Bittel could do nothing but call for the gendarmes. The situation remained critical until Bittel found out the reason for the uprising and promised immediate redress. There was a short, violent argument with Zia Bey who asserted that he no longer knew what the world was coming to. Then a settlement was made: wages were increased to fifty kuruş per day and handed to each worker individually on payday.

Although the first excavation was only intended to check on previous work, the expedition soon ran into the kind of good luck which Winckler had enjoyed on this same spot: a clay-tablet archive was discovered. The initial yield was some 350 cuneiform texts in the Akkadian and Hittite languages—both of which were readable, the former since the nineteenth century and the latter since Hrozný's decipherment. After such a find it was obvious that the digging had to be continued. But at this point the Danat Bank in Berlin closed its doors—a signal that the German economic crisis was approaching its climax. Suddenly the expedition was without funds. It had begun work on 3,000 marks; it continued on an emergency budget of 1,000 marks contributed by the Archæological Institute. But in spite of these grave financial difficulties, all of Bittel's excavations up to the outbreak of the Second World War were enormously successful.

Unlike his predecessors at Boghazköy, Bittel's interests were not one-sided. He had no preconception of what he wanted to find, but rather was trying to obtain a picture of the whole. Neither was he greedy for undivided glory; before writing up the results of his work, he consulted experts in other fields—biologists, zoologists, chemists—and in this way clarified problems which were outside the province of an archæologist working alone.

As a result, there gradually formed a rounded picture of the historical origins of Hattusas. In the course of time five cultural strata were distinguished. The oldest, Layer IV, dated probably from the first centuries of Hittite domination; Layer III marked the apex of Hittite power—around the time of Suppiluliumas, the middle of the fourteenth century B.C., when the mighty citadel walls and

temples were built; Layer IIIb preserves a picture of Hattusas from the reign of Tudhaliyas IV to the city's destruction by the big fire. Layers II and I show signs of Phrygian
and early Hellenistic influence.

Bittel took fresh photographs of both the buildings in

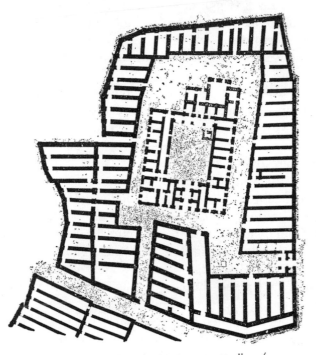

GROUND-PLAN OF TEMPLE I AT BOGHAZKÖY (HATTUSAS),
WHICH CONTAINED MORE THAN SEVENTY STORAGE ROOMS.

Hattusas itself and the rock temple of Yazilikaya, near
Boghazköy. The new excavations showed that Büyükkale
(the citadel) had been a closed area at the time of Suppiluliumas, and it became apparent that the huge complex
of buildings at the King's Gate, which Puchstein had half
excavated in 1907 and taken for a palace, must in reality

have been a temple. The proportions of the structure were stupendous: some 200 x 200 feet of wall enclosing more than sixty rooms.

Undoubtedly the clay-tablet archives were Bittel's most important find. In 1952 he found 832 cuneiform texts to add to his first 350 tablets, and a year later he turned up 5500! He also discovered those bilingual seals we have already mentioned which provided *proof* that the first hypothetical readings of Hittite hieroglyphs had indeed been correct.

Bittel worked on the interpretation of his material for nine years. He became Director of the German Archæological Institute in Istanbul—but every year as soon as the rainy season was over he promptly went out to the citadel of Boghazköy. A cluster of mud huts about a spring formed his permanent living quarters. For anybody but an archæologist, the ruins of Boghazköy are a barren place. The daily routine went on, with scarcely a variation, from year to year. It amounted to a sensation when a solitary wolf was sighted now and again. What entertainment there was came from watching the circling of gigantic eagles and the languorous swoopings of the vultures. For light conversation there were always events about the camp, such as someone having to shake one of the common and dangerous green scorpions out of his bed. 1938 was a lively year in this respect for no less than five species of weasel-spiders (Galeodes) were encountered. Dirty tan and long as a finger, this poisonous spider is probably the most repulsive insect of the Near East. When danger threatens, it throws up its head and prepares to meet the enemy with a pair of open claws. Plagued by such vermin, amidst surroundings as monotonous as those of a penal colony, Bittel worked away as happy as only a devoted scholar can be.

. . .

Soon we shall set off for Karatepe, where Professor Bossert leads the most important of the postwar expeditions into Hittite territory. But before we go, we feel we should equip ourselves, as all good travelers do, with certain general ideas on the historical role of this mysterious people. These ideas are not easy to come by. They do not exist ready-made, since the best minds working in this field disagree radically with one another, not only on details but on broad interpretation. Therefore we cannot

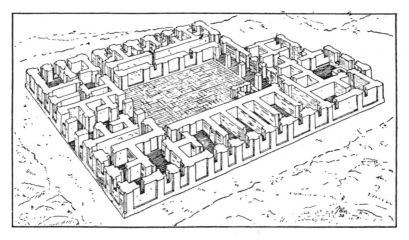

RECONSTRUCTION OF THE STONE PLINTH OF TEMPLE I AT BOGHAZKÖY.

look to the authorities for an "official" theory of the role of the Hittites in world history. What follows is strictly my own provisional interpretation, which I put forward in the hope that it will help us in our journey.

Let us sum up what we have learned of the history of the Hittites as disclosed by their cuneiform documents and monumental structures.

First: By the second millennium B.C. the Hittites had already been a Great Power for several hundred years.

They conquered and maintained their position by superiority in the strategy and implements of warfare and by remarkable skill in diplomacy.

Second: The government was a federal state under centralized administration. The kingdom consisted not of a single Hittite nation, but of numerous peoples of diverse psychology united by contractual ties and held in line by the military and economic dominance of the Hittites. The kingdom must be considered a constitutional rather than an absolute monarchy, the king being largely responsible to a council of nobles known as the *Pankus*. It is significant that their role in the government was based upon a *concept* of the state, not upon a chance rising to power of a caste of nobles.

Third: The social order was not rigid; classes were not divided by insurmountable walls. A feudal system prevailed under which even the slave had definite rights. Moral and ethical obligations of the propertied class were clearly recognized. For the second millennium B.C. the Hittite kingdom represented a distinctly progressive (in the Occidental sense) social structure.

Fourth: The social order was founded on a code of law which differed from all other known Oriental legal codes in its humaneness. The principle of an eye for an eye had no place in this code. We may say that the guiding principle throughout was reparation rather than the then prevailing *lex talionis* or law of retaliation.

These characteristics of the Hittite Empire contrast very strongly with other Oriental political structures of the second millennium B.C. Even if we judge the Hittite Empire in Occidental terms rather than in terms of cultural relativity, our verdict is a very favorable one. There has been, consequently, a tendency to ascribe these "progressive" characteristics to the fact that the Hittite ruling class was Indo-European.

But certain other significant traits are equally important for a proper evaluation of these people.

Fifth: The Hittite nation was not united by a single language; in Boghazköy alone traces of eight languages have been found. Of these at least four were widespread. The Hittite nation also had no unified script. The hieroglyphs employed during the imperial period exclusively

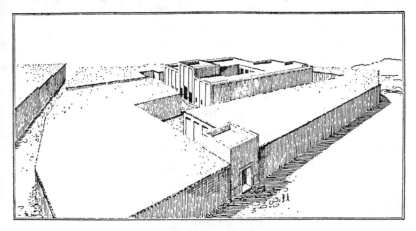

TENTATIVE RECONSTRUCTION OF THE GREAT TEMPLE DISTRICT AT BOGHAZKÖY (HATTUSAS).

for royal and religious inscriptions apparently arose among the Hittites themselves, were even developed into a simple, cursive form of writing, but these hieroglyphs were employed mainly in the surviving city-states after the fall of the Empire. The cuneiform script the Hittites employed for ordinary purposes was borrowed from the Assyrians.

Sixth: The Hittite Empire was not spiritually united by a single religion. ("The Hittites have a thousand gods.") There were many religions side by side, mingled with innumerable national and local cults. The Hittites' primary attitude toward religion was tolerance—wise from a political point of view; unfortunate from a cultural point of view, for it prevents the creation of a homogeneous spiritual substructure.

Seventh: The plastic art of the Hittites in the imperial period manifested tendencies toward monumentality, but no tendencies toward form. The sculptors were frivolously experimental; if the material did not yield easily to their chisels, they left it and attacked another stone. Half-finished and finished, old and new work were jumbled together. The ornamental properties of script were never conceived of—when inscriptions were required, they were carved wherever there happened to be room for them. That is true even of the temple of Yazilikaya where, at least in the procession of the gods, an impulse toward form can be sensed. But this temple may have been mainly the work of Hurrians; at any rate several of the hieroglyphs give Hurrian names. And Yazilikaya, situated as it was near the capital city, was unique, not typical. Normally Hittite art has no *style,* although it has distinct crude characteristics (which show traces of Hurrian and later of Assyrian influences).

Eighth: The architecture of the Hittites differs in intent from that of all the other architectures of their era. Other peoples built everything around their temples. But the militaristic Hittites in Boghazköy and elsewhere plainly made the walled citadel their central architectural feature. At the same time, the Hittite architects were peculiarly foolish in the construction of their citadel. At the cost of gigantic toil they piled stone blocks upon a natural cliff which in any case defied ascent. And on the opposite side, where the slope was far less steep, they covered the outside of their walls with stucco. During my second visit to Boghazköy I watched some Turkish boys who for a small *baksheesh* will perform the feat of climbing these stuccoed walls. The irregularities of the stucco offer a thousand toe holds, and barefooted soldiers would have had no trouble storming the citadel. Then there are the militarily senseless poternes—tunnels through the 230-foot breadth of the wall out into the plain—and the inviting stairways. The arrangement of the citadel of Boghazköy is just as frivolous, just as little governed by a guiding idea and style, as the reliefs on the gatehouses and the sculptures at the portals.

I should add that no thorough investigation of the military importance of Hittite fortifications has as yet been published. (Kampman, the Dutch archæologist who has made a stab at it, has confined himself to generalized descriptions.) Nor has anyone as yet pointed out the curious disproportion between the gigantic stone foundations of such buildings as Temple I at Boghazköy and the limited architectural possibilities of erecting upon them an organic superstructure of other materials.

Ninth: With the exception of the astonishing *Prayers in Time of Plague* of Mursilis we nowhere encounter anything like a Hittite literature. It may be objected that perhaps we have not found it since the Hittites wrote not only upon stone and clay, but also upon wood, lead, and silver which would be lost beyond recovery. But this theory will not hold water. If there had been a literature, we should at least have some mention of it in the vast number of documents that have turned up. Fragments of the Gilgamesh epic were found in Boghazköy, for example—but that epic is not Hittite.

Tenth: We must put in the proper light one point that specialists in prehistory are fond of making. It must be remembered that the division of early history into the Stone Age, the Bronze Age, and so on, is outmoded now that the concept of cultural history has come to the fore. Therefore it is of no great historical importance to note that the Hittites knew *iron* at a very early period, perhaps as early as the time of Labarnas. Around 1600 B.C. they appear to have had a certain monopoly in the manufacture of iron. But it is wrong to imagine, as older writers have done, that in those ancient times a material had only to be invented or discovered for it to start affecting history. If *amutum* in the Kültepe texts has been correctly read and interpreted as the word for "iron"—and the evidence is strong—then in early Hittite history *iron was five times more expensive than gold, forty times dearer than silver*. For centuries it must have been the rarest of luxuries. And in fact the Pharaohs wrote letters to the Hittite kings begging for some iron—requests that were haughtily rejected. Iron was a precious metal from which ornaments, not weapons, were made. And it seems likely that the first iron weapons were qualitatively by no means equal to the tried and true stone and bronze weapons. The actual "iron age" came many centuries later; it was probably introduced by the "peoples of the sea" whose iron weapons overthrew the Hittite Empire and blotted it from history for hundreds of years.

LION HEAD FROM THE GATE AT BOGHAZKÖY.

When we try to fashion for ourselves a picture of the Hittite nation, we can easily be led astray by the fact that most of the sculptures which bring it to life for us date

from a period when the Empire had already been dead
for five hundred years. For the most vivid pictures of Hittite life are to be found not in the monuments from the
Imperial Age, but in the innumerable reliefs and sculptures in the city-states which survived the fall of the Empire: Carchemish, Zinjirli, and Karatepe too. These works
of art belong in the era 800 to 700 B.C. We must under no
circumstances follow the lead of earlier archæologists who
imagined that those neo-Hittite sculptures were characteristic of the Hittite people. They were not at all!

What we are seeing when we look at these sculptures
is the provincial reflection of one-time Hittite greatness.
The sculptors of the city-states pictured comfortable rulers and contented subjects, paunchy, smug people who
took things easy and lived well, whether they were masters or servants. In no other art memorials of the ancient
Orient do we encounter so many children and animals;
the reliefs swarm with them. King Asitawandas who appears on a relief at Karatepe is a genial reveler, a lover of
wine, women, and song, the very model of a father to his
people, but not one inch a real ruler. Can Mursilis, who
conquered Babylon, or Suppiluliumas, who forged the
Empire, or Muwatallis, who defeated Ramses, ever have
looked like that?

It is interesting to read that an expedition in which
Americans and Germans co-operated at Nimrud-Dagh
in Commagene has made finds which show continuing
traces of Hittite influence upon the plastic art of this
vicinity as late as the first century B.C. But the true nature
of the Hittites emerges only from the productions of the
Empire itself, which dominated Asia Minor from 1800 to
1200 B.C.; the art and architecture of later periods are mis-
leading.

These ten points lead us to the following conclusions
about the real historical role of the Hittites:

In the second millennium B.C. there existed a Hittite Empire, but no Hittite culture. The Hittites were a master race whose energies were bent on dominating and leading the heterogeneous tribes of Asia Minor.

It is worth noting that two Englishmen, Wright and Sayce, were the first to apply to the Hittite government the word *empire*. With the example of British nineteenth-century imperialism before their minds, they instinctively chose this term. Had they been men of the twentieth century, they might more accurately have spoken of a *commonwealth*.

If we survey the approximately six hundred years of Hittite domination with these points in mind, we find we cannot speak of Hittite history. History is organic growth,

TENTATIVE RECONSTRUCTION OF THE CITADEL OF BOGHAZKÖY (HATTUSAS), THE RESIDENCE OF THE HITTITE KINGS. VIEW FROM THE NORTHWEST.

spiritual unity, progress in the striving for form and style; it is linked up with a distinctive culture such as we find contemporaneously in Egypt and Babylonia. This type of culture was not present in the Hittite Empire. Over a span of six hundred years we find characteristics and variants, but not a trace of organic development.

The Hittite Empire of the second millennium B.C. was

the most splendid and amazing political phenomenon of ancient history. In the first flush of enthusiasm over its discovery, many scholars believed that this people would prove to be the link between Mesopotamia and Greece. It has since developed that the Empire made no such lasting cultural contributions. The Hittites passed on to the Greeks only the names of a few gods, perhaps also the form of their military helmets, and possibly a musical instrument. That does not amount to much. (It should be added that Professor Helmuth T. Bossert takes a different view of the matter. He believes that the influence of the Hittites upon early Greece was very considerable.)

Anything, absolutely anything, might have come of this Empire if it had not been shattered by the wave of migrations that began around 1200 B.C. But of what value are such historical "ifs"?

Part IV

THE MYSTERY OF THEIR
SURVIVAL

BRONZE STATUETTE OF A BULL.

XI

THE FINDS ON THE BLACK MOUNTAIN

IN THE LATE SUMMER of 1945 a small group of travelers crossed the Taurus Mountains from north to south. The party consisted of Professor Helmuth T. Bossert and three ladies, Dr. Halet Çambel, Nihal Ongunsu, and Muhibbe Darga, his assistants. Sponsored by the University of Istanbul, they were hunting for traces of any ancient Anatolian civilization in regions which had scarcely been explored—almost trackless wastes that were by no means without their perils.

One day they rested in the tiny village of Feke, in the remote southeastern part of present-day Turkey. Several Yürüks, the last nomads of this region, told them about a "lion stone" which was to be found "in the black mountains," beyond the nearby town of Kadirli. The story was confirmed by some of the villagers, which made it more than an idle rumor.

The news excited Bossert—the lion is one of the typical symbolic beasts of the Hittites. But it turned out that Kadirli could not be reached—the roads were already impassable and the expedition could not take the time to make a lengthy detour.

In February Bossert came again, accompanied by Dr.

Halet Çambel. He was advised against the expedition; it was too early in the year, he was told; there had been rains only recently and the vicinity of Kadirli would be a dreadful bog. But Bossert had taken it into his head to follow up this clue in spite of any obstacles. Such strong-mindedness was characteristic of the man. People who know Bossert only from his publications, as the brilliant co-decipherer of Hittite hieroglyphs, know only one side of this versatile personality. Born in 1889 in the small town of Landau in the Rhineland, he studied art history, archæology, Germanic philology, and mediæval history, specializing in paleography, the study of ancient writing. During the First World War he became an army officer and by the end of the war was serving in the War Ministry. After the armistice, when both the military and the academic careers held out few prospects in Germany, he entered the big German art-publishing house of Wasmuth as an apprentice. A few years later he was a director of the firm. He published a six-volume *History of Handicrafts* which has become the standard work in this field. On the side he pursued his studies of the subjects later to become his specialties: cuneiform and hieroglyphic writing. He was one of a group of Berlin scholars who gathered around the Assyriologists Ernst F. Weidner and Bruno Meissner.

But these were not the only irons he had in the fire. While he was already working out his first contribution to decipherment (it was published in 1932 under the title of *Santas und Kupapa*), he entered the book publishing branch of the *Frankfurter Zeitung*. Here he published such different works as *The Beginnings of Photography*,[1] and two picture books, *Buddies in the West* [2] and *Defenseless Behind the Lines*.[3] These last, vividly projecting the

[1] *Die Anfänge der Fotografie.*
[2] *Kamerad im Westen.*
[3] *Wehrlos hinter der Front.*

sufferings of the civilian population in a future war, were thrown into the bonfires during the first Nazi book-burnings in Berlin, and Bossert's name was entered on the storm troopers' blacklist.

For a man of such energy and principle it was un-doubtedly fortunate that he was able to stay out of Nazi Germany. In the fall of 1933 the Turkish Minister of Pub-lic Instruction urged him to remain in Turkey. (At the time he had already made a trip to Boghazköy where he worked with Kurt Bittel on the rock inscriptions and ac-quired experience in field archæology.) He accepted the offer, and in April 1934 was appointed Professor at the University of Istanbul and Director of the Archæological Institute of that city. With typical consistency, he ac-quired Turkish citizenship and a Turkish wife.

This man, having made up his mind to investigate the mysterious "lion stone," could not be deterred by a warn-ing that the roads would be bad. His determination was matched by his assistant, Halet Çambel, who, in spite of a high fever, insisted that she was not going to be left behind. She was later to be Bossert's most energetic asso-ciate, with sufficient daring to stay on alone at Karatepe for a time—a solitary woman in charge of the rough work-men. Her name is quaintly appropriate to her character, for it means "pine tree at the little pass."

On February 27, 1946, at one o'clock in the afternoon, they set out in a *tash arabasi*, a horse-drawn wagon with-out springs of a kind which has been in use for centuries in Turkey. Kadirli is a provincial capital, but to this day it does not have electric light, and it was not until 1954 that a hard road to the nearest village was completed. Be-fore the building of that road the town was completely cut off during the rainy periods in spring and fall. This had its points for the people of the countryside; during those months there was no government.

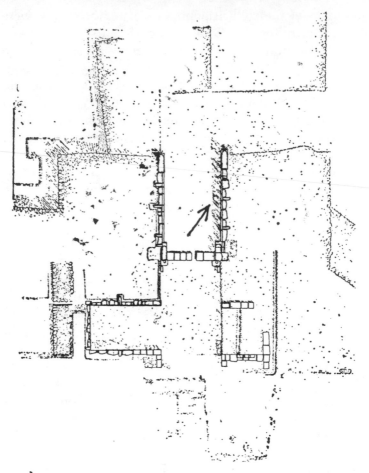

BIRD'S-EYE VIEW OF THE EXCAVATIONS OF THE NORTH GATE
AT KARATEPE. THE ARROW INDICATES THE VIEW SHOWN IN
PLATE 19.

In Kozan, Bossert and Madame Çambel were joined
by the museum director of Adana, Naçi Kum. The party
had gone a little way beyond Kozan when they bogged
down in a pathless waste of mud. The horses collapsed
from exhaustion. In the village of Köseli they were forced

to make a halt. The driver, who it now turned out had no idea of their route and had chosen the most unlikely team for a trip of this sort, was sent back to Kozan. But in these parts a traveler is always hospitably received and aided; with the help of the villagers another driver with a pair of powerful horses was obtained. The party set out again, but were overtaken by darkness. The mud became bottomless. Even the fresh horses bogged down; the travelers had to get out and walk. Finally horses and wagon were trapped in a ditch. "But," Bossert writes laconically, "through a labyrinth of cart tracks the driver finally brought us safe and sound to Kadirli."

It was late in the evening. Since they were expected, an excellent dinner awaited them, tendered by the *kaymakam* (the district chief), the mayor, and other dignitaries. Bossert was grateful but impatient; he was burning to find out more about the stone. A "lion stone" near Kadirli? None of those present had ever heard of it. Bossert persisted with his questioning. Was there anyone around who knew the region very well, who for one reason or another had ridden and tramped about the vicinity?

Villagers were sent for. By eleven o'clock at night some ten persons turned up in the town hall with the strangest stories about the countryside; but none of them knew anything at all about "lion stones." They had never seen or heard of sculptures, old walls in the woods, or stones covered with inscriptions. But then the schoolteacher, Ekrem Kuşçu came in. To everyone's surprise he declared that he had not only seen the stone once, but four times since 1927 in his rides about the neighborhood. He would be glad to lead the travelers to the spot. Tomorrow would surely be a fair day, he thought; they could look forward to a pleasant ride of only five or six hours.

"We spent a very restful night at Kadirli," Bossert

THE FIRST COLUMN OF PHŒNICIAN SCRIPT FROM THE NORTH
GATE AT KARATEPE. IT STANDS UPON TWO ORTHOSTATS, ONE
WIDE AND ONE NARROW, AND CONTAINS TWENTY-ONE LINES.
THE BLACK SPOTS DO NOT INDICATE PLACES WHERE THE
WRITING HAS BEEN WORN AWAY, BUT FAULTS IN THE STONE
WHICH THE HITTITE SCULPTOR LEFT BLANK. SIMILAR BLANKS
CAN BE SEEN ON THE NARROW ORTHOSTAT (LEFT), FOR
EXAMPLE IN LINES SEVEN AND EIGHT.

wrote. He had no suspicion of what awaited him at Karatepe.

At eight-thirty the following morning the horses were ready. It was indeed a fair day. Their road led across a plain, then twisted slowly up into the gloomy mountains. To the east stood the snow-capped peaks of the Anti-Taurus. The group slowly approached the towering mountain ridge known as Karatepe—the Black Mountain. After a ride of several hours the jungle of prickly broom proved such hard going for the horses that they dismounted and scrambled on foot along an ancient shepherds' path. When they reached the top and took their first look around, they saw an endless chain of dim valleys and hills. Below them, muddy yellow and foaming wildly, winding in loop upon loop, ran a river. It was the Ceyhan, known in ancient days as the Pyramus.

And finally, when they tore their eyes away from the vistas of broom and scree and giant rocks, they saw the lion stone! And more. For this lion stone had obviously been the pediment for a statue. The statue lay beside it, badly damaged, armless and headless—but with an *inscription* on it.

As soon as Bossert saw the symbols, he recognized them as Semitic. For a moment he was troubled—were these merely the debris of some Semitic settlement which had somehow been brought to this place?

At the moment of discovery, by the way, it is very hard to know what you have found. An archæologist must be extremely cautious about his first statements. An instructive example of the danger of rash judgments occurred in 1954 when inexperienced Egyptian archæologists sent out such excited reports on new finds at Gizeh and Sakkara (funerary ships and a pyramid grave with a sarcophagus) that newspapers throughout the world carried sensational stories—until closer study revealed that from the scientific point of view the finds were extremely mediocre.

When Bossert considered the size of the stone he thought that it must have been worked on the spot, or very close by. On the other hand, the stone was dark, porous basalt; there was a great deal of rock round about, but none of it basalt of this color. Finally, the statue and the pediment were indubitably Hittite in character, but

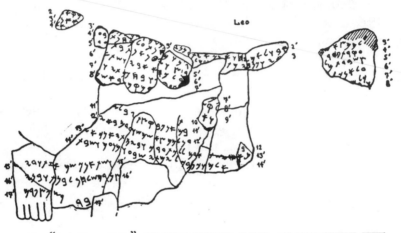

THE "PAPER LION." ON THE NORTH GATE AT KARATEPE THE PHŒNICIAN INSCRIPTION BEGINS ON A LION. RESTORATION WAS IMPOSSIBLE; BOSSERT THEREFORE MERELY PUT THE FRAGMENTS OF SCRIPT TOGETHER ON PAPER AND OBTAINED SEVENTEEN LINES.

the inscription was certainly Semitic. At the time Bossert thought the language must be Aramaic; it later turned out to be Phœnician.

While Halet Çambel took photographs and prepared an impression, Bossert struggled through the thick brushwood to examine the general area around the stone. He found several fragments of reliefs, among which a man's head and a half-human figure were recognizable. Finally he found other fragments, unfortunately quite small, which bore hieroglyphic symbols.

A sudden idea flashed through his mind. Here was a Semitic inscription upon a piece of Hittite sculpture, and here were signs in hieroglyphic script. If these hieroglyphs were unquestionably Hittite the possibility existed —since these two scripts were lying about side by side— that he had at last found what for decades archæologists had been dreaming of: a bilingual. But no—it was too much to hope for. Bossert dismissed the thought. He and his colleague had been here at Karatepe only three hours; they had not turned up so much as a spadeful of earth. Any interpretation on the basis of such superficial impressions was premature.

Reluctantly, they left in order not to be overtaken by darkness in this wilderness. After a ride of an hour and a half they reached Kizyusuflu, the nearest village. While they sat at their campfire that night, surrounded by farmers who had assembled to see the strangers, Bossert already planned a return to Karatepe.

Perhaps the schoolmaster, Ekrem Kuşçu, should be called the actual discoverer of Karatepe—on Bossert's recommendation he later received from the Turkish Historical Society a reward in appreciation of his services. But Ekrem freely admits that he had first heard of the existence of the lion stone in 1927 from an eighty-year-old inhabitant of Kizyusuflu named Abdullah. Abdullah had told him, moreover, that the monuments had been known for many years; living villagers had seen the stones standing upright. In the interval they had probably been knocked over by nomads hunting for treasure.

How far back ought the trail be pursued? The question at issue is the old one: to know something is good, but to recognize its meaning is knowledge of a different order. Helmuth T. Bossert and his assistant Madame Halet Çambel (Naçi Kum had only come along as an interested guest) were the discoverers of Karatepe because they were the first interpreters of the site.

On March 15, 1947 Bossert reached Karatepe for the second time. Now he was accompanied by "Brave Rainbow"—that is the literal translation of the name of Bahadir Alkim. Dr. Alkim was one of Professor Bossert's students. Born in Izmir in 1915, educated at the University of Istanbul, he had already had experience in archæological expeditions at Alaja Hüyük and other sites. For a time he visited Sir Leonard Woolley at Alalakh. He was one of that generation of clever, polyglot, and cosmopolitan-minded young scholars who grew up in Turkey after the reforms of Kemal Atatürk. At the time he was assisting Bossert he had already been appointed to a teaching post at the University of Istanbul.

This first joint excavation lasted only a month, from March 15 to April 15, 1947. In that short time they chalked up extraordinary results. They had few workmen, only the simplest tools, no decent shelter. Since the weather was abysmally bad they dwelt in a tent, the guests of the last nomads who lived along the *akyol* (the "White Road"), that ancient caravan highway which for centuries has connected the east with the west and south. (In 1951 Muhibbe Darga—she was one of Bossert's most capable assistants—was our guide to the black tents of this nomad settlement. The men were out guarding their herds; we sat with the numerous women around the fireplace where from morning to night *yuffka* is baked—a paper-thin flatbread. From the dirt-crusted, crooked fingers of an aged grandmother we received the guest's due of crumbly goat cheese, and ate it. The lady-archæologist and myself had to represent ourselves as man and wife. We threw in six sons for good measure. Unless married—

THE FOURTH COLUMN OF SCRIPT FROM THE STATUE OF THE
GODS—BOSSERT'S RECONSTRUCTION OF THE TEXT IN 1953
AFTER HE HAD INSERTED THE SMALL FRAGMENTS.

and therefore the proud parents of several sons—a man
and woman could not have been accepted into the nomads' tents. The other alternative was to be brother and

sister, but this would have been difficult to carry off, since I did not understand a word of the Yürük Turkoman dialect.)

In these tents Bossert and "Brave Rainbow" put up for three weeks. They were surrounded by innumerable crawling infants and incredible filth and lived on cheese and yuffka. But day after day they were on the Black Mountain. They detected fortification walls—so there must have been a citadel here. Inside the citadel they exposed the remains of building walls—so there must have been a temple or a palace there. When they dug trial shafts they came across well-preserved reliefs showing human and animal figures more than a yard high, chiseled in dark-gray basalt slabs and standing upright *"in situ"*— that is to say, exactly where they had first been placed thousands of years ago.

Bossert also found the beginning of a long Phœnician inscription—how long, he did not yet suspect. And on one of the last days Bossert thought he had found something he had been on the lookout for all those weeks: more pieces of a Hittite hieroglyphic inscription. He had kept the matter to himself—what was the sense of voicing his wild hope that they might discover a bilingual?

He had been scratching away with hand and trowel at the upper corner of a relief. There was no time left to dig this relief out now; he merely intended to determine the course of future excavation. But what he saw made his heart leap—for here were Phœnician signs and Hittite hieroglyphs. The Hittite symbols were barely recognizable—but is it any wonder that, with the dream of all Hittitologists for decades uppermost in his mind, all his doubts vanished and he became certain that he had discovered a bilingual? (For the Phœnician script was readable.)

It is one of the most dramatic twists in the whole history of the discovery of the Hittite Empire that Bossert was wrong about *this*—and that he was nevertheless right!

The first full-fledged expedition to Karatepe started work in September 1947. It was financed by the Turkish Historical Society, the University of Istanbul, and the Department of Museums and Antiquities. It was supplied with the essential equipment and had the funds to hire a good-sized team of workmen.

Bossert has a flair for dramatic effects and enjoys springing surprises on his colleagues. Therefore he skillfully arranged matters so that at the start of the first day's digging the company would be standing near the spot where he had discovered the hieroglyphs. The place differed in no respect from any other location in the area, for Bossert had carefully covered up all traces of his previous probing. In the most casual tone he announced that this was as good a place to begin digging as any. With sly satisfaction he listened to the cries of wonder and admiration from his colleagues when the removal of a few shovelfuls of earth and sand exposed a relief covered with lines of Phœnician writing. Feeling completely sure of himself, he meant to repeat his triumph by conjuring the hieroglyphic inscription out of the debris in a similar miraculous fashion. He told his associates to dig a few yards away from this first find. Sure enough, they uncovered another relief and Bossert was about to point out the hieroglyphs on this new slab—when he realized that he had been mistaken.

It had been late afternoon when he had fleetingly glimpsed the markings that he took for hieroglyphs. Now, in the glaring light of the morning sun, he saw that these marks were nothing but the runes of time, script-like scratches worn into the stone.

It is hard to describe the intense disappointment he felt at that moment. Of course this was a good place to dig, since a relief had been turned up. His associates were delighted at having made a significant find so promptly, but Bossert could not share their enthusiasm. Glumly he stared at the gray stone which was rapidly emerging from the ground where it had lain so long. He had placed his hopes on finding a long, coherent hieroglyphic inscription, and all summer long he had been obsessed by the rash thought that perhaps such an inscription, together with the Phœnician fragments they had found, would provide the long-desired bilingual key to the Hittite hieroglyphs.

At such times the advances of science are a question of character. Bossert ordered the diggers to go on. He had them probe here and there and, though it sounds absolutely incredible, a yard away from the pseudo-hieroglyphs he found the actual hieroglyphic inscription he had been dreaming of.

Those excavations in the fall of 1947 proved to be the most successful ever undertaken at Karatepe. A great many finds were made later; the entire vicinity was carefully investigated and first Hittite, then Roman fortifications were discovered on the Domuztepe, the "mountain of the swine." But the results of this one autumn's dig surpassed everything that came after.

On October 1, 1951 the late Father P. T. O'Callaghan, two German students, and myself succeeded, with the aid of the Kaymakam of Kadirli, in chartering a jeep to take us to Karatepe. Father O'Callaghan was a big, cheerful, and devout man who in the most charming manner combined within himself the most contradictory elements. He was an American, a Jesuit, a professor of Orientalogy at the Bible Institute in Rome. He was fluent in a great many living and dead languages, was fond of singing old German folk songs, and would several times a day abruptly withdraw from his companions and with profound absorption read his Latin breviary.

The two students were eager for adventure, curious, and impatient. It was due to their impatience that we disregarded the advice of Bossert who had warned us under no circumstances to risk a ride or a drive to Karatepe after dark. We started out at seven o'clock in the evening, just as twilight was falling. On the other hand, had it not been for the impatience of the students, we would have missed an unforgettable impression.

After half an hour's ride across a trackless plain it became clear that the Turkish driver had lost his way. We headed straight for the black mountains. A jeep is the perfect vehicle for such excursions, but this one was about ready for the junkyard. Night fell. One of the jeep's headlights was out of commission; the other threatened to give out any minute. There was a full moon, but most of the time the sky was mantled by clouds. The ride was hairraising. We plunged across rushing brooks, bounced over rocks, were uneasily aware of black abysses yawning on both sides of the road we'd taken. Suddenly the driver braked sharply, stalling the roaring motor; and in the stillness of the mountain night we heard strange noises—clumping, heavy footsteps, gentle snorting, angry hisses, panting breaths. Then, into the cone of light from our one-eyed jeep came a procession of heavily-laden camels—a caravan. With unhurried step the procession passed, the men muffled in their burnooses uttering throaty cries to the camels but not deigning to glance at us. They behaved as though the presence of a jeep on this road in the middle of the night were quite in the nature of things. Our driver spoke three or four words with them—shouts of recognition, rather, like a solitary sailor hailing a passing ship.

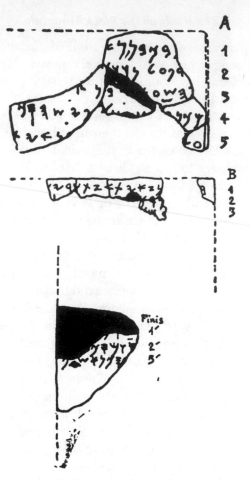

FRAGMENTS OF PHŒNICIAN TEXT WHICH WERE FOUND IN 1953 SCATTERED IN THE THICKETS OR NEAR THE SURFACE BELOW THE SOUTH GATE. INSCRIPTION A, BOSSERT BELIEVES, FORMS THE CONTINUATION OF THE INSCRIPTION ON ORTHOSTAT I. IF NEW FINDS SHOULD PROVE THAT INSCRIPTIONS A, B AND FINIS FORM A SINGLE TEXT, THEY WOULD CONSTITUTE A NEW BILINGUAL—THE KEY TO THE STILL UNDECIPHERABLE PORTIONS OF THE HITTITE HIEROGLYPHIC TEXT OF THE SOUTH GATE.

But after the fantastic camel train had passed and we bumped on with gasping motor up the rocky slope of the Black Mountain, we suddenly felt a sense of approaching our destination. We had come upon the *akyol,* the age-old caravan route, and our driver now thought he knew the direction.

After another hour or two we stopped again. The night was darker than ever. We were on a tiny plateau which narrowed up ahead of us into a footpath. One of the students rushed forward—and promptly vanished from sight. Our driver gabbled something ·at us; he was so excited we could not understand a word. Father O'Callaghan gripped my arm and pointed into the darkness. In front of us, with glowing eyes, fascinated by the headlight of the jeep, stood a wolf-like animal. Drawn by the light and at the same time blinded by it, it began slinking in a wide circle around our car. It was one of those wild dogs that roam everywhere in this area; in packs they can be a real menace.

I arranged signal calls with Father O'Callaghan and then set out in the direction in which our young student had disappeared. And then I had the wonderful experience which is ordinarily reserved for the field archæologist. The strange, remote world which I knew only from my studies of the literature rose up before me, and the unexpected physical presence of it was overwhelming.

With only my flashlight to illuminate the darkness, I followed the narrow, stony footpath that began at the edge of the plateau. Suddenly the path widened out, and before me I saw steps. Involuntarily I paused. And as if at this moment nature decided to produce a thrilling theatrical effect, the clouds scattered and the moon showered its silvery light upon a stately outside stairway built of weather-beaten slabs of stone. It curved gently as I climbed it, broadened out, and then to my right and left

I saw a series of upright stone plaques, nearly the height of a man, with wonderfully distinct carvings. Since these were bas-reliefs, the moonlight created a beautifully life-like play of shadows across them. I saw the faces of men and animals staring at me. Were these gods, kings? Why, of course, how could I have failed to recognize it? I had seen it in photographs. This was the famous "Feast of Asitawandas," the relief immortalizing the lord of Kara-tepe not as ruler and warrior, but as a genial patriarch and gourmand. I looked into his face. There he sat with a peaked cap on his head, his large eyes gazing expect-antly at the servants who were bringing him food and drink. His huge hooked nose, his receding forehead and receding chin, gave him a look of mildness—and yet he was not without lordly dignity. His full lips reached out slightly toward the fine dishes being offered to him, and in the shimmer of pallid moonlight they might have been about to open.

At the top of the stairway two dark figures awaited me. They responded to my call with a silent gesture. Min-utes later I stepped into the circle of light cast by a power-ful acetylene lamp in Professor Bossert's hand. Hearing our calls, he had come forward to show us the way. The lost student had been found, and Father O'Callaghan soon joined us. We sat down to supper with Bossert and his assistants on the thatch-roofed "terrace" of the small stone house that he had built since his first expedition. The table was crude, the chairs rickety, the conversation good. From the darkness round about sounded the wail-ing howl of the jackals and the distant barking of the wild dogs—the expedition's regular serenade.

At seven the following morning we breakfasted. At seven-thirty the day's work began—and for us the first tour of the site.

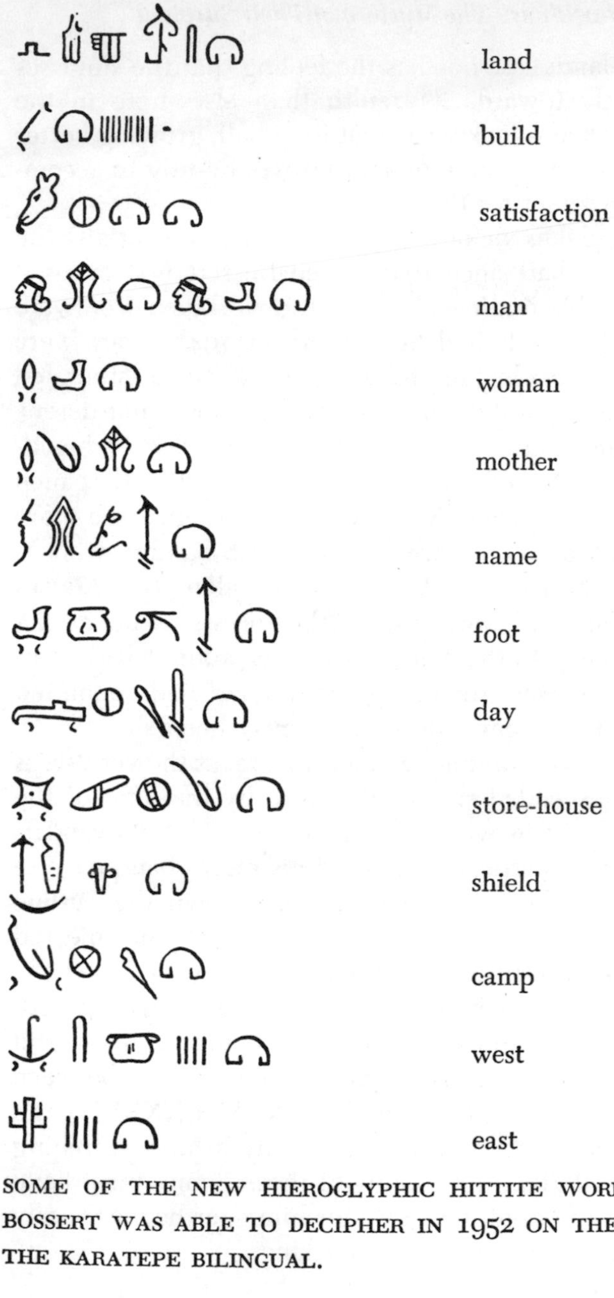

land

build

satisfaction

man

woman

mother

name

foot

day

store-house

shield

camp

west

east

SOME OF THE NEW HIEROGLYPHIC HITTITE WORDS WHICH BOSSERT WAS ABLE TO DECIPHER IN 1952 ON THE BASIS OF THE KARATEPE BILINGUAL.

In this landscape one has the feeling that the sun rises more swiftly towards its zenith than elsewhere in the world. One keeps looking at that fiery ball, growing hotter and yellower every minute, and hurries unduly to accomplish the tasks set for the day.

The citadel as we now saw it presented essentially the aspect it had had since 1947, when Bossert first exposed its recognizable outlines. Most of the workmen who were now plying shovels had been there in 1947. They were smiling, harmless-looking fellows, and we were astounded to learn that among them were several known murderers. In this region feuds are common and the law of blood-vengeance still holds; it was an axiom of life that men would kill for revenge. Moreover, all of them were more or less related to the large numbers of bandits who as recently as the 1930's had spread terror along the caravan route, around Karatepe, and in the forests as far as the plain of Adana. In the course of conversation it was casually mentioned that the first guard Bossert had appointed after his initial excavation had recently been shot.

We began our tour at the South Gate, at the very steps that I had ascended the night before by the light of the moon. Once again we lingered in front of Asitawandas, the King of Karatepe, and studied his merry banquet. We walked along the citadel walls, were shown the outline of the bastions and of the defense towers which projected sharply from the fortification walls. Then we crossed the peak of the mountain, approached the lower-lying North Gate, and found ourselves abruptly before a wonderful view of the tremendous Ceyhan Valley. Here, between the two lions of the gate (see Plates XXXVI-XXXVII) the king may have stood watching enemy armies marching toward his citadel. The coming of those armies must have spelled the end of all his glory for him—for he was surely by temperament no great warrior-king.

As we walked past the numerous upright reliefs which lined the entrance of the North Gate as well as the walls of two chambers directly adjoining the gatehouse, we received an impression of the luxuriant formlessness of this Late Hittite culture, this surviving provincial culture of a great empire. Lumped together without the slightest logical or artistic connection were sculptures of men and animals, heraldic groups, processions, genre pictures, representations of gods, ritualistic scenes, pictures of hunts on water and land, scenes of music-making and dancing, and finally a chariot and a boat side by side. Interspersed among these sculptures were the inscriptions, some massed on special steles, others helter-skelter. Phœnician and hieroglyphic Hittite inscriptions were set down in any old place; the only principle seemed to be: get writing in wherever there happened to be room. There were script symbols on the reliefs, on single figures, even on the belly of the great lion at the gate. Bossert had already determined that nowhere was there the slightest connection between the content of the inscriptions and the reliefs or sculptures on which they were scribbled.

As we climbed back to the expedition's camp we talked about the mystery of this strange survival of a cultural form in Carchemish, Zinjirli, and here at Karatepe— a form that had never actually been a real form even in the imperial period, that had never become a great characteristic style, and that had nevertheless gone on influencing the art of the region for a good five hundred years—or shall we say half a millennium, as that better renders the significance of such a span of time.

At this point there is a great gap in our knowledge of history. Those five hundred years between 1200 B.C., when Hattusas was burned and the Hittite Empire collapsed, and about 700 B.C., when the last Hittite city-states were absorbed by the Assyrian Empire, are at present quite obscure to us. It is very rare indeed for an empire to break down while its culture goes on persisting—on a provincial level, but still persisting—for five hundred years among isolated racial groups surrounded by extremely different peoples and exposed to numerous alien cultural influences.

"Some day we will understand all the interrelationships," Bossert said to me. He carefully unfolded a large, stiff sheet of paper covered with Hittite hieroglyphs, an impression that had just been taken. "If by using the Karatepe bilingual key we can learn to read the Karatepe hieroglyphs, we will straightway be able to read all the hieroglyphs of the imperial age!"

These words bring us to the most exciting chapter of the Karatepe excavation—the decipherment of the bilingual. In our discussion of deciphering we left the story at the point the decipherment of the Hittite hieroglyphs had reached an impasse. Here at Karatepe the work was finally carried to a triumphant conclusion. And yet even after Bossert had discovered the genuine hieroglyphic inscription, he could not prove immediately that it was the twin of the Phœnician inscription. For first it was necessary to *prove* that what he had found was really a bilingual, not simply two different inscriptions in two different languages.

It is curious, in fact almost unbelievable, that one of Bossert's associates succeeded in working out this proof in his sleep!

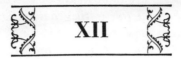

XII

ASITAWANDAS SPEAKS

THE PHŒNICIAN TEXTS unearthed in the excavation of 1947 called for immediate translation. Phœnician is a very ancient language; the task was one for specialists. Bossert, burning with eagerness to know what he had found, sent careful copies of the inscriptions to several important Semitic scholars: Johannes Friedrich in Berlin, R. D. Barnett in London, Dupont-Sommer in Paris, and Father O'Callaghan in Rome. These inscriptions came from the statues—those same statues whose base, the "lion stone," had brought the archæologists to long-lost Karatepe in the first place. That stone had since become famous indeed. One of the Turkish workmen, Kemal Deveci, composed for better or worse a pæan of twelve stanzas to it. A typical sample is the following stanza:

> *"Great old Hittites left this here,*
> *How long ago is still unknown.*
> *The world is breathless, that is clear.*
> *There's nothing like the lion stone!"*

And at night the stone was serenaded in a song almost equally long, composed by the ten-year-old child of a workman, Mehmet Kisti. This one climaxed in the stanza:

"When Little Mehmet hears of the lion stone
He is filled all full with great delight.
Sing a song to praise the lion stone
That wins all hearts by day and night."

It is certainly odd that in the meantime Professor H. G. Güterbock, come from Ankara on a visit to the site, discovered that the "lions" were in reality a pair of bulls.

The experts pored over the four columns of text from the statue. Johannes Friedrich of Berlin was the first to send Bossert the translation. The written passages were full of gaps, the statue having suffered from the tooth of time, and therefore the translation does not read very fluently. In any case, the principal value of the Karatepe inscriptions was not their content, but the fact that they constituted the longest Old Phœnician running text that had so far been discovered, and that they also held the probability that the hieroglyphics were a Hittite version of that same text.

We learn that the author of the inscription was a king whose name in the vowelless Semitic script was written "'ztwd." Later, on the basis of the hieroglyphs, Bossert was able to expand this name to "Asitawandas." The fact that, as Friedrich remarks, the language was "pure Old Phœnician without any Aramaic admixture" permits us to date this king; it is certain that he lived in the eighth century B.C., and evidence from other finds makes the date 730 B.C. probable. It was during his lifetime that Karatepe was conquered and destroyed by enemies. Compared to the kind of self-glorification conventional in the Orient, Asitawandas displayed a perhaps typical Hittite modesty. "And I built this city and gave it the name Asitawanda. . . . And I built strong fortifications everywhere on the borders and in the places where bad men were the leaders of robber bands." He calls himself "Ruler of the Daniuna";

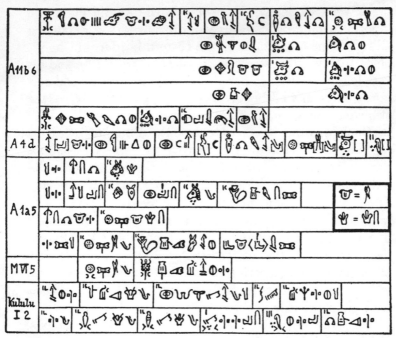

A 11 b 6:   But for them among these gods will be bled, for an-
            nual food:
            to the god Karhuha one steer and one sheep;
            to the goddess Küpapa one steer and one sheep;
            to the divinity Sarku one sheep;
            and a kutupalis sheep to the male divinities.

A 4 d   Also to this god A. among the gods (I will? . . . verb
            broken off) as

A 1a5   And who (is appointed to supply) a sheep
            now for this hero (?) he shall "sacrifice" a sheep to
            the god!
            But whosoever is (appointed to supply) his food
            he shall (they shall) "bring" food and drink to him

Kululu I 2: And these I had set up for the tarhunds of the under-
            derworld. I shall "sacrifice" to him year after year
            with a steer (and) three sheep.

A HIEROGLYPHIC HITTITE SACRIFICE FORMULA TRANSLATED
BY H. T. BOSSERT IN 1953 ON THE BASIS OF THE PHŒNICIAN-
HITTITE BILINGUAL FOUND AT KARATEPE.

these were, we know, the people of the Adana Plain. He reports that he pacified his western border by deporting all rebellious inhabitants to the eastern border, but he repeatedly lays great stress on the statement that he and his people always lived in happiness and prosperity. And certainly one can well believe that the rotund fellow we see at his feast was fond of good and easy living.

Such was the basic content of the Phœnician text as reproduced in Friedrich's translation. The translations that came in from Paris and Rome differed in some details, but in no essential points, from Friedrich's version. Then the translation from London arrived.

Not only was it different from the others; in the fifth line the translator had arrived at an entirely different meaning. To put the matter briefly, he had discovered another king in the inscription in addition to Asitawandas, a King Anek. Understandably enough, all the participants were tremendously excited by the news.

Professor Barnett's reasoning was extremely ingenious, and his conclusions were supported by two other Semitic scholars whom he had consulted, Jacob Leveen and Cyril Moss.

The inscription begins with the Phœnician word *'nk,* which is unquestionably the personal pronoun of the first person singular—in other words, *I.* In the fifth line the same sign occurs again, but in such a grammatical relationship that it is really impossible to read it as *I.* Professor Barnett therefore advanced a theory which was supported by the ninth line of the third column. If *'nk* was to be read as *I,* then the text would be saying "for the sons and daughters of I"—which, as the scholar remarked, is "a thing as absurd in translation as it is in Phœnician."

This being so, Barnett discarded the reading of *I* for *'nk.* Instead he took the symbols as the name of another king, *Anek*—or possibly *Inak,* since the vowels are wanting. He and his two colleagues proposed extraordinarily clever arguments, sought out the most remote historical points of reference, indulged in speculations on the possible kinships of this King Anek or Inak, and even ventured to draw certain definite conclusions.

Their brilliant guesswork, however, was based upon a false assumption. King Anek or Inak never existed.

THE "PEOPLE OF THE SEA," AN EGYPTIAN REPRESENTATION. WITH THEIR FAMILIES AND THEIR CHARIOTS THEY MOVED THROUGH ASIA MINOR AND SYRIA, BURNING AND PILLAGING, UNTIL BROUGHT TO A HALT BY THE EGYPTIAN BORDER FORTIFICATIONS. THIS INVASION SMASHED THE HITTITE EMPIRE. THE SMALL DRAWING HAS ITS PLACE IN THE HISTORY OF ARCHÆOLOGY. IT WAS MADE UNDER THE DIRECTION OF CHAMPOLLION, THE DECIPHERER OF THE EGYPTIAN HIEROGLYPHS, IN THE COURSE OF THE ONLY EGYPTIAN JOURNEY (1828–29) THAT BRILLIANT ARMCHAIR ARCHÆOLOGIST WAS ABLE TO TAKE BEFORE HIS PREMATURE DEATH.

There was in fact a genuine problem concealed within the use of the pronoun *'nk*, but Friedrich had coped with the matter in his first translation; he had proposed a solution in a footnote, and the other translators—aside from Barnett, Leveen, and Moss—came to the same conclusion as he.

"The author of the inscription," he wrote, "has the

barbarous habit of using *'nk* with the third person singular masculine form of the perfect (instead of with the first person singular verb)."

Thus a new king was born of the slanginess of a scribe who wrote 2700 years ago—was born and died with great promptness.

In the development of any young science such mistakes are inevitable. They may cause a great deal of trouble, impeding progress for a long time. Such was the case with Jensen's reading of the name "Syennesis" in a hieroglyphic Hittite inscription. He justified this interpretation so cleverly that all other scholars went along with it. In reality, as Bossert proved, the name should have been read Uarpalauas—Urballa in Assyrian. On the other hand, when an error is corrected by other scholars immediately after publication, as was the case with Barnett's King Anek, it may do no harm.

Now that the Phœnician text had been interpreted, the time had come to compare the hieroglyphic words with the Phœnician text. There seemed a good prospect that this procedure would at last lead to the decipherment of hieroglyphic Hittite.

In fact the task was far more difficult than the archæologists imagined in the first flush of enthusiasm. It turned out that they could not even prove they really had a bilingual. For there were three Phœnician inscriptions, accompanied by two hieroglyphic Hittite texts, and all were scattered in such random fashion about the gate and the buildings that there was no saying where the hieroglyphic Hittite text even began. The inscriptions often jumped wantonly from stone to stone. At this time, moreover, the scholars had so limited a vocabulary—for example they knew only a single verb, the symbol for "to make"—that they had nothing to fasten on when it came to demonstrating that the inscriptions were identical in content. If they had only been able to discover the name of Asitawandas in the hieroglyphic Hittite text, the evidence

VOTIVE STELE FROM MARASH.

that here was a genuine bilingual would be enormously strengthened.

When the problem reached this impasse a student of Bossert's, twice in succession, had the incredible good fortune of finding and recognizing the solution in a literally somnambulistic manner.

Franz Steinherr is an outsider in the academic world. If you meet him today in the offices of the German Embassy at Ankara, where he translates and checks over commercial treaties between Turkey and the German Federal Republic, you would never dream of the arcane matters he deals with in his spare time.

He was born in 1902 in Landshut, near Nuremberg, Germany. The education he received was nondescript and he began his career as a bookkeeper's apprentice. He then became in turn correspondent for a shipping line, a bank, a rayon manufacturer, and a construction company. It was as representative of the latter that he was first sent to Istanbul. Because of his wholly remarkable grasp of languages, he filled all sorts of functions in the Turkish capital. Meanwhile he was busy writing. One of the first things he published was a study entitled: "On the Colloquial Speech and Thieves' Cant of Istanbul."

He had taught himself Turkish at the age of fifteen. At seventeen he had taken up Arabic, at eighteen Japanese, and at nineteen Russian. "After a while," he has remarked in conversation, "when you have learned a number of languages you develop a certain technique for learning more." It need scarcely be mentioned that he speaks fluent French and English in addition to his German. In 1939 he happened to meet Professor Bossert, who convinced him that such an extraordinary gift for languages ought to be put to use in the service of archæology. For that purpose he would have to learn Latin and Greek, which he had missed out on.

Under the rules of German universities (which were followed in Turkey), a student must have passed his *Abitur* in order to qualify for matriculation. The *Abitur* is far more difficult than American college entrance examinations, and Steinherr was at this time thirty-seven years old. He took two hours of tutoring in mathematics daily and finished the course in two months. Then he reviewed all of his secondary-school studies and went back to his old school in Munich to take his examination. He passed with flying colors, returned to Istanbul, and registered at the University as a student of Bossert's. Bossert arranged the schedule of his lectures to suit this extraordinary student.

And so Steinherr, who was at this time business manager and bookkeeper of the German Hospital in Istanbul, also acquired his Ph.D. and was invited to be a guest of the Karatepe expedition of 1947.

On that expedition he was man of all work. Since at first there was a shortage of workmen, he himself pitched in, erecting tents, arranging the camp, taking photographs, scouting the terrain, cleaning reliefs, copying inscriptions, and sorting, or rather trying to sort, the rapidly swelling collection of hieroglyphic Hittite texts that were coming to light.

One evening after the day's work was done he stood looking at a well-preserved sphinx that had just been dug up. Idly, his hand passed over the encrusted surface, and as it did so the thin layer of sand upon the sphinx was brushed off. "Then I became aware that the body was covered with Hittite hieroglyphs. I at once tried to read the hieroglyphs my hand had exposed, and I was overcome by great excitement as I realized that they formed the name of King Asitawandas who is mentioned in the Phœnician text. The style was, to be sure, unusual . . . but the interpretation was corroborated by the other signs. . . . That evening this important find was suitably celebrated by all the members of the expedition. Muhibbe Darga solemnly presented me with a chain of those blue beads common in these parts—I still have it in my possession as a memento."

It was established now that the inscriptions in the two

different scripts dealt with the same king. However, a reading at least a sentence long was needed to prove that the substance as well as the subject of the texts were identical, that one was a translation of the other.

When Steinherr was once more back at his desk in the German Hospital in Istanbul, he spent every night for weeks working on the texts, comparing, sorting, copying. "In this way whole passages of the text in both languages became firmly embedded in my memory, so that I could have committed them to paper at any time."

One afternoon he attended a lecture of Bossert's during which the professor discussed a part of the Phœnician text in which there occurred the phrase: ". . . and I made horse [go] with horse, and shield with shield, and army with army . . ."

That evening Steinherr worked until late at night. At last he went to bed exhausted, but in that state of mental excitement which often carries over into dreams. Suddenly he awoke, sat up, and saw with the greatest clarity before his mind's eye a piece of the hieroglyphic inscription in which there were two horses' heads in succession. He also saw the signs for *I made* which up to this moment neither he nor anyone else had detected in the context. We will remember that "to make" happened to be the one known verb in hieroglyphic Hittite. What was that Phœnician text Professor Bossert had discussed during the afternoon? ". . . and I made horse [go] with horse . . ."

Here was unequivocal proof! A hieroglyphic Hittite sentence had been found that corresponded word for word with a Phœnician sentence. The Karatepe inscription was certainly a bilingual!

Now that the first parallel between the two inscriptions had been found, Bossert in his turn had a sudden insight and discovered where the hieroglyphic Hittite inscription started. Thanks to his archæological finds, he had at his disposal an amount of material greater than any other scholar and was now able to attack the final decipherment of hieroglyphic Hittite with every prospect of success. As these lines are being written, early in 1955, it can be stated with certainty that hieroglyphic Hittite, the unknown language of an unknown people written in an unknown script, is now readable. The discovery of the bilingual at Karatepe, the Black Mountain by the Ceyhan River, provided the key to the enigma over which scholars labored for three generations and almost seventy years.

Bossert is still digging at Karatepe, accompanied by "Brave Rainbow"—Bahadir Alkim—as well as by the latter's wife, Madame Handan (which means "She Who Smiles Sweetly"). His own Turkish wife and his former colleagues and students often join him at his labors on the Black Mountain. They are concerned now with restoration, with putting together the innumerable fragments of sculptures and inscriptions. They are also mindful of the necessity of preserving their finds which are weathering rapidly from being exposed to the burning sun of summer and the torrential rains of winter. Bossert has always had to contend with the problem of obtaining funds for his field work. The day of great philanthropists who backed such expeditions is gone, and the Turkish scientific societies have limited means. Bossert and his colleagues financed one of the recent excavations out of their own savings. That particular expedition—the campaign of 1953—provided another surprise, one no one had seriously expected, although the way for it had been prepared by careful reasoning and diligent desk-work.

In comparing all the inscriptions found at Karatepe in recent years, Bossert had become more and more aware of certain gaps. Numerous incomplete sentences indicated that the inscription on the South Gate must have been much longer than he and his colleagues had originally supposed. Bossert suggested searching for missing fragments on the slope that fell sharply away from the South Gate—a toilsome and time-consuming job because of all the rocks and prickly shrubs, and not without its dangers, for snakes and scorpions apparently considered this slope their private Eden. But it was worth the effort, for Bossert's guess was right. He found a large number of fragments which when put together yielded a new bilingual with a completely new text.

The work at Karatepe, like Bittel's excavations at Boghazköy, is still going on. Asitawandas has much more to tell us of his vanished times. It struck me as wholly appropriate that after dark one evening in 1951, while I was a guest of the expedition, we formed a procession and proceeded solemnly to view the relief of Asitawandas. Our only illumination was the glaring acetylene lamp in Bossert's hand. With swarms of insects buzzing around us and the mysterious night noises of the Black Mountain ringing in our ears, we marked the close of a season's excavation by paying humblest homage to King Asitawandas, who had ruled here two thousand seven hundred years ago, and who had so recently deigned to speak to us.

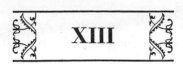

THE FUTURE

FIELD WORK is continuing, and not only at Karatepe and Boghazköy. Nor are Westerners monopolizing the research. Kemal Attatürk founded the departments of language, history, and geography at the University of Ankara, the capital he himself had built, and brought in the young German scholars Landsberger and Güterbock to teach the language and history of the Hittites. Bossert had already come to Istanbul by this time, and the German and British Archæological Institutes had long influenced cultural life in Istanbul and Ankara. Under the ægis of these scholars and societies, the first generation of Turkish Hittitologists grew up. Among them were Bahadir Alkim, the co-excavator of Karatepe; Tahsin Özgüç and his wife Nimet, who dug successfully at Kara Hüyük, Dündartepe, and Kültepe; and Remzi Oguz Arik, the co-director of the Alaja Hüyük excavation.

Other young Turks were studying abroad. Energetic, multilingual Halet Çambel went to Paris and was, after her return, an assistant of Kurt Bittel as well as Bossert. Hamit Zübeyr Koşay studied in Budapest, later became director general of the Turkish museums and a skillful excavator. Professor Ekrem Akurgal, now Director of the School of Fine Arts, University of Ankara, and Professor Sedat Alp attended the University of Berlin.

Kemal Atatürk died in 1938. In his will he had bequeathed to the Turkish Historical Society a trust fund which provided 125,000 Turkish pounds annually for a systematic program of research in Anatolia. Atatürk may well be considered not only the "Father of the Turks," but also the father of a new generation of Turkish scholars.

The work goes on. Field archæologists are digging, and will continue to dig for a long time, at many sites between Boghazköy and Hamath, between Smyrna and Tell Halaf. Every new hieroglyphic inscription that turns up is readable now and will help paint the history of the Hittite Empire, that first great Indo-European state, in richer and truer colors. The new evidence is throwing light not only on the period of the Empire but also—as is shown by the results of the most recent excavations in Ugarit by Claude Schaeffer, the French archæologist—upon the political interrelationships of the petty states of the later Hittite era. Perhaps these discoveries will ultimately solve the mystery of the Hittites' survival.

Seventy years ago the Hittites and their Empire were unknown. Our schools still teach that the Mesopotamian and Egyptian kingdoms alone shaped the political and military history of the second millennium B.C. in Asia Minor and the Near East. But for a while the Hittite Empire was their equal, and the Hittite capital of Hattusas matched Babylon and Thebes—not in culture, but in armed might and political importance.

And so we come to the end of our history of the discovery of this Empire, of its many languages and scripts, its rise and its fall. There is a beautiful inevitability in the line of development that stretches from the earliest to the latest discovery, from the year 1834, when Charles Texier stood all unsuspecting above the ruins of Boghazköy, to the year 1947 when the bilingual inscription found at Karatepe provided the needed key to our knowledge of the Hittite people and their Empire. The line runs straight from the "Narrow Gorge" to the "Black Mountain."

CHRONOLOGICAL TABLE,
BIBLIOGRAPHY, AND INDEX

CHRONOLOGICAL TABLE OF
THE HITTITE EMPIRE

(ALL DATES B.C.)

THE DATES for the reigns of the kings are based upon papers by Dr. Sidney Smith and Professor Albrecht Götze. For the reconstructed dates I follow Dr. O. R. Gurney; where definite dates cannot be determined he reckons with the average length of a generation. According to Gurney, the dates from 1590 to 1335 B.C. are assured. All other dates must be regarded as approximate; it is, however, not likely that future correction of errors will decisively alter the general picture. Kings about whom very little is known are indicated by italics.

Tribal migrations in Asia Minor, in the course of which bands of Indo-Europeans descend upon Anatolia from the northwest or northeast, subjugate the natives (Proto-Hattians), and create the first city-states, among them Hattusas near present-day Boghazköy, in the great bend of the Halys River.

Pitkhanas of Kussara
Anittas of Kussara
  (circa 1900)
Tudhaliyas I (1740–
  1710)
*Pu-sarrumas (1710–
  1680)*
Labarnas (1680–1650)

King Anittas conquers Hattusas, destroys the city, and places a curse upon it. Nevertheless it is reconstructed; new rulers trace their ancestry back to the House of Kussara. (Feudalism; electoral kingship.)

Labarnas must probably be considered the founder of the Hittite Empire. He unites the city-states into a federal government with centralized leadership and extends the Hittite power eastward and westward. The king, although still answerable to the *Pankus,* the council of nobles, is accorded the right of naming his successor. Subsequently the name Labarnas becomes a title.

Hattusilis I (1650–1520)

Hattusilis is the first to practice imperialistic policies. He marches across the Taurus Mountains as far as Aleppo. Shortly before his death he disinherits his foster son and appoints as his successor Mursilis I.

Mursilis I (1620–1590)
Hantilis I (1590–1560)
Zidantas I (1560–1550)

Mursilis repeats the Aleppo campaign, advances still farther and conquers Babylon. The Hittite Kingdom becomes the leading Great Power of the Near East.

Ammunas (1550–1530)
Huzziyas I (1530–1525)

Mursilis is assassinated. Incompetent successors to the kingship lose what he has won. Sharp conflicts arise between the nobility and the kings. Fathers and brothers are murdered for the crown. Telipinus

Telipinus (1525–1500)

succeeds in forcing through the needed constitutional reform, establishing strict rules of hereditary succession. This brings about new consolidation of royal rule and

Alluwamnas (1500–1490)
Hantilis II (1490–1480)
Zidantas II (1480–1470)

strengthening of the Hittite power against external enemies. In this period a Hittite code of law is drawn up. In contrast to the Oriental prin-

Huzziyas II (1470–1460)

Tudhaliyas II (1460–1440)

Arnuwandas I (1440–1420)

Hattusilis II (1420–1400)

Tudhaliyas III (1400–1385)

Arnuwandas II (1385–1375)

Suppiluliumas I (1375–1335)

Arnuwandas III (1335–1334)

Mursilis II (1334–1306)

ciple of an eye for an eye it is characterized by distinctly humane penal provisions. Although the Hurrian Kingdom of Mitanni on the east of the Hittite Kingdom now displays vigorous political and cultural growth and significantly influences the Hittites, three kings, Tudhaliyas II, Hattusilis II, and Tudhaliyas III succeed in consolidating Hittite power as far south as the Syrian border. In Suppiluliumas the Hittites produce a great ruler who combines military with political genius. He smashes the Kingdom of Mitanni and extends the borders of his kingdom as far as Lebanon, but does not enslave the conquered peoples. Instead he makes them his vassals, in part by a policy of clever marital alliances. So formidable does he seem to his contemporaries that the Egyptian queen, widow of Tutankhamen, asks him for one of his sons whom she may take for a husband and set upon the throne of the Pharaohs. After the brief but ill-starred reign of the invalid Arnuwandas III, Mursilis II proves a worthy successor to Suppiluliumas. He consolidates his father's conquests, wages numerous border wars, but interests himself also in religious and artistic matters. His *Prayers in Time of Plague* and his *Annals* are significant literary and historical documents.

Muwatallis (1306–1282)   The decisive conflict with Egypt comes to a head under his son Muwatallis. At Kadesh on the Orontes in 1296 Pharaoh Ramses II is defeated by the Hittites and barely escapes with his life.

Urhi-Teshub (1282–1275)
Hattusilis III (1275–1250)

After a brief reign of the rightful heir the throne is usurped by Hattusilis III, the brother of Muwatallis. He concludes an "everlasting peace" with Egypt, sealing the peace treaty by the marriage of one of his daughters to Ramses. His *Life* is the first example in literature of a self-critical autobiography.

Tudhaliyas IV (1250–1220)
Arnuwandas IV (1220–1190)
Suppiluliumas II (c. 1190)

Gradually the Empire falls apart. In west and east allies of the Hittites revolt. New migrating races pour in across the borders; the Hittite Empire collapses.

Around 1200 Hattusas is burned. Hittite culture, with distinctive use of the Hittite hieroglyphic script, is preserved in city-states in North Syria (Carchemish, Zinjirli, etc.) and Cilicia (Karatepe) until about 700 B.C. In Commagene, at the northern reaches of the Euphrates, Hittite cultural influences (hieroglyphic symbols) have been found dating from as late as the first century A.D.

BIBLIOGRAPHY

Because Hittitology is one of the youngest offshoots of archæology, there have been few comprehensive studies of the entire field. Not many scholars have ventured to write a history of the Hittites. The sum total of some seventy years of scholarly labors is scattered among innumerable professional journals and yearbooks. For this reason I have not attempted a complete, authoritative bibliography, such as was once begun by Contenau but never finished. Such a bibliography would, at a conservative estimate, prove to be at least five times as long as this one.

I have made a point of listing as far as possible every piece of writing which is still of value at the present stage of Hittitology, or which contributed significantly to the development of the science. Much more material fell into these categories than I had anticipated. The result—a happy one, I trust—has been a bibliography that is probably the most extensive *modern* list of Hittite studies.

The arrangement of the six subject groups follows the structure of this book.
1. *General* (Fundamental works on the history of Asia Minor and the Hittite Kingdom; bibliographies; works on related subjects).
2. *Discovery* (The first travelers' reports; first finds; theories up to the year 1912).
3. *Languages and Writings* (Deciphering; Karatepe inscriptions; cf. Group 5).
4. *History* (Hittite politics, religion, art and general culture down to the collapse of the Empire about 1200 B.C.; also reports of excavations after 1912).
5. *The Petty Kingdoms* (Especially material on Karatepe and the bilingual found there; to the absorption of the Hittite state into the Assyrian Empire).
6. *Translations from Hittite Literature* (Including copies and transcriptions).

1. *GENERAL* (Fundamental works on the history of Asia Minor and the Hittite Kingdom; bibliographies; works on related subjects).

Albright, W. F.: "New Light on the History of Western Asia in the Second Millennium B.C." *Bulletin of the American Schools of Oriental Research*, Nos. 77, 78. 1940.

Baikie, J.: *The Amarna Age.* London, 1926.
Bilabel, F.: *Geschichte Vorderasiens und Ägyptens vom 16.—11. Jahrhundert v. Chr.* Heidelberg, 1927.
Bittel, Kurt: *Grundzüge der Vor- und Frühgeschichte Kleinasiens.* Second edition. Tübingen, 1950.
Bossert, H. T.: *Altanatolien.* Berlin, 1942.
Boveri, Margret: *"Der Trojanische Krieg fand statt. Neues aus dem Reich der Hethiter."* *Wirtschafts-Zeitung,* Stuttgart, April 16, 1949.
Breasted, J. H.: *A History of Egypt.* Second edition. New York, 1909.
Cavaignac, E.: *Les Hittites.* Paris, 1950.
———: *Le problème hittite.* Paris, 1936.
Contenau, G.: *Éléments de bibliographie hittite.* Paris, 1922.
———: *"Supplément aux Éléments de bibliographie hittite."* *Babyloniaca,* X,1–3. Paris, 1927.
———: *La civilisation des Hittites et des Hurrites du Mitanni.* Paris, 1948.
Daniel, Glyn E.: *A Hundred Years of Archaeology.* London, 1950.
Delaporte, L.: *Les Hittites.* Paris, 1936.
———: *"Eine periodische Bibliographie."* *Revue Hittite et Asianique.*
Erman, Adolf: *Die Literatur der Ägypter.* Leipzig, 1923.
Erman, Adolf, and Ranke, Hermann: *Ägypten und ägyptisches Leben im Altertum.* Tübingen, 1923.
Friedell, Egon: *Kulturgeschichte Ägyptens und des Alten Orients; Leben und Legende der vorchristlichen Seele.* Third edition. Munich, 1951.
Garstang, John: *The Land of the Hittites. An account of recent explorations and discoveries in Asia Minor, with descriptions of the Hittite monuments.* London, 1910.
———: *The Hittite Empire. A survey of the history, geography and monuments of Hittite Asia Minor and Syria.* London, 1929.
Götze, A.: *"Das Hethiter-Reich."* *Der Alte Orient,* Vol. 27. Leipzig, 1928.
———: *"Kleinasien."* *Handbuch der Altertumswissenschaft* III, 1. Munich, 1933.
———: *Hethiter, Churriter und Assyrer. Hauptlinien der Vorderasiatischen Kulturentwicklung im II. Jahrtausend v. Chr.* Oslo, 1936.
———: *"The Present State of Anatolian and Hittite Studies."* *The Haverford Symposium,* 1938.
Gurney, O. R.: *The Hittites.* London, 1952.
Güterbock, H. G.: *"Die Neuaufstellung der hethitischen Denkmäler in Ankara."* *Archiv für Orientforschung,* XIII, 6. Berlin, 1941.
———: *Guide to the Hittite Museum in the Bedesten at Ankara.* Istanbul, 1946.
Hardy, R. S.: *"The Old Hittite Kingdom."* *American Journal of Semitic Languages,* LVIII, 1941.

Hogarth, D. G.: "The Empire of the Hatti." *Illustrated London News*, June 1911.
———: "The Hittites of Asia Minor." *Cambridge Ancient History*. Cambridge, 1931.
Hrozný, Bedrich (Friedrich): "Hittites." Article in *Encyclopædia Britannica*, 1929 to 1950.
Johnson, Frederick: "Radiocarbon Dating." *Society for American Archaeology Memoir*, July 8, 1951.
———: *See also* Libby, Willard F.
Johnson, J. A.: *The Life of a Citizen at Home and in Foreign Service*. (Reminiscences on the first discovery of hieroglyphic Hittite inscriptions.) New York, 1915.
Keith, Arthur: *A New Theory of Human Evolution*. London, 1948.
King, L. W.: "Note on the Hittite Problem." *Journal of Egyptian Archaeology*, 1917.
Knudtzon, J. A., and Weber, O.: "*Die El-Amarna-Tafeln.*" *Vorderasiatische Bibliothek*, Vol. II. Leipzig, 1915.
Lange, Kurt: *König Echnaton und die Amarna-Zeit. Die Geschichte eines Gottkünders*. Munich, 1951.
Laroche, E.: "*La Bibliothèque de Hattusa.*" *Archiv Orientalni*, XVII, 1949.
———: "*Dix Ans d'Études Asianiques.*" *Conférences d'Institut de Linguistique de l'Université de Paris*, IX, 1949. Paris, 1950.
Libby, Willard F.: *Radiocarbon Dating*. (Contains Frederick Johnson's "The Significance of the Dates for Archaeology and Geology.") The University of Chicago Press. Chicago, 1952.
Mansel, A. M.: "*Türkiyenin Arkeoloji.*" *Epigrafi ve Tarihi Cografyasi için Bibliyografya. Türk Tarih Kurumu Yayinlarindan, 12. Seri, I*. (Contains a bibliography of archæological research in Turkey up to 1939.) Ankara, 1948.
Mayer, L. A., and Garstang, John: *Index of Hittite Names*. British School of Archaeology in Jerusalem, Suppl. papers. Volume 1, 1923.
Mercer, S. A. B.: *The Tell El-Amarna Tablets*. Toronto, 1939.
Messerschmidt, Leopold: *Die Hethiter*. Second edition. *Der Alte Orient*, IV, I, Leipzig, 1903.
———: *Zur Technik des Tontafelschreibens*. Expanded reprint from the *Orientalistische Litteratur-Zeitung* 1906. Berlin, 1907.
Meyer, Eduard: *Reich und Kultur der Chetiter*. Berlin, 1914.
———: *Geschichte des Altertums*, I–V. Stuttgart and Berlin, 1926–31.
Moortgat, Anton: *Die bildende Kunst des alten Orients und die Bergvölker*. Berlin, 1933.
Naumann, Rudolf: *Die Hethiter*. Berlin, 1948.
O'Callaghan, R.: "Aram Naharaim, A Contribution to the History of Upper Mesopotamia in the Second Millennium B.C." *Analecta Orientalia*, 26. Rome, 1948.
Oppeln-Bronikowski, Friedrich von: *Archäologische Entdeckungen im 20. Jahrhundert*. Berlin, 1931.

Parrot, André: *Archéologie Mésopotamienne*, I–II. Paris, 1953.
————: *Mari, une ville perdue—et retrouvée par l'archéologie française*. Paris, 1936.
————: *Mari, Documentation photographique de la mission archéologique de Mari*. Paris, 1953.
Perrot, Georges, and Chipiez, Charles: *Histoire de l'art dans l'antiquité*. Vol. IV: *Judée, Sardaigne, Syrie, Cappadoce*. (Book 6 contains a section entitled: *"Les Hétéens."*) Paris, 1887.
Pope, Hugh: "Mari: A long lost city." *The Dublin Review*, II. Dublin, 1939.
Riemschneider, Margarete: *"Die Welt der Hethiter." Grosse Kulturen der Frühzeit*. Edited by Prof. Dr. Helmuth T. Bossert. (Contains the finest collection of illustrations of Hittite monuments.) Stuttgart, 1954.
Sayce, A. H.: *The Hittites. The Story of a Forgotten Empire*. Fifth edition. London, 1910.
————: *Reminiscences*. 1923.
————: "Hittite and Mitannian Elements in the Old Testament." *Journal of Theological Studies*, XXIX, 1928.
Schaeffer, C. F. A.: *Stratigraphie comparée et chronologie de l'Asie occidentale*. London, 1948.
Scharff, Alexander, and Moortgat, Anton: *Ägypten und Vorderasien im Altertum*. In the series entitled *Weltgeschichte in Einzeldarstellungen*. Munich, 1950.
Schefold, Karl: *"Orient, Hellas und Rom in der archäologischen Forschung seit 1939." Wissenschaftliche Forschungsberichte, 15*. Bern, 1949.
Schmökel, Hartmut: *Die ersten Arier im Alten Orient*. Leipzig, 1938.
Schott, Siegfried: *Altägyptische Liebeslieder. Mit Märchen und Liebesgeschichten*. (Contains the account of the arrival of the Hittite princess at the court of Ramses II.) Zurich, 1950.
Schwartz, B.: *The Hittites. A list of references in the New York Public Library*. New York, 1939.
Sommer, Ferdinand: *Hethitisches I und II. Boghazköi-Studien, 4 und 7*, Leipzig, 1920 and 1922.
————: *Hethiter und Hethitisch*. Stuttgart, 1947.
Spengler, Oswald: *Zur Weltgeschichte des zweiten vorchristlichen Jahrtausends. Reden und Aufsätze*. Third edition. Munich, 1951.
————: *Achäerfragen*. Ibid.
Vietta, Egon: *"Der Weg zu den Hethitern." Frankfurter Allgemeine Zeitung*, Oct. 25, 1951.
————: *"Die Heiligtümer der Hethiter."* Ibid., Nov. 5, 1951.
Vieyra, Maurice: *Hittite Art 2300–750 B.C.* London, 1955.
Wachsmann, Felix: *Die radioaktiven Isotope und ihre Anwendung in Medizin und Technik*. Munich, 1954.
Wegner, Max: *"Die Musikinstrumente des Alten Orients." Orbis Antiquus 2*, Münster, 1950.

Woolley, Sir Leonard: *Digging Up the Past*. Penguin Books, Harmondsworth (repr. 1952).

———: *A Forgotten Kingdom*. Penguin Books, London, 1953.

Worrell, W. H.: *A Study of Races in the Ancient Near East*. Cambridge, 1927.

Wright, William: *The Empire of the Hittites* (with decipherment of Hittite inscriptions by Prof. A. H. Sayce, a map by Col. Sir Charles Wilson, and a complete set of Hittite inscriptions, revised by W. H. Rylands). London, 1884.

2. *DISCOVERY* (The first travelers' reports; first finds; theories up to the year 1912).

Anderson, J. G.: "Exploration in Asia Minor during 1898." *Ann. of Brit. Sch. at Athens*, IV, 1899.

Ball, C. J.: "The Letter of the King of Arzapi to Amenophis III." *Academy*, Nov. 1889.

Barth, H.: *"Über die Ruinen bei Uejuk im alten Kappadocien."* *Archäologische Zeitung*, 1859.

Breasted, J. H.: "When Did the Hittites Enter Palestine?" *American Journal of Semitic Languages and Literatures*, XXI, 1904.

Burckhardt, J. L.: *Travels in Syria and the Holy Land*. London, 1822.

Campbell, J.: *The Hittites, Their Inscriptions and Their History*, I and II. London, 1891.

"Carchemish": *The London Times*, August 1880.

Chantre, E.: *Recherches archéologiques dans l'Asie Occidentale. Mission en Cappadoce, 1893–4*. Paris, 1898.

Conder, C. R.: "The Decipherment of the Hittite Hieroglyphs." *Academy*, March 1887.

Davis, E. J.: *Anatolica, or the journal of a visit to some of the ancient ruined cities of Caria, Phrygia, Lycia and Pisidia*. London, 1874.

———: "On a New Hamathite Inscription at Ibreez." *Transactions of the Society for Biblical Archaeology*, IV. 1876.

Garstang, John: "Dr. Winckler's Discoveries of Hittite Remains at Boghazkeui." *Annals of Archaeology and Anthropology*, I. Liverpool, 1908.

———: "Excavations at Sakje-Geuzi in North Syria." Ibid., I,V.

Halévy, J.: *"Sur la langue des Hétéens."* *Bull. Acadm. Inscr.*, XV, 1887.

Hamilton, W. T.: *Researches in Asia Minor, Pontus and Armenia, with some account of their antiquities and geology*. London, 1842.

Hirschfeld, G.: *Die Felsenreliefs in Kleinasien und das Volk der Hethiter. Zweiter Beitrag zur Kunstgeschichte Kleinasiens*. Berlin, 1887.

Humann, K., and Puchstein, O.: *Reise in Kleinasien und Nord-Syrien*. Berlin, 1890.

Jensen, P.: "The So-called Hittite Inscriptions." *Academy*, XLVI, 1894.

——: "*Grundlagen für eine Entzifferung der (hatischen oder) cilicischen (?) Inschriften.*" *Zeitschrift der Deutschen Morgenländischen Gesellschaft*, XLVIII, 1894.

Knudtzon, J. A.: *Die zwei Arzawa-Briefe. Die ältesten Urkunden in indogermanischer Sprache. Mit Bemerkungen von Sophus Bugge und Alf. Torp.* Leipzig, 1902.

Koldewey, Robert: *Die hethitische Inschrift gefunden in der Königsburg von Babylon am 22. August 1899 und veröffentlicht mit einer Abbildung und drei Tafeln.* Leipzig, 1900.

Luschan, F. von, and others. *Ausgrabungen in Sendschirli*, I–V. Berlin 1893, 1898, 1902, 1911, 1943.

Macridy Bey: "*La porte des sphinx à Euyuk. Fouilles du Musée Impérial Ottoman.*" *Mitteilungen der Vorderasiatisch-Ägyptischen Gesellschaft*, XIII. 1908.

Messerschmidt, Leopold: "*Hethitische Fälschungen.*" *Orientalistische Literaturzeitung* III. 1900.

Mordtmann, A. D.: "*Boghasköi und Uyük.*" *Sitzungsberichte der Königlich Bayerischen Akademie der Wissenschaften.* 1861.

Peiser, F. E.: *Die hethitischen Inschriften. Ein Versuch ihrer Entzifferung nebst einer das weitere Studium vorbereitenden methodisch geordneten Ausgabe.* Berlin, 1892.

Perrot, Georges, Guillaume, Edmond, and Delbet, Jules: *Exploration archéologique de la Galatie et de la Bithynie, d'une partie de la Mysie, de la Phrygie, de Cappadoce et du Pont, exécutée en 1861.* I–II. (Vol. I, a volume of pictures, was published in 1862. Volume II ten years later. This accounts for the differing publication dates assigned to this important book in various encyclopedias.) Paris, 1872.

Puchstein, O.: *Boğhazköi, die Bauwerke (Deutsche Orientgesellschaft Nr. 19).* Leipzig, 1912.

Rylands, W. H.: "Engraved gem from Nineveh." *Proceedings of the Society for Biblical Archaeology*, VI, 1884.

Sayce, A. H.: "On the Hamathite inscriptions." *Transactions of the Society for Biblical Archaeology*, V. 1877.

——: "The Hittites in Asia Minor." *Academy*, Nov. 1879.

——: "The bilingual Hittite and cuneiform inscription of Tarkondêmos." *Transactions of the Society for Biblical Archaeology*, VII. 1882.

——: "The inscriptions of Tarkondêmos." *Proceedings of the Society for Biblical Archaeology*, VII. 1885.

——: "The Hittite inscription discovered by Sir W. M. Ramsay and Miss Bell on the Kara-Dagh." *Proceedings of the Society for Biblical Archaeology*, XXI. 1909.

Texier, Charles: *Description de l'Asie Mineure, faite par ordre du Gouvernement français de 1833–37, et publiée par le Ministère de l'Instruction Publique, Beaux-arts, monuments historiques, plans et topographie des cités antiques, gravures de Lemaître.* 3 volumes. Paris, 1839–1849.

Thompson, R. C.: "A Journey by some Unmapped Routes in the Western Hittite Country between Angora and Eregli." *Proceedings of the Society for Biblical Archaeology,* XXXII, 1910; XXXIII, 1911.

Winckler, Hugo: *Der Tontafelfund von Tell el-Amarna.* Berlin, 1890.

————: *"Vorläufige Nachrichten über die Ausgrabungen in Boghazköi im Sommer 1907. Die Tontafel-Funde." Mitteilungen der Deutschen Orientgesellschaft,* XXXV, 1907.

————: Two addresses in memory of Hugo Winckler. Delivered on July 2, 1913 by A. Jeremias and O. Weber. Together with a bibliography of Winckleriana by O. Schroeder. *Mitteilungen der Vorderasiatisch-Ägyptischen Gesellschaft,* Vol. 20, I.

————, and Puchstein, Otto: "Excavations at Boghaz-Keui in the summer of 1907." *Smithsonian Report for 1908.*

Wright, William: "The Decipherment of the Hittite Inscriptions." *British Weekly.* March, 1887.

3. *LANGUAGES AND WRITINGS* (Deciphering; Karatepe inscriptions; cf. Group 5).

Albright, W. F.: "Hittite Scripts." *Antiquity,* VIII. 1934.

Andrae, W.: *"Hethitische Inschriften auf Bleistreifen aus Assur." Mitteilungen der Deutschen Orient-Gesellschaft,* Vol. 46. 1924.

Barnett, R. D.: "Hittite Hieroglyphic Texts at Aleppo." *Iraq,* X. London, 1948.

Bittel, Kurt: *"Bemerkungen über einige in Kleinasien gefundene Siegel." Archiv für Orientforschung,* XIII, 6. Berlin, 1941.

Bonfante, G.: "Hieroglyphic Hittite, Indo-Hittite, and the linguistic method." *Journal of American Oriental Society,* LXV. 1945.

————: "Indo-Hittite and Areal Linguistics." *American Journal of Philology,* LXVII. 1946.

————, and Gelb, I. J.: "The Position of 'Hieroglyphic Hittite' among the Indo-European Languages." *Journal of American Oriental Society,* LXV. 1945.

Bopp, Franz: *Vergleichende Grammatik des Sanskrit, Zend, Griechischen, Lateinischen, Litthauischen, Gothischen und Deutschen,* 5 Abt. Berlin, 1833–49.

Bossert, H. T.: *"Šantaš und Kupapa. Neue Beiträge zur Entzifferung der kretischen und hethitischen Bilderschrift." Mitteilungen der Altorientalischen Gesellschaft,* VI, 3. Leipzig, 1932.

————: "Nischan-Tepe und Nischan-Tasch." Archiv für Orientforschung, IX, 4. Berlin, 1934.

————: Ein hethitisches Königssiegel. Berlin, 1944.

————: "Das hieroglyphenhethitische Zahlwort 'Fünf.'" Archiv Orientalni, XVIII. 1950.

————: "Zu drei hieroglyphen-hethitischen Inschriften." Jahrbuch für Kleinasiatische Forschung, I (2). Heidelberg, 1950.

————: "Schreibstoff und Schreibgerät der Hethiter." Belleten, XVI, Ankara, 1952.

————: "Wie lange wurden hethitische Hieroglyphen geschrieben?" Die Welt des Orients, Wissenschaftliche Beiträge zur Kunde des Morgenlandes, Göttingen, 1952.

Cowley, E.: The Hittites. Schweich Lectures, London, 1920.

Delaporte, L.: Manuel de la langue hittite. Paris, 1929–33.

————: Pour lire le hittite cunéiforme. Paris, 1935.

————, and Meriggi, Piero: "L'inscription hittite hiéroglyphique du Soultan han." Revue hittite et asianique, II, 1932–34.

Forrer, Emil O.: "Die acht Sprachen der Boghazköi-Inschriften." Sitzungsberichte der Preuss. Akad. d. Wiss., 1919.

————: "Die Inschriften und Sprachen des Hatti-Reiches." Zeitschrift der Deutschen Morgenländischen Gesellschaft, LXXVI, 1922.

Friedrich, Johannes: Kleinasiatische Sprachdenkmäler. Berlin, 1932.

————: Kleine Beiträge zur churritischen Grammatik. Leipzig, 1939.

————: Hethitisches Elementarbuch I. und II. 1940 and 1946.

————: Hethitisches Wörterbuch. Heidelberg, 1952–54.

————: Eine hethitische Keilschrifttafel mit minoischen Linearzeichen. Minos, III, Salamanca, 1954.

Gelb, Ignace J.: Hittite Hieroglyphs. I, II, III, Chicago, 1931, 1935, 1942.

————: Inscriptions from Alishar and vicinity. Oriental Inst. Publ. of the Univ. of Chicago, XXVII, 1935.

————: Hittite Hieroglyphic Monuments. Ibid. XLV, 1939.

————: Hurrians and Subarians. Chicago, 1944.

————: "A contribution to the Proto-Indo-European question." Jahrbuch für Kleinasiatische Forschung, II/1, Heidelberg, 1951.

Götze, Albrecht: "Hittite and the Indo-European Languages." Journal of American Oriental Society, LXV, 1945.

Güterbock, Hans Gustav: "Siegel aus Bogazköy," I–II. Archiv für Orientforschung, Beihefte 5 und 7, 1940, 1944.

————: "Die Elemente MUWA und ZITI in den hethitischen Hieroglyphen." Symbolae Hrozný III. Archiv Orientalni, XVIII, 1, 1950.

Hrozný, Bedrich (Friedrich): "Die Lösung des hethitischen Problems." Mitteilungen der Deutschen Orientgesellschaft, LVI, 1915.

————: *Die Sprache der Hethiter, ihr Bau und ihre Zugehörigkeit zum indogermanischen Sprachstamm. Ein Entzifferungsversuch* I, Leipzig, 1917.

————: *"Über die Völker und Sprachen des alten Chatti-Landes." Boghazköi-Studien* 5, 1920.

————: *"Etruskisch und die hethitischen Sprachen." Zeitschrift für Assyriologie,* XXXVIII, 1928.

————: *Les Inscriptions Hittites Hiéroglyphiques I–III.* Prague, 1933–37.

Jensen, P.: *"Ziffern und Zahlen in den hittischen Hieroglypheninschriften." Zeitschrift für Ethnologie,* LXIV, 1933.

Jones, Sir William: *Grammar of the Persian Language.* 1771.

Jonkees, J. H.: *"Zur Transcription des Lydischen." Mnemosyne,* VII, 1939.

Juret, A.: *Esquisse d'un vocabulaire étymologique de la langue hittite.* Paris, 1940.

Kahle, P. and Sommer, F.: *"Die lydisch-aramäische Bilingue." Kleinasiatische Forschungen,* I, 1927.

Keith, A. B.: *"The Relation of Hittite, Tocharian and Indo-European." Indian Historical Quarterly,* XIV, 1938.

Laroche, E.: *"Hattic Deities and their Epithets." Journal of Cuneiform Studies,* I, 187–216, 1947.

————: *"Études proto-hittites." Revue d'Assyriologie,* XLI, 1948.

————: *"Problèmes de la linguistique Asianique." Conférences de l'Institut de Linguistique de l'Université de Paris,* IX, 1949. Paris, 1950.

————: *"Une conjuration bilingue Hatti-Hittite." Jahrbuch für Kleinasiatische Forschung,* I/2, Heidelberg, 1950.

————: *"Importations mycéniennes à Boghaz-Köy?" Minos,* III, Salamanca, 1954.

Lesný, V.: *"The language of the Mitanni chieftains, a third branch of the Aryan group." Archiv Orientalni,* IV, 1932.

Meillet, A.: *"La Chronologie des langues indo-européennes et le développement du gendre féminin." Comptes Rendus de l'Académie des Inscriptions et des Belles Lettres,* 1930.

————: *"Essai de chronologie des langues indo-européennes." Bulletin de la Société Linguistique de Paris,* XXXII, I–28, 1931.

Meriggi, Piero: *"Die «hethitischen» Hieroglypheninschriften, I. Die kürzeren Votiv- und Bauinschriften." Wiener Zeitschrift für die Kunde des Morgenlandes,* XL, 1933, II. *"Die längeren Votiv- und Bauinschriften."* Ibid. XLI, 1934.

————: *"Die hethitische Hieroglyphenschrift." Zeitschrift für Assyriologie,* XXXIX, N. F. V., 1930.

Messerschmidt, Leopold: *"Corpus Inscriptionum Hettiticarum." Mitteilungen der Vorderasiatisch-Ägyptischen Gesellschaft* 5, 7, 11 (1900, 1902, 1907).

Otten, H.: *"Zum Paläischen." Zeitschrift für Assyriologie,* XLVIII, 1944.

Parrot, A. and Nougayrol, J.: "*Un Document de fondation hurrite.*" *Revue d'Assyriologie*, XLII, 1948.

Pedersen, H.: *Hittitisch und die anderen indo-europäischen Sprachen*. Copenhagen, 1938.

————: *Lykisch und Hittitisch*. Copenhagen, 1945.

Petersen, W.: "Hittite and Tocharian." *Language*, IX, 1933.

Pisani, V.: "*La Question de l'indo-hittite et le concepte de parenté linguistique.*" *Archiv Orientalni*, XVII, 1949.

Rosenkranz, B.: "*Die Stellung des Luwischen im Hatti-Reiche.*" *Indogermanische Forschungen*, LVI, 1938.

Sayce, A. H.: "The decipherment of the Hittite hieroglyphic texts." *Journal of the Royal Asiatic Society of Great Britain and Ireland*, 1922.

————: "Proto-Hittite." *Journal of Royal Asiatic Society*, 1924.

————: "The hieroglyphic inscription on the seal of Subbiluliuma." *Archiv für Orientforschung*, VII, 1931/32.

————: "Indians in Western Asia in the fifteenth century B.C." *Oriental Studies in Honour of Cursetji Erachji Pavry*, London, 1933.

Smith, S.: "The Greek Trade at Al Mina." *Antiquaries' Journal*, XXII, 1942.

Speiser, E. A.: "Introduction to Hurrian." *Annual of American Schools of Oriental Research*, XX, 1941.

Steinherr, Franz: "Hittite hieroglyphic «all, every, whole»." *Oriens*, I, 1948.

————: "Proposal for a new reading of the Hittite Hieroglyphic «tar»." *Oriens*, II, 1, 1949.

————: "*Zu einer neuen hieroglyphenhethitischen Studie.*" *Orientalia* 20/1, Rome, 1951.

————: "*Zu den neuen karischen Inschriften.*" *Jahrbuch für Kleinasiatische Forschung I*, 1951.

————: "*Minoisch und Hieroglyphenhethitisch.*" *Minos*, III, Salamanca, 1954.

Sturtevant, E. H.: "The Relationship of Hittite to Indo-European." *Transactions of American Philological Association*, LX, 1929.

————: *A Comparative Grammar of the Hittite Language*. Philadelphia, 1933 and 1951.

————: *A Hittite Glossary*. Philadelphia, 1936, Supplement 1939.

————: *The Indo-Hittite Laryngeal*. Philadelphia, 1942.

————: "Hittite and Areal Linguistics." *Language*, XXIII, 1947.

Thompson, R. Campbell: "A new decipherment of the Hittite hieroglyphs." *Archaeologia*, LXIV, Oxford, 1913.

Tritsch, F. J.: "Lycian, Luwian and Hittite." *Archiv Orientalni*, XVIII, 1950.

Weidner, Ernst F.: *Studien zur hethitischen Sprachwissenschaft I*. *Leipziger Semitist. Stud.*, VIII, Leipzig, 1917.

4. *HISTORY* (Hittite politics, religion, art, and general culture down to the collapse of the Empire about 1200 B.C., and reports of excavations after 1912).

Akurgal, Ekrem: *Remarques stylistiques sur les reliefs de Malatya.* Ankara, 1946.
———: *Späthethitische Bildkunst.* Ankara, 1949.
Albright, W. F.: "The Anatolian Goddes Kubaba." *Archiv für Orientforschung,* V, Berlin, 1929.
———: "A Third Revision in the Early Chronology of Western Asia." *Bulletin of the American Schools of Oriental Research Nr. 88,* 1942.
Alt, A.: "Zur Topographie der Schlacht bei Kades." *Zeitschrift des deutschen Palästina-Vereins,* LV, 1932.
Anstock-Darga, Muhibbe: "*Ein Relief aus dem Bertiz-Tal.*" *Jahrbuch für Kleinasiatische Forschung,* I/1, Heidelberg, 1950.
Balkan, K.: *Ankara arkeoloji müzesinde bulunan Boğazköy tabletleri.* Istanbul, 1948.
Barnett, R. D.: "The Epic of Kumarbi and the Theogony of Hesiod." *Journal of Hellenic Studies,* XLV, 1945.
Bittel, Kurt: "*Vorläufiger Bericht über eine Grabung auf Büyük Kale, der Akropolis von Bogazköy.*" *Archäologischer Anzeiger, Beiblatt zum Jahrbuch des Deutschen Archäologischen Instituts, Band 46,* I–II, Berlin, 1931.
———: "*Die Felsbilder von Yazilikaya. Neue Aufnahmen der deutschen Boghazköy-Expedition 1931.*" *Istanbuler Forschungen.* Bamberg, 1934.
———: "*Die Ruinen von Boğazköy, der Hauptstadt des Hethiterreiches.*" *Kurze Beschreibung.* Berlin and Leipzig, 1937.
———: "*Boğazköy, Die Kleinfunde der Grabungen 1906–12.*" *Deutsche Orientgesellschaft, Nr. 60.* Leipzig, 1937.
———: "*Die Reliefs am Karabel bei Nif (Kemal Paşa). Nebst einigen Bemerkungen über die hethitischen Denkmäler Westkleinasiens.*" *Archiv für Orientforschung,* XIII, 4–5, Berlin, 1940.
———: "*Bemerkungen zu dem auf Büyükkale (Boğazköy) entdeckten hethitischen Siegeldepot.*" *Jahrbuch für Kleinasiatische Forschung,* I/2. Heidelberg, 1950.
Bittel, Kurt and Güterbock, H. G.: "*Vorläufiger Bericht über die dritte Grabung in Boğazköy.*" *Mitteilungen der Deutschen Orient-Gesellschaft, Nr. 72,* 1933.
———: "*Boğazköy, neue Untersuchungen in der hethitischen Hauptstadt.*" *Abhandl. der Preuss. Akademie der Wissensch.,* 1935, 1. Berlin, 1935.
Bittel, Kurt and Naumann, Rudolf: "*Boğazköy II., Neue Untersuchungen hethitischer Architektur.*" *Abhandlungen der*

Preussischen Akademie der Wissenschaften, 1938, 1. Berlin, 1938.

Bittel, Kurt, Naumann, Rudolf and Otto, H.: *"Yazilikaya, Architektur Felsbilder, Inschriften und Kleinfunde."* Wissenschaftliche Veröffentlichung der Deutschen Orient-Gesellschaft 61. Leipzig, 1941.

Bittel, Kurt and Naumann, Rudolf (with contribution by Sophie Ehrhardt and Richard Vogel): *"Boğazköy-Hattuša. Ergebnisse der Ausgrabungen des Deutschen Archäologischen Instituts und der Deutschen Orient-Gesellschaft in den Jahren 1931–1939 (I. Architektur, Topographie, Landeskunde und Siedlungsgeschichte)."* Wissenschaftliche Veröffentlichung der Deutschen Orient-Gesellschaft, Stuttgart, 1952.

Böhl, F. M. T.: *"Tud'alia I, Zeitgenosse Abrahams um 1650 v. Chr."* Zeitschrift für Alttestamentliche Wissenschaft, Neue Folge I, 1924.

Boissier, A.: *Mantique babylonienne et mantique hittite.* Paris, 1935.

Bossert, Helmuth T.: *"Zur Chronologie der Skulpturen von Malatya."* Felsefe Arkivi, 1947.

———: *"Das hethitische Felsrelief bei Hanyeri (Gezbeli)."* Orientalia, Commentarii Periodici Pontificii Instituti Biblici, Vol. 23, Fasc. 2. Rome, 1954.

Brandenstein, C. G.: *"Hethitische Götter nach Bildbeschreibungen in Keilschrifttexten."* Mitteilungen der Vorderasiatisch-Ägyptischen Gesellschaft, XLVI (2), 1943.

Breasted, J. H.: *The Battle of Kadesh, a study in the earliest known military strategy.* Univ. of Chicago Dexennial Public. V. Chicago, 1903.

Burne, A. H.: *"Some Notes on the battle of Kadesh."* Journal of Egyptian Archaeology, VII, 1920.

Calder, W. M.: *"Notes on Anatolian Religion."* Journal of the Manchester Egyptian and Oriental Society, XI, 1924.

Cavaignac, E.: *"L'Égypte, le Mitanni et les Hittites de 1478 à 1350."* Revue Hittite et Asianique, I, 1931.

———: *Subbiluliuma et son temps.* Paris, 1932.

———: *"L'Affaire de Iaruvatta."* Revue Hittite et Asianique, I, 1932.

———: *"Synchronismes assyriens, égyptiens et hittites (14e–13e siècles)."* Ibid., II, 1933.

———: *"La Date et l'ordre des campagnes de Mursil."* Ibid., II, 1934.

———: *"Hittites et Achéens."* Ibid., III, 1935.

———: *"L'Histoire politique de l'orient de 1340 à 1230, succession des événements."* Ibid., III, 1935.

———: *"La lettre de Ramsès II au roi de Mira."* Ibid., III, 1935.

————: *"La Maison de Subbiluliuma."* Ibid., III, 1936.
————: *"La question hittito-achéenne après les dernières publications."* *Bulletin de Correspondence Hellénique*, LXX, 1946.
Collinet, P.: *"Droit babylonien, droit assyrien, droit hittite."* *Journal des Savants*, 1932.
Couissin, P.: *"Le dieu épée de Iasili-Kaia et le culte de l'épée dans l'antiquité."* *Revue Archéologique*, V, 27, 1928.
Cuq, E.: *Études sur le droit babylonien, les lois assyriennes et les lois hittites.* Paris, 1929.
Delaporte, L.: *"Les Hittites sont-ils nommés dans la Bible?"* *Revue Hittite et Asianique*, IV, 1938.
————: *Arslantepe I, La Porte des Lions.* Paris, 1940.
Dussaud, R.: *"Un Point de chronologie hittite et assyrienne."* *Syria*, XVI, 1935.
————: *"Datation des reliefs de Malat-ya."* *Comptes rendus de l'Académie des Inscriptions et des Belles Lettres*, 1945.
Forrer, Emil O.: *"Vorhomerische Griechen in den Keilschrifttexten von Boğhazköy."* *Mitteilungen der Deutschen Orientgesellschaft*, LXIII, 1924.
————: *"Die Griechen in den Boğhazköy-Texten."* *Orientalistische Literaturzeitung*, 1924.
————: *"Ergebnisse einer archäologischen Reise in Kleinasien, 1926."* *Mitteilungen der Deutschen Orientgesellschaft*, LXV, 1927.
————: *"Für die Griechen in den Boghazköi-Inschriften."* *Kleinasiatische Forschungen*, I, 1929.
————: *"La Découverte de la Grèce Mycénienne dans les textes cuneiformes de l'empire hittite."* *Revue des Études Grecques*, XL, 1930.
————: *"The Hittites in Palestine,"* *Palestine Exploration Quarterly*, LXVIII, and LXIX, 1936–37.
Franz, L.: *"Die Muttergöttin im Vorderen Orient und in Europa."* *Der Alte Orient*, XXXV, 3, Leipzig, 1937.
Friedrich, Johannes: *"Staatsverträge des Hattireichs."* *Mitteilungen der Vorderasiatisch-Ägyptischen Gesellschaft* 31, 1926 and 34, 1930.
————: *"Werden in den hethitischen Keilschrifttexten die Griechen erwähnt?"* *Kleinasiatische Forschungen*, 1929.
Furlani, G.: *La Religione degli Hittiti.* Bologna, 1936.
————: *"The Basic Aspect of Hittite Religion."* *Harvard Theological Review*, XXXI, 1938.
Garstang, John: *"The Sun-Goddess of Arinna."* *Annals of Archaeology and Anthropology*, VI, 1914.
————: *"The Winged Deity and other Sculptures of Malatia."* Ibid.
————: *"Excavations at Mersin, 1938–39. The historic periods."* Ibid., XXVI, 1940.

————: "Notes on a Journey through Asia Minor." Ibid., I, 1–12.
————: "Hittite Military Roads in Asia Minor." *American Journal of Archaeology*, XLVII, 1943.
de Genouillac, H.: *Céramique cappadocienne*. Paris, 1926.
Götze, Albrecht: *"Zur Schlacht bei Quades."* Orientalistische Literaturzeitung, XXXII, 1929.
————: *The Hittite Ritual of Tunnawi* (in cooperation with E. H. Sturtevant). American Oriental Society, New Haven, 1938.
————: *Kizzuwatna and the problem of Hittite Geography*. New Haven, 1940.
————: "The Linguistic Continuity of Anatolia as Shown by Its Proper Names." *Journal of Cuneiform Studies*, VIII, 2, 1954.
Goldmann, H.: "Excavations at Tarsus." *American Journal of Archaeology*, XXXIX, 1935, 526–49; XLI, 1937, 262–86; XLII, 1938, 30–54; XLIV, 1940, 60–86.
Gurney, O. R.: "Hittite Prayers of Mursilis II." *Annals of Archaeology and Anthropology*, XXVII, Liverpool, 1940.
Güterbock, H. G.: *"Die historische Tradition und ihre literarische Gestaltung bei Babyloniern und Hethitern bis 1200."* Zeitschrift für Assyriologie XLII, 1933, and XLIII, 1934.
————: *"Neue Ahhijawā-Texte."* Zeitschrift für Assyriologie, XLIII, 1934.
————: *"Siegel aus Boğazköy."* I and II, Archiv für Orientforschung, 1940 and 1944.
————: *"Hethitische Götterdarstellungen und Götternamen."* Belleten, Ankara, 1943.
————: "The Hittite version of the Hurrian Kumarbi Myths, Oriental Forerunners of Hesiod." *American Journal of Archaeology*, LII, 1948.
————: "The Song of Ullikummi." *Journal of Cuneiform Studies* 5, 1951, and 6, 1952.
Hall, H. R.: "Mursil and Myrtilos." *Journal of Hellenic Studies*, XXIX, 1909.
Hanfmann, G. M. A.: "Archaeology in Homeric Asia Minor." *American Journal of Archaeology*, 52, 1948.
Hogarth, D. G.: *Hittite seals with particular reference to the Ashmolean Collection*. Oxford, 1920.
Hogarth, D. G. and Woolley, C. L.: *Carchemish, Report on the excavations at Djerabis on behalf of the British Museum*. London, I, 1914, II, 1921.
Holt, J.: *"Quelques interprétations du Code Hittite."* Archiv Orientalni, XVII, 1950.
Hrozný, Bedrich (Friedrich): *"Über die Völker und Sprachen des alten Chatti-Landes."* Boghazköi-Studien, 5, Leipzig, 1920.
————: *"Nâram-Sin et ses ennemis d'après un texte hittite."* Archiv Orientalni, I, 1929.
————: *"Sur un paragraphe du Code Hittite."* Archiv Orientalni, XVI, 1947.

Jirku, A.: *"Eine hethitische Ansiedlung in Jerusalem zur Zeit von El-Amarna."* Zeitschrift des deutschen Palästina-Vereins, XLIII, 1920.

Kampman, A. A.: *"De Historische Beteekens der Hethietische Vestingbouwkunde."* Med. en Verh. Ex Oriente Lux 7. Leiden, 1947.

Korošec, V.: *"Hethitische Staatsverträge, ein Beitrag zu ihrer juristischen Wertung."* Leipziger Rechtswissenschaftliche Studien 60, 1931.

———: *"Beiträge zum hethitischen Privatrecht."* Zeitschrift der Savigny-Stiftung, LII, 1932.

———: *"Raub- und Kaufehe im hethitischen Recht."* Studi in Onore di Salvatori Riccobono I. Palermo, 1932.

———: *"Einige Beiträge zum hethitischen Sklavenrecht."* Festschrift P. Koschaker, III.

Kosay, Hamit Zubeyr.: "A Great Discovery." (Excavations at Alaja Hüyük.) *Illustrated London News,* July 1945.

Koschaker, P.: *"Fratriarchat, Hausgemeinschaft und Mutterrecht in Keilschriftrechten."* Zeitschrift für Assyriologie, XLI, 1933.

———: *"Zum Levirat nach hethitischem Recht."* Revue Hittite et Asianique, II, 1933.

Krause, K.: *"Boğazköy Tempel V, Ein Beitrag zum Problem der hethitischen Baukunst."* Istanbuler Forschungen, II, 1940.

Kuentz, C.: *"La Bataille de Qadech."* Mémoires de L'Institut Français d'Archéologie Orientale, LV, 1934.

Landsberger, Benno: *"Assyrische Königsliste und dunkles Zeitalter."* Journal of Cuneiform Studies, VIII, 1–3, 1954.

Laroche, E.: *"Un point d'histoire: Ulmi-Teššub."* Revue Hittite et Asianique, VIII, 1947–48.

———: *Recherches sur les noms des dieux hittites.* Paris, 1947.

———: *"Teššub, Hebat et leur cour."* Journal of Cuneiform Studies, II, 1948.

Leonhard, W.: *Hettiter und Amazonen.* Leipzig, 1911.

Lesky, A.: *"Ein ritueller Scheinkampf bei den Hethitern."* Archiv für Religionswissenschaft, XXIV, 1927.

Lewy, J.: *"La Chronologie de Bithana et d'Anitta de Kussara."* Revue Hittite et Asianique III, 1934.

Naumann, Rudolf: "Bogazköy." *Archiv für Orientforschung,* XIII, 4–5. Berlin, 1940.

Noth, M.: *"Die Stadt Kadesh am Orontes in der Geschichte des zweiten Jahrtausends v. Chr."* Die Welt des Orients, 1948.

Oppenheim, M., Baron von: *Tell Halaf, a new culture in oldest Mesopotamia.* London, 1933.

Osten, H. H. von der: *Explorations in Central Anatolia, season of 1926.* Univ. of Chicago, Or. Inst. Publ. V, 1929.

———: *Explorations in Hittite Asia Minor, 1927–29.* Univ. of Chicago, Or. Inst. Comm., 6 and 8. 1929–30.

———: *Four Hittite Rhytons.* Parnassus, New York, 1932.

276 *Bibliography*

―――: *Discoveries in Anatolia,* 1930–31. Univ. of Chicago, Or. Inst. Comm., 14, 1933.

―――: *The Alishar Hüyük. Seasons of 1930–32.* Univ. of Chicago, Or. Inst. Publ. XXVIII, XXIX, XXX, 1937.

Otten, H.: *"Ein Bestattungsritual hethitischer Könige." Zeitschrift für Assyriologie,* XLVI, 1942.

―――: *"Die hethitischen Königslisten und die altorientalische Chronologie." Mitteilungen der Deutschen Orient-Gesellschaft* 83, 1951.

Özgüç, T.: "Where the Assyrians built a commercial empire in second millennium Anatolia: excavating the ' «karum» of Kanes.' " *Illustrated London News,* January 1950.

Phythian-Adams, W. J.: "Hittite and Trojan Allies." *Bulletin of British School of Archaeology in Jerusalem,* I, 3–7, 1922.

Poisson, G.: *"Tantale, roi des hittites." Revue Archéologique,* Serie 5, XXII, 1925.

Prentice, W. K.: "The Achaeans." *American Journal of Archaeology,* XXXIII, 1929.

Price, J.: "The so-called Levirate-Marriage in Hittite and Assyrian Laws." *Oriental Studies,* Baltimore, 1926.

Puchstein, Otto: *Boğhazköy, die Bauwerke. Wissenschaftliche Veröffentlichung der Deutschen Orient-Gesellschaft* 19, Leipzig, 1912 *(unter Mitwirkung von H. Kohl und D. Krencker).*

Puukko, A. F.: *"Die altassyrischen und hethitischen Gesetze und das alte Testament." Studia Orientalia,* I, 1925.

―――: *"Die Leviratsehe in den altorientalischen Gesetzen." Archiv Orientalni,* XVII, 1949.

Ransome, H. M.: *Sacred Bee in Ancient Times and Folklore.* London, 1937.

Rosenkranz, B.: *"Zur Chronologie der hethitischen Gesetze." Zeitschrift für Assyriologie,* XLIV, 1938.

San Nicolò, M.: *"Zur Frage der Schriftlichkeit des Abschlusses von Rechtsgeschäften bei den Hethitern." Zeitschrift der Savigny-Stiftung,* LVI, 1936.

Sayce, A. H.: "Perseus and the Achaeans in the Hittite tablets." *Journal of Hellenic Studies,* XLV, 1925.

Schachermeyr, F.: *"Hethiter und Achäer." Mitteilungen der Altorientalischen Gesellschaft,* IX, 1/2, Leipzig, 1935.

Schaeffer, C. F. A.: *Stratigraphie Comparée et Chronologie de l'Asie Occidentale.* London, 1948.

Schroeder, O.: *"Uria der Hettiter." Zeitschrift für Alttestamentliche Wissenschaft,* XXXV, 1915.

Shewan, A.: "Hittite Names." *Classical Review,* XLV, 2–4, London, 1931.

Smith, S.: *Alalakh and Chronology.* London, 1940.

―――: "Amarna Letter 170 and Chronology." *Halil Edhem hâtira kitabi,* Ankara, 1947.

Sommer, Ferdinand: *"Die Ahhijavā-Urkunden."* *Abhandlungen der Bayrischen Akademie der Wissenschaften, Neue Folge* 6, 1932.
————: *"Ahhijavā und kein Ende?"* *Indogermanische Forschungen,* LV, 169–297, 1937.
Sommer, F. and Falkenstein, A.: *"Die hethitisch-akkadische Bilingue des Hattusili I* (Labarna II)." *Abhandlungen der Bayrischen Akademie der Wissenschaften, Neue Folge,* XVI. Munich, 1938.
Strong, H. A. and Garstang, J.: *The Syrian Goddess.* London, 1913.
Sturm, J.: *"Wer ist Piphururias?"* *Revue Hittite et Asianique,* II, 1933.
————: *"Der Hettiterkrieg Ramses' II."* *Wiener Zeitschrift für die Kunde des Morgenlandes,* 1939.
Tenner, E.: *"Tages- und Nachtsonne bei den Hethitern."* *Zeitschrift für Assyriologie,* XXXVIII, 1929.
Vaughan, D.: *"Notes on the Dado Sculptures of Sakjegeuzi."* *Annals of Archaeology and Anthropology,* XXI, Liverpool, 1934.
Virolleaud, C.: *"Suppiluliuma et Niqmad d'Ugarit."* *Revue Hittite et Asianique,* V, 1939.
Weber, Otto: *Die Kunst der Hethiter.* Orbis Pictus 9, Berlin, 1922.
Weidner, Ernst F.: *Der Zug Sargons von Akkad nach Kleinasien, die ältesten geschichtlichen Beziehungen zwischen Babylonien und Hatti. Boghazköi-Studien,* 6. Heft, Leipzig, 1922.
————: *Politische Dokumente aus Kleinasien. Boghazköi-Studien,* 8. Heft, 1923.
Weill, R.: *"Les Achéens d'Asie Mineure et les problèmes de l'arrivée achéenne sur la Méditerranée au IIe millénaire."* *Journal Asiatique,* CCXVI, 77–108, 1930.
Wilson, J. A.: *"The Texts of the Battle of Qadesh."* *American Journal of Semitic Languages,* XLIII, 1927.
Wohler, L.: *"Die altrömische und die hethitische evocatio."* *Archiv für Religionswissenschaft,* XXV, 1928.
Woolley, C. Leonard: *"Hittite burial customs."* *Annals of Archaeology and Anthropology,* VI, 1914.
————: *"New Clues to Hittite History in Asia."* *Illustrated London News,* October 1937.
————: *"Gaps filled in Syrian History of 3500 years ago: New discoveries at Atchana, near Antioch."* *Ibid.,* September 1938.
————: *"Excavations at Atchana-Alalakh."* *Antiquaries Journal,* XIX, 1939, and XXVIII, 1948.
Yeivin, S.: *"Canaanite and Hittite Strategy in the Second Half of the Second Millennium B. C."* *Journal of Near Eastern Studies,* IX, Chicago, 1950.

5. *THE PETTY KINGDOMS* (Especially material on Karatepe and the bilingual found there; to the absorption of the Hittite state into the Assyrian Empire).

Alkim, U. Bahadir: *"Les résultats archéologiques des fouilles de Karatépé."* *Revue Hittite et Asianique*, IX, 1948/49.
————: "Excavations at Karatepe." *Belleten*, XII, Ankara, 1948.
————: "Third Season's Work at Karatepe." *Belleten*, XIII, Ankara, 1949.
————: "Karatepe: Fourth and Fifth Campaigns." *Belletin*, XIV, Ankara, 1950.
————: "Karatepe: Seventh and Eighth Campaigns." *Belleten*, XVI, Ankara, 1952.
Alt, Albrecht: *"Die geschichtliche Bedeutung der neuen phönikischen Inschriften aus Kilikien."* *Forschungen und Fortschritte*, Heft 11/12, Berlin, 1948.
Barnett, R. D.: "A lost language found." *The Spectator*, April 1949.
————: "Karatepe, the key to the hittite hieroglyphs." *Journal of the British Institute of Archaeology at Ankara*, Vol. III, 1953.
Barnett, R. D., Leveen, I., and Moss, C.: "A Phoenician Inscription from Eastern Cilicia." *Iraq* X, 1948.
Bissing, Fr. W. Freiherr von: *"Zu zwei in Karatepe zutage gekommenen Reliefs mit «BES»-Figuren."* *Jahrbuch für Kleinasiatische Forschung*, II/1, Heidelberg, 1951.
Bossert, Helmuth T.: *"Meine beiden ersten Reisen zum Karatepe."* *Orientalia*, XVII, 4, Rome, 1948.
————: "Found at last: a bi-lingual key to the previously undecipherable Hittite Hieroglyphic inscriptions." *Illustrated London News*, May 1949.
———— (with U. B. Alkim, H. Çambel, N. Ongunsu and Ü. Süzen): *Die Ausgrabungen auf dem Karatepe. Erster Vorbericht*, Ankara, 1950.
————: *"Die phönizisch-hethitischen Bilinguen von Karatepe."* *Oriens* I, 1948, *Oriens* II, 1949, *Archiv Orientalni* 18, 1950, *Jahrbuch für Kleinasiatische Forschung* I, 1950/51, and II, 1952/53.
————: *"Die phonizischen Inschriften vom Karatepe nach dem Stande von Herbst 1953."* *Belleten*, XVII, 66, Ankara, 1953.
————: *"Die Hieroglyphen-Hethitischen Inschriften vom Karatepe nach dem Stand vom Herbst 1953."* *Belleten*, XVIII, 69, Ankara, 1954.
Bossert, Helmuth T. and Alkim, U. Bahadir: *Karatepe, Kadirli and its Environments, First and second preliminary reports.* Publications of the University of Istanbul, 1946 and 1947.
Bossert, Helmuth T. and Çambel, Halet: *Karatepe, A preliminary report on a new Hittite site.* Faculty of the University of Istanbul, Publ. of the Inst. for Research in Ancient Oriental Civilisations, Nr. 1, Istanbul, 1946.
Çambel, Halet: *"Archäologischer Bericht aus Anatolien."* *Orientalia*, XVII, 2, Rome, 1948.
————: "Karatepe, an archaeological introduction to a recently dis-

covered Hittite site in southern Anatolia." *Oriens* 1, 1948.

Dunand, M.: *"Les inscriptions phéniciennes de Karatépé." Bulletin du Musée de Beyrouth*, VII, 1948.

Dupont-Sommer, A.: *"Azitawadda, roi des Danouniens." Revue d'Assyriologie*, XLII, 1948.

———: *"Le déchiffrement des hiéroglyphes hittites et les inscriptions bilingues de Karatépé." Revue historique*, 1949.

Friedrich, Johannes: *"Eine altphönizische Inschrift aus Kilikien." Forschungen und Fortschritte*, Heft 7/8, Berlin, 1948.

Gelb, Ignace J.: "The Contribution of the new Cilician Bilinguals to the Decipherment of Hieroglyphic Hittite." *Bibliotheca Orientalis*, VII, 1950.

Gordon, C. H.: "Azitawadda's Phoenician Inscription." *Journal of Near Eastern Studies*, VIII, 1949.

Güterbock, Hans Gustav: *"Die Bedeutung der Bilinguen vom Karatepe für die Entzifferung der hethitischen Hieroglyphen." Eranos*, XLVII, Gotenburg, 1949.

Hogarth, D. G.: *Carchemish*. Report on the excavations at Djerabis on behalf of the British Museum, conducted by C. L. Woolley and T. E. Lawrence. London, 1914. (*See* Woolley, C. L.: *Carchemish II.*)

Hogarth, D. G., Woolley, C. L., and Barnett, R. D.: *Carchemish III*. London, 1953.

Honeyman, A. M.: *"Epigraphic Discoveries at Karatepe." Palestine Exploration Quarterly*, 1949.

Kum, Naçi: *"Karatepe harabeleri—Kâşif kimdir?" Türk Sözü*, Adana, January 1949.

Landsberger, B.: *"Sam'al. Studien zur Entdeckung der Ruinenstätte Karatepe*. Turkish Historical Society, 1948.

Marcus, R. and Gelb, I. J.: "A Preliminary Study of the new Phoenician Inscription from Cilicia." *Journal of Near Eastern Studies*, VII, 1948.

———: "The Phoenician Stele Inscription from Cilicia." *Journal of Near Eastern Studies*, VIII, 1949.

del Medico, H. E.: *"Déchiffrement et lecture des hiéroglyphes néohittites." Revue Hittite et Asianique*, X, 1949.

Obermann, J.: "New discoveries at Karatepe." A complete text of the Phoenician royal inscription from Cilicia. *Transactions of the Connecticut Academy of Arts and Sciences*, XXXVIII, 1949.

O'Callaghan, R. T.: "The Great Phoenician Portal Inscription from Karatepe." *Orientalia*, XVIII, Rome, 1949.

———: "An Approach to some Religious Problems of Karatepe." *Archiv Orientalni*, XVIII, 1950.

———: "The Phoenician Inscription on the King's Statue at Karatepe." *The Catholic Biblical Quarterly*, XI, Rome, 1949.

Steinherr, Franz: "Karatepe, the Key to the Hittite Hieroglyphic." *Archaeology*, II, 4, 1949.

Woolley, C. L.: *Carchemish*. Report on the excavations at Jerablus on behalf of the British Museum, conducted by C. L. Woolley, with T. E. Lawrence and P. L. O. Guy, Part II, "The town defences." London, 1921.

6. *HITTITE LITERATURE* (Translations, copies, and transcriptions).

Barton, George A. and Weitzel, Baruch: *A Hittite Chrestomathy with Vocabulary*. Hittite Studies Nr. 2, Paris, 1932.
Bossert, H. T.: *Die Bleibriefe aus Assur. Bibliotheca Orientalis*, VIII, Nr. 4, Leiden, 1951.
Cavaignac, E.: *Les annales de Subbiluliuma*. Strasbourg, 1931.
Friedrich, Johannes: "*Aus dem hethitischen Schrifttum.*" *Der alte Orient*, XXIV and XXV, 1925.
————: "*Staatsverträge des Hatti-Reiches in hethitischer Sprache.*" *Mitteilungen der Vorderasiatisch-Ägyptischen Gesellschaft*, XXXI (1926) and XXXIV (1930).
————: "*Die hethitischen Bruchstücke des Gilgames-Epos.*" *Zeitschrift für Assyriologie*, XXXIX, 1930.
————: "*Ein hethitischer Brief aus Tell Atchana.*" *Orientalia*, VIII, 1939.
————: "*Der churritische Mythus vom Schlangendämon Hedammu in hethitischer Sprache.*" *Archiv Orientalni*, XVII, 1949.
————: "*Churritische Märchen und Sagen in hethitischer Sprache.*" *Zeitschrift für Assyriologie*, XLIX, 1950.
Friedrich, J. and Zimmern, H.: "*Hethitische Gesetze aus dem Staatsarchiv von Boğhazköi (um 1300 v. Chr.).*" *Der Alte Orient*, 23. Jhg., Heft 2, Leipzig, 1922.
Forrer, Emil O.: *Die Boghazköi-Texte in Umschrift*, I and II, 41 and 42. *Wissenschaftliche Veröffentlichung der Deutschen Orientgesellschaft*. Leipzig, 1922 and 1926.
Götze, Albrecht: "*Madduwattas.*" *Mitteilungen der Vorderasiatisch-Ägyptischen Gesellschaft*, XXXII, 1928.
————: "*Die Pestgebete des Mursilis.*" *Kleinasiatische Forschungen*, I, 1929.
————: "*Verstreute Boghazköi-Texte.*" Marburg, 1930.
————: "*Die Annalen des Mursilis.*" *Mitteilungen der Vorderasiatisch-Ägyptischen Gesellschaft*, XXXVIII, 6, 1933.
————: "*Cuneiform Inscriptions from Tarsus.*" *Journal of the American Oriental Society*, LIX, 1939.
————: "*A new letter from Ramesses to Hattusilis.*" *Journal of Cuneiform Studies*, I, 1947.
Gurney, O. R.: "*Mita of Pahhuwa.*" *Annals of Archaeology and Anthropology*, XXVIII, 1948.
Güterbock, Hans Gustav: "*Kumarbi.*" *Istanbuler Schriften*, Nr. 16, 1946.

————: *"Neue Texte zur Geschichte Suppiluliumas."* Indo-germanische Forschungen, LX, 1950.

Hrozný, Bedrich (Friedrich): *Hethitische Keilschrifttexte aus Boghazköi. In Umschrift, mit Übersetzung und Kommentar.* Boghazköi-Studien 3, Leipzig, 1919.

————: *Code Hittite provenant de l'Asie Mineure.* Hethitica I, Paris, 1922.

————: *"La deuxième lettre d'Arzawa et le vrai nom des hittites indoeuropéens."* Journal Asiatique, CCXVIII, 1931.

Keilschrifttexte aus Boğhazköy. Wissenschaftliche Veröffentlichung der Deutschen Orient-Gesellschaft, Nr. 30, 1–4, 1916–1923; and Nr. 36, 1–2, 1921.

Keilschrifturkunden aus Boğhazköy. Herausgegeben von den Staatlichen Museen zu Berlin, Vorderasiatische Abteilung, Berlin, 1921–34.

Langdon, S. H.: *"Letter of Ramesses II to a king of Mirā."* Journal of Egyptian Archaeology, VI.

Luckenbill, D. D.: "Hittite Treaties and Letters." *American Journal of Semitic Languages,* XXXVII, 1921.

Meier, G.: *"Ein akkadisches Heilungsritual aus Boğazköy."* Zeitschrift für Assyriologie, XLV, 1942.

Müller, W. Max: *"Der Bündnisvertrag Ramses' II. und des Chetiterkönigs, im Originaltext herausgegeben und übersetzt."* Mitteilungen der Vorderasiatisch-Ägyptischen Gesellschaft, Band 7, V. Leipzig, 1902.

Neufeld, E.: *The Hittite Laws, translated into English and Hebrew with Commentary.* London, 1951.

Otten, H.: *Mythen vom Gotte Kumarbi, neue Fragmente. Deutsche Akademie der Wissenschaften zu Berlin, Institut für Orientforschung,* 3, 1950.

Pritchard, J. B.: *Ancient Near Eastern Texts relating to the Old Testament.* Princeton University Press, 1950. (Translations of A. Götze's Hittite texts.)

Roeder, Günther: *"Ägypter und Hethiter."* Der Alte Orient, 20. Jhg., Leipzig, 1919.

Sommer, F. and Ehelolf, H.: *Das hethitische Ritual des Papanikri von Komana. Boghazköi-Studien,* 10, 1924.

Sturtevant, E. H.: *"Selections from the Code."* See Sturtevant and Bechtel: *A Hittite Chrestomathy.* Philadelphia, 1935.

Szemerenyi, O.: *"Der Vertrag des Hethiter-Königs Tudhaliya IV. mit Istarmuwa von Amurru."* Acta Societatis Hungaricae Orientalis, IX, 1945.

Vieyra, M. M.: *"Un Recueil de présages accado-hittites tirés des éclipses solaires."* Revue de l'Histoire des Religions, CXVI, 1937.

Weidner, Ernest F.: *Politische Documente aus Kleinasien.* Boghazköi-Studien, 8–9, 1923.

INDEX

Arnuwandas III, 163, 259
Arnuwandas IV, 65, 196–7, 260
Arsawa. *See* Arzawa
Artaxerxes III, 143
Arthaud, G., 108
Aryan, 85
Arzawa, 32, 47–8, 58, 67, 163, 196
Asia, 3, 5, 76, 156, 167, 178
Asia Minor, 3, 5–8, 12, 21–3, 27,
    32–3, 38, 46–7, 88, 90–2, 121,
    123, 131, 136, 213–14, 245, 254,
    257
Asitawanda (city; Karatepe), 242
Asitawandas (King), 213, 236,
    238, 242, 244, 249–50, 252
Asshur. *See* Assur
Assur, 6, 138
Assurbanipal, 64, 142
Assyria(n), 6, 13, 19, 26–7, 30,
    41, 47, 55, 78, 81, 87, 93–4, 123,
    128, 136, 139, 142–3, 145–7,
    149, 196, 209, 210, 240, 246
Atatürk. *See* Kemal Atatürk
Atchana. *See* Alalakh
Athens Museum, 103
Aton (Sun God), 31
Attila, 167

Baal, 177, 178, 180, 182, 184
Babylon(ian), 30, 46, 49–50, 55,
    58–9, 66, 78, 81, 87, 93, 123,
    127, 132, 136–8, 140, 142–3,
    145–7, 150, 154, 213, 214, 254,
    258
Bad-tibira, 137
Balawat, 30
Balkans, 92
Ball, C. J., 108
Barnett, R. D., 241, 244–6
Barth, H., 13
Basque, 77
Bedouins, 147, 172
Belzoni, Giovanni Battista, 59
Bentesina, 170, 186–7, 189
Berlin-to-Bagdad Railway, 44
Berlin Museum, 29, 67

Berlin Orient Committee, 34, 55
Berlin, University of, 200, 253
Bethel, 4
Bible, 4, 21, 22, 23–5, 47, 48, 91,
    143, 156
Bible Institute (Rome), 232
Biredjik, 124
Bit Gabbari. *See* Zinjirli
Bittel, Kurt, 101, 111–12, 130, 135,
    199–206, 221, 252, 253
Black Mountain (Karatepe), 225,
    251–2, 254; *see also* Karatepe
Black Sea, 7, 93, 125
Blegen, Carl William, 103
Bogaskoi. *See* Boghazköy
Bogazköy. *See* Boghazköy
Boghaz Keui. *See* Boghazköy
Boghazköy (Hattusas), 6, 9–13,
    25, 32, 44, 47, 52–5, 59, 60,
    64–7, 72, 77, 79, 81, 84, 87, 89–
    94, 101, 111–13, 121–2, 129–
    30, 135, 148, 190, 199, 201–7,
    209–12, 214, 221, 252–4, 257;
    see also Hattusas
Bopp, Franz, 76
Bosporus, 92
Bossert, Helmuth T., 110, 115, 207,
    215, 219–43, 246–53
Botta, Paul Émile, 13
Brahe, Tycho, 131
"Brave Rainbow" (Dr. U. Bahadir
    Alkim), 228–30, 251
British Empire, 197, 214
*British and Foreign Evangelical
    Review*, 22
British Museum, 18–19, 67, 100
Bruno, Giordano, 131
Bulaq, 29, 58
Bulgarmaden, 95
Burckhardt, Johann Ludwig, 15–
    16
Büyükkale, 205

Cairo, 15, 28, 29
Calderon de la Barca, Pedro, 131

Index

v